IMAGES
of America

NEWPORT AND JACKSON COUNTY

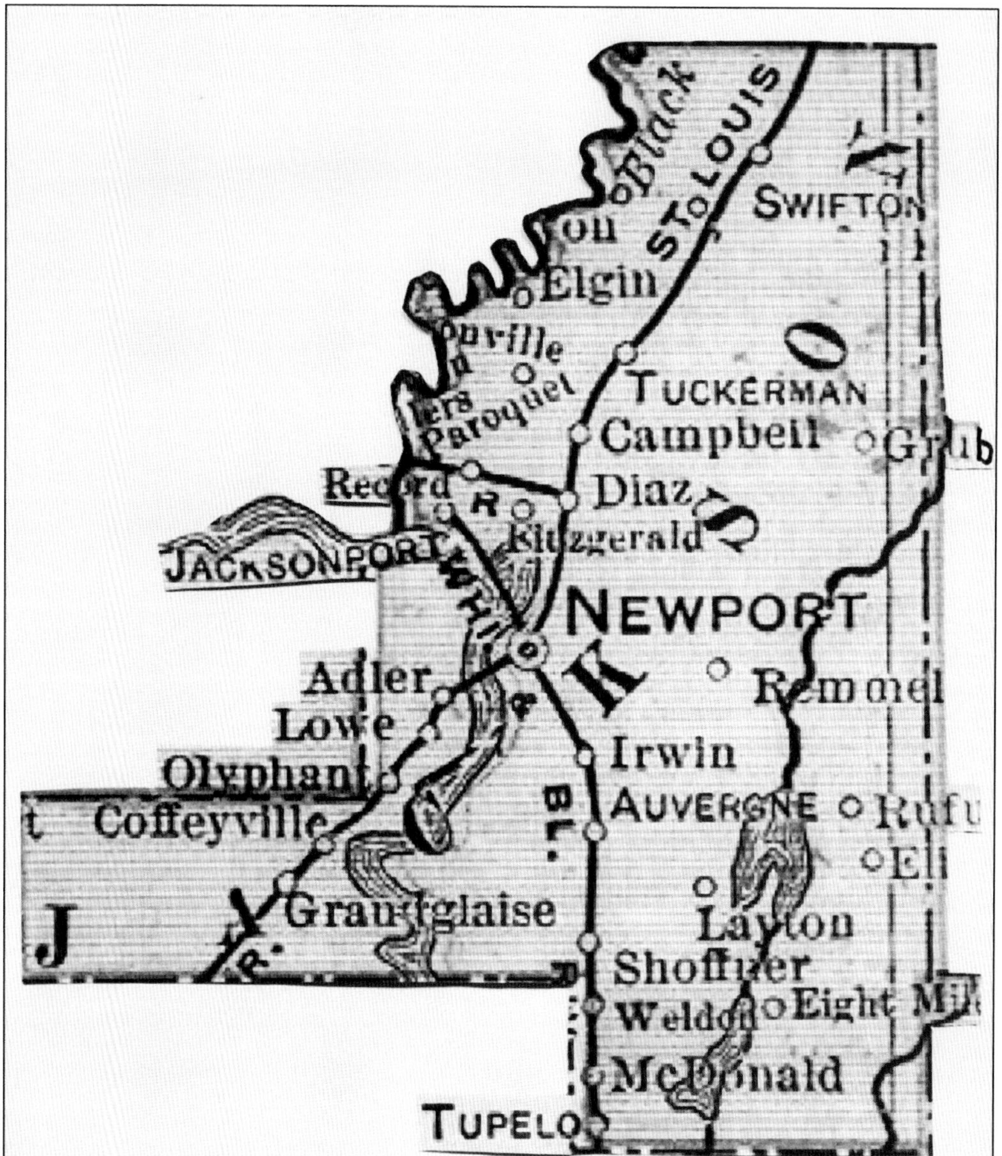

Jackson County was created by act of the Arkansas Territorial Legislature on November 5, 1829, seven years before the territory became the state of Arkansas. The old Southwest Trail that ran from St. Louis to Texas traversed the county from the northeast to the southwest, and settlement had developed along the White and Black Rivers, which were navigable all the way to the Mississippi. (Courtesy of Hearthstone Legacy Publications.)

On the Cover: Miss Newport Betty Castleberry waves to an admiring crowd in a Fourth of July parade in a neighboring town in 1951. Her costume tied her to the Southern Belle heritage of the Mississippi Delta region and resonated with her audience in this traditional Southern town. Eleanor Parish Jowers, a descendant of a pioneer Jackson County family, drives the car, enjoying herself immensely, as she always did. (Courtesy of Cindy Lamkin.)

IMAGES
of America

NEWPORT AND JACKSON COUNTY

Tim Watson and Betsy Jacoway Watson

ARCADIA
PUBLISHING

ISBN 978-1-4671-1585-8

Published by Arcadia Publishing
Charleston, South Carolina

Printed in the United States of America

Library of Congress Control Number: 2015957480

For all general information, please contact Arcadia Publishing:
Telephone 843-853-2070
Fax 843-853-0044
E-mail sales@arcadiapublishing.com
For customer service and orders:
Toll-Free 1-888-313-2665

Visit us on the Internet at www.arcadiapublishing.com

We dedicate this book to Lady Elizabeth Watson Luker, whose love of Jackson County led her to create the Jackson County Historical Society, the Jacksonport Courthouse Museum, and the Mary Woods No. 2 Steamboat Museum. Without her devotion to these projects, Jackson County would undoubtedly have lost much of its heritage.

CONTENTS

ACKNOWLEDGMENTS

Many people have contributed to the creation of this book, most notably Lady Elizabeth Watson Luker, James Logan Morgan Jr., Charlotte Plegge, Robert Craig, and Wayne Boyce, whose devotion to Jackson County history laid the foundation from which all subsequent work must proceed.

Frank Plegge has worked tirelessly to restore old photographs from the Jacksonport Museum collection for us, and we are deeply indebted to him for sharing his time so generously and always in such good humor.

Angela Gibbs has been most generous in helping us obtain suitable images from the collections at Jacksonport State Park.

Many other people have shared from their own collections, often devoting extensive time to finding the images we requested; among these are Phil McDonald, Cindy Lamkin, Lindley Hodges, Camille Murray, Jane Parnell, Henry Boyce, John Minor, Jean Boyce, Ray Hanley and AnnaMarie Sullivan, John Purdy, Luckett McDonald, J.W. Hulen, Larry Bright, Ann Hout, Tara Byrd, Rex Wilmans, Harold Erwin, Ollie and Debbie Brown, Joe and Darlene Black, the staff at the W.A. Billingsley Library in Newport, and the staff at the Butler Center for Arkansas Studies in Little Rock, especially Linda McDowell.

Our contacts at Arcadia Publishing, Sarah Gottlieb and Julia Simpson, have guided and encouraged us from the start and helped to make this project an enjoyable adventure.

To our sons, Tim Watson Jr. and Todd Watson, we offer hearty thanks for listening to our many stories and sharing our enthusiasm for this project.

Unless otherwise noted, all images appear courtesy of the collections of Jacksonport State Park.

INTRODUCTION

The region now comprising Jackson County in northeastern Arkansas is mostly flat bottomland, and it was heavily forested until the middle of the 19th century. Home to many Native American tribes, the land teemed with wild game of all kinds, and its many old horseshoe lakes offered an excellent source of fish and turtles.

Arkansas was a part of the Louisiana Purchase, and Congress created the Territory of Arkansas in 1819. Early settlers began arriving in the 1820s, attracted by the lure of rich soil and vast tracts of virgin timber. By 1829, a sufficient number of settlers had established homesteads, so the territorial assembly created Jackson County on November 5 that year. Jackson County thus predates the state of Arkansas by seven years. The county was named for Andrew Jackson, then president of the United States.

The county is home to three major rivers—the White, the Black, and the Cache—plus numerous other streams, and upwards of 40 lakes of all sizes, created by changes in the courses of the rivers over time. The existence of the rivers led to the early expansion of settlement, hastened by the coming of the steamboat in the early 1830s. The White River, especially, with its year-round deepwater navigation, created ideal locations for early towns along its banks, including Elizabeth, Augusta, Jacksonport, Grand Glaize, and Newport, from which farm produce, fur pelts, timber, and other products of the area could be shipped all the way to Memphis, New Orleans, and beyond. The county became prosperous; in the 1850s, Jacksonport became one of the leading small cities in the state.

Immigrants from other Southern states—principally Tennessee, Kentucky, Virginia, and the states of the Deep South—settled Jackson County, and they brought their slaves with them. When the Civil War broke out, Arkansas seceded by act of the general assembly on May 6, 1861. So high were the Southern sympathies in Jackson County that the first contingent of volunteers to the Confederate cause left Jacksonport for the eastern theater on May 5, 1861, the day before the state actually seceded.

Following the war, Jacksonport slowly recovered, and the long-planned new courthouse finally opened in 1871. This magnificent structure still stands in old Jacksonport, and is now the hub of Jacksonport State Park. The coming of the railroad through the county bypassed Jacksonport and ran closest to the White River at the old ferryboat town of New Port, three miles downstream.

Newport (as it came to be called) had long been overshadowed by the major river ports of Elizabeth and Jacksonport, both county seats in succession, but the location of the railroad created a transportation opportunity that was the basis of the spectacular growth of Newport in the 1870s and 1880s. Newport became the county seat in 1892, with its own beautiful new courthouse.

The turn of the 20th century saw continuing growth in Jackson County. The Iron Mountain Railway had given birth to many new towns along its right-of-way, from Olyphant and Coffeeville in the southwest part of the county to Campbell Station, Tuckerman, and Swifton on the line northeast of Newport. A second major railroad, the Chicago, Rock Island and Pacific, acquired a line from Newport south, and the towns of Erwin Switch, Auvergne, Weldon, Shoffner and Tupelo sat strategically along its right-of-way, giving farmers in those areas ready access to markets beyond Jackson County.

Large forests had now been logged, leaving thousands of acres of excellent soil for the production of the principal crop, cotton, with other acres planted in corn and winter wheat. But cotton was king, and the county was covered with cotton gins. Front Street in Newport, parallel to the railroad and the new Iron Mountain Depot, was clogged with cotton wagons during the harvest, where cotton buyers took samples of the white fiber and struck deals with the growers and the mills the buyers represented.

The First World War inspired the patriotic county to send many soldiers to war and played havoc with the price of farm products, as it did elsewhere. The depression in the farm community following the war presaged the larger Depression of the 1930s, but the county persevered, still almost wholly agricultural. With the discovery of pearls in the mussels of the White River, a new industry sprang up almost overnight. Jewelry markets prospered from the new interest in pearls, buttons emerged from the mussel shells, and shell factories gave employment to hundreds of workers and profits to many entrepreneurs.

The Second World War brought the Depression to an end, and the county became the home of a major military installation from 1942 to 1945, a vast Army airfield located three miles east of Newport. Thousands of GIs passed through this base and contributed greatly to the local economy and especially to the new phenomenon of the juke joint. After the repeal of Prohibition in 1933, Jackson County had voted to go "wet," meaning the sale and consumption of alcoholic beverages were allowed, and Jackson County was surrounded by dry counties. As a result, several dance halls/saloons opened in the county, and the patronage of the soldiers from the airfield was critical to their success.

In the mid-1950s, rock and roll came to Jackson County, as Newport and the surrounding towns became a major destination for the new performers coming out of Sam Phillips's Sun Record Company in Memphis, just 90 miles away. The 1950s brought another new phenomenon to the county, the assembly line factory. Several such businesses opened, most of them at the now defunct airbase, providing a new source of employment for hundreds of farm laborers who were losing their agricultural jobs because of farm mechanization.

The 1960s saw the beginnings of the movement of commerce in Newport eastward. New businesses opened on Highway 67 east of town, and what had been open country for the most part now became the location of new housing additions to the city. As a consequence, the old residential areas of Newport between Third Street and Remmel Avenue began an inexorable decline.

Smaller communities around the county lost not only their local schools but also much of their population. The large new combines, bigger and more powerful tractors, and the mechanical cotton pickers displaced large numbers of farm laborers who had lived and shopped in these small communities. With jobs, stores, and schools gone, there was nothing to keep workers and their families in these rural hamlets. As a result, little towns like Estico, Centerville, Kenyon, and many others simply disappeared. Rice production was replacing cotton as the "cash" crop of the county, and new rice dryers replaced century-old cotton gins. The farming of rice required fewer field hands than cotton, and the switch caused the loss of even more agricultural jobs.

The 1970s brought the arrival of the shopping center in Newport, theretofore a big-city phenomenon. The Village Mall opened in 1972, anchored by one of the first Walmart stores, and included several of the former "downtown" businesses. The growth of new residential areas continued along Highway 67, now no longer "east" of town but almost its center. Integration of the public schools, long overdue, finally came to the remaining school districts in Jackson County, without incident. New factories moved in, and industrial employment reached an all-time high, while agricultural work continued to diminish. By the end of the 1970s, the whole county was in transition. The towns of Tuckerman, Swifton, Grubbs, Weldon, and Tupelo lost significant population, while Olyphant, Shoffner, and others virtually ceased to exist.

Over the relatively short span of 100-plus years, Jackson County had grown from a frontier territory offering unlimited opportunity into a modern, bustling agricultural and industrial player on the American landscape. The stories of that adventure are not unlike those of a thousand other American towns, where small-town living preserved gracious traditions and demonstrated that the American Dream was a reality that, with hard work and determination, could be achieved.

One

A New Beginning

The 1870s and 1880s

From the late 1840s, the river-port town of Jacksonport flourished at the head of deepwater navigation on the White River, evolving from a rowdy pioneer town into a wealthy one with a distinctly Old South elegance and tone. The Civil War interrupted the affluence of Jacksonport, but it was the coming of the railroad that killed the town. In the early 1870s, a group of railroad entrepreneurs approached Jacksonport's leaders and offered to alter the route of their planned line if the town would give an easement of land. The leaders refused, and the St. Louis, Iron Mountain, and Southern Railway Company bypassed Jacksonport entirely, laying its tracks through the tiny ferry settlement three river-miles south that had long been called New Port.

Situated on a bluff on the left bank of the White River and therefore somewhat protected from the frequent flooding in an area with no levees, the town of Newport prospered. The 1870s and 1880s saw a mass emigration from the older town to the new, and by 1892 even the county seat had moved to Newport. In time, Jacksonport became a virtual ghost town. Newport developed rapidly as the principal market town in this northeast Arkansas county. Steamboats and railroad cars transported millions of dollars of lumber and cotton out of virgin hardwood forests and newly cleared fertile land as Newport developed into a promising new town with its roots deep in the Southern past. Elsewhere in the county, the towns of Swifton and Tuckerman (as railroad towns on the new Iron Mountain line) and Weldon, Shoffner, and Grubbs (as rural centers of agricultural enterprises) sprang up as the population of the county rapidly increased. As with the rest of the Old South, cotton was king, and cotton gins sprang up all over the county, as did sawmills to service the booming logging companies. Jackson County was on its way to becoming one of the wealthiest agricultural producers in the country, and it attracted many investors from outside the region who saw the opportunities developing in what had been, just a few years before, an untouched wilderness.

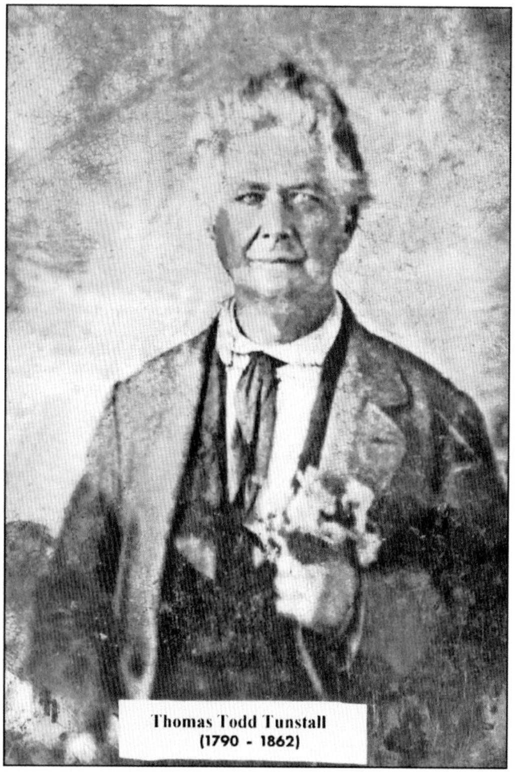

Thomas Todd Tunstall (1790–1862) is generally acknowledged as the founder of Jacksonport. Tunstall brought the second steamboat up the White River in 1833 and stopped at the mouth of Jack's Creek, later renamed Jacksonport. Captain Tunstall and his son William laid out the town, built a sawmill, hotel, and several business houses along the river front, and accumulated great wealth. The town of Jacksonport was incorporated in 1852, and in 1854 it became the county seat of Jackson County.

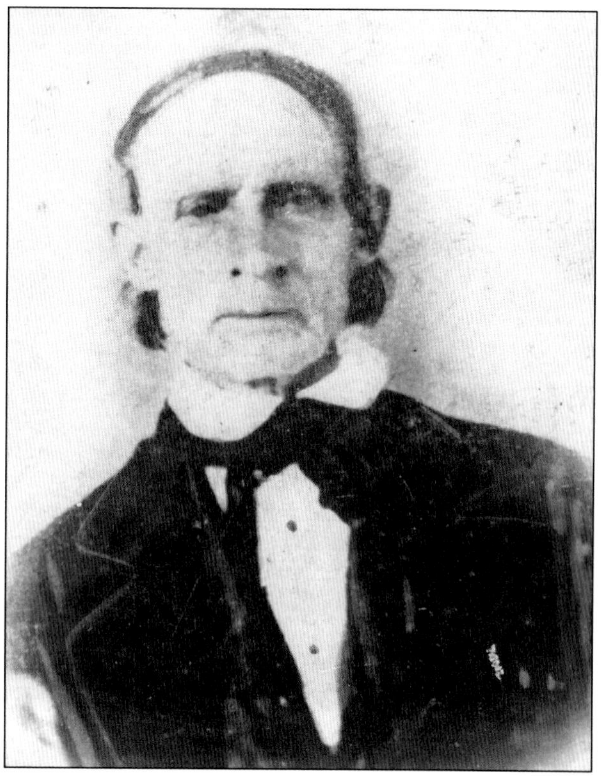

Judge John Robinson (1748–1832) came to Jackson County from Kentucky in 1831, leading a party of 200 people, each of whom received 1,000 acres of land, purchased for $1 an acre. Robinson and his wife had five sons. His sister married his wife's brother, and they had five daughters. The five sons married the five daughters, and these six couples became the progenitors of much of the future leadership of Jackson County. (Courtesy of C. Phillip McDonald.)

Isabella Means Harrison (1821–1892) moved with her family to Jacksonport in 1849. She brought her slave Pal (short for Palestine) Louisa. An ancestor of the prominent Boyce family of Tuckerman, Harrison represents much of the pioneer spirit that moved America west in the mid-19th century. Obviously a woman of culture, refinement, and wealth, Harrison brought her love of books and fine things and planted them as a family inheritance in northeast Arkansas. (Courtesy of Wayne Boyce.)

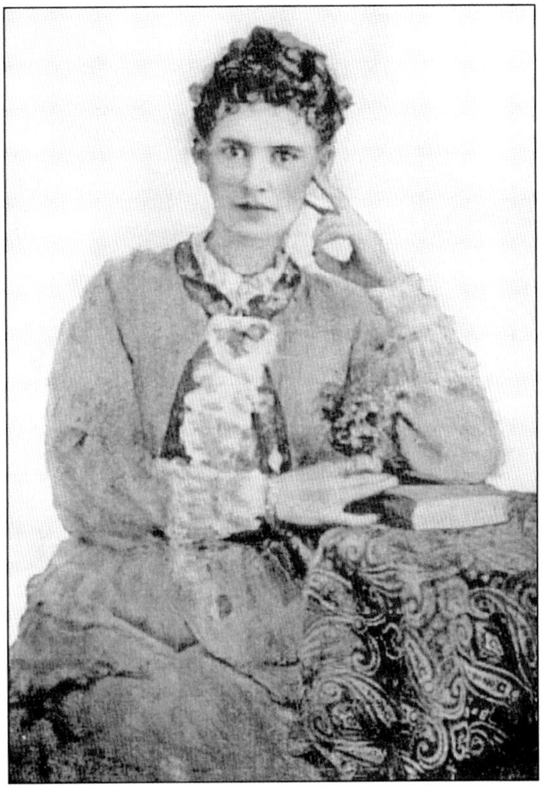

Said by residents to be the original Tunstall Tavern in Jacksonport, renamed the Robert E. Lee Saloon after the Civil War, this was a favorite gathering place and watering hole for the men of the town. The outside stairway, large central chimney, and upper gallery place it architecturally in the 1840s, which was when Tunstall was buying and building properties all over the new town.

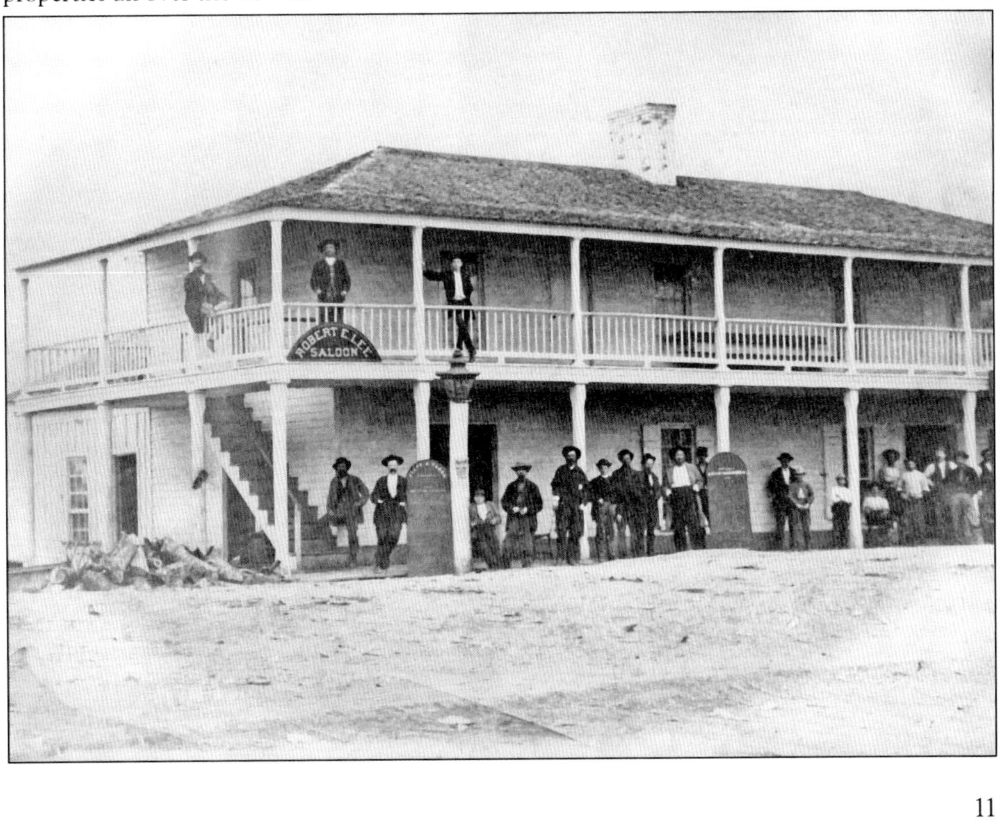

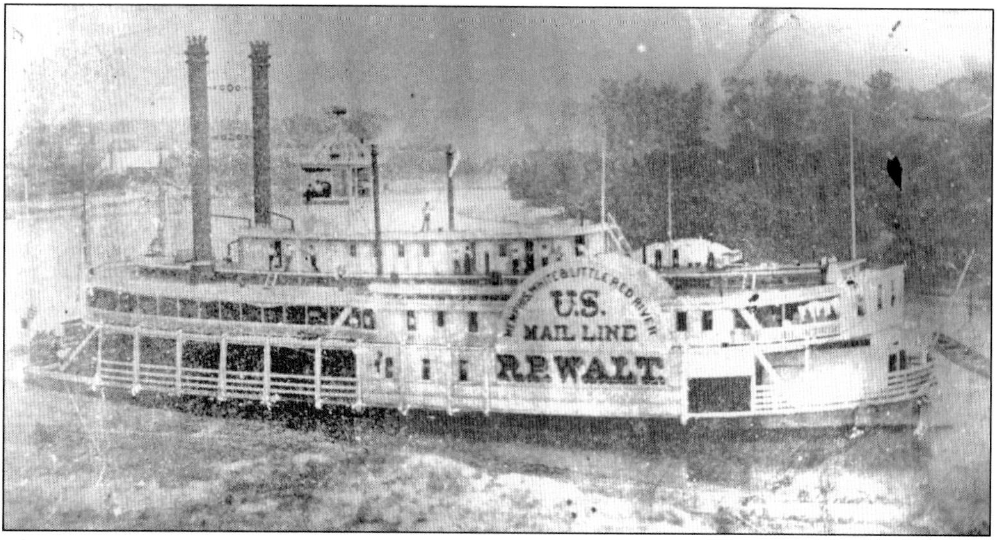

The steamboat *Walt* was a truly elegant steamer. Its 43 staterooms were lavishly furnished, but the 10 set aside for women were fitted like rooms in a fine hotel, with imported furnishings. The cabin was covered with the finest velvet carpet, with all furniture richly and ornately carved. This sleek steamer departed Memphis for Jacksonport in 1870, and parties were held at every town along the way.

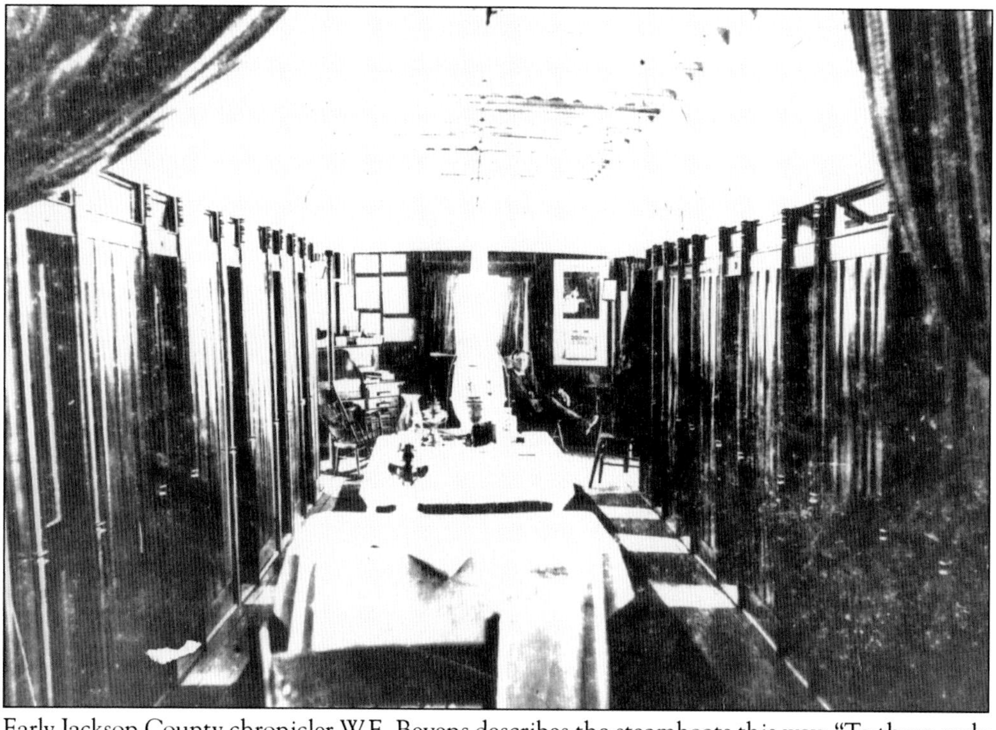

Early Jackson County chronicler W.E. Bevens describes the steamboats this way: "To those early pioneers, so long forced to do without luxuries, they seemed the acme of elegance, with their bands of music, their calliopes, handsome cabins, tables adorned with shining silver, glass and linen, loaded with everything good to eat and drink. The arrival of a big steamboat was always the occasion for much social activity."

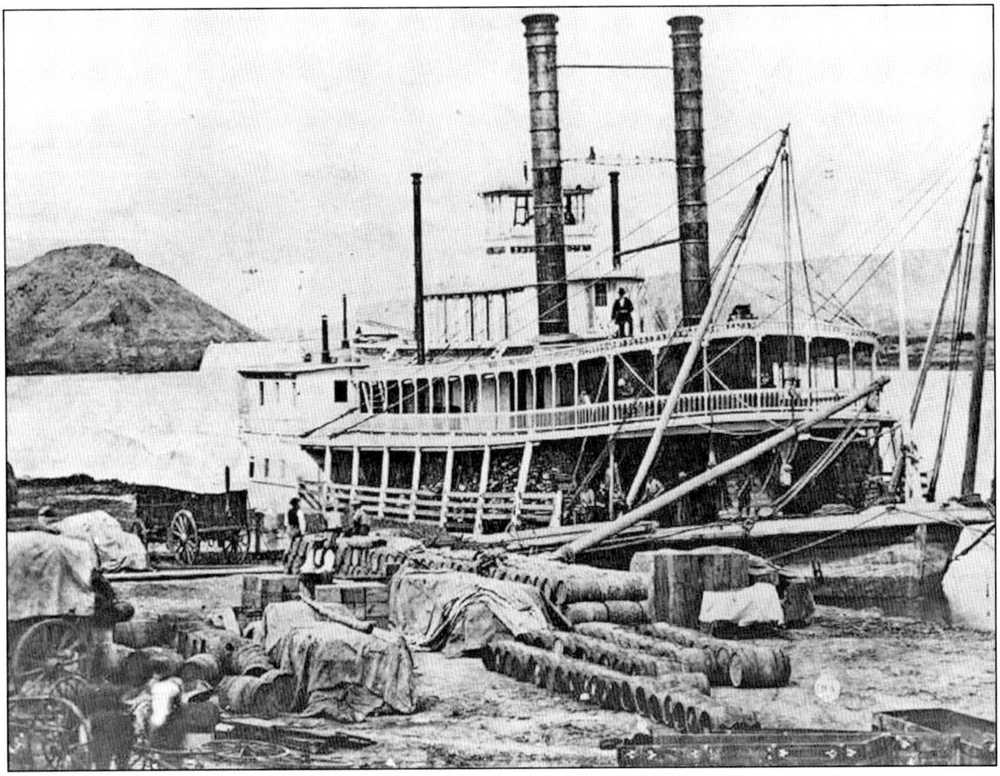

Some steamboats carried as many as 125 passengers and 2,000 bales of cotton. When they came up the river, they carried thousands of sacks of salt along with cargo of sugar, molasses, and dry goods, which they could trade in the backcountry, before loading up with cotton bales for the return trip. The steamer *DeSmet* was typical of river traffic in the 1870s.

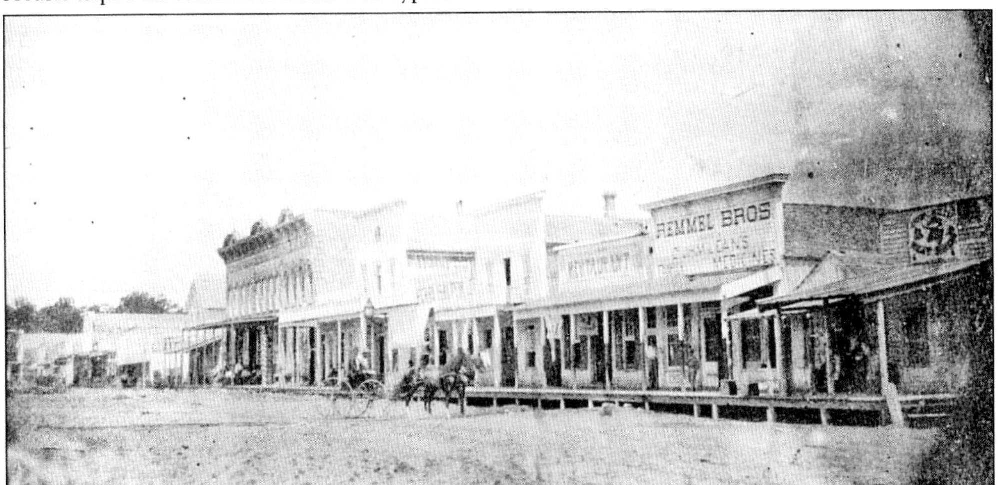

This photograph of the Remmel Brothers Lumber Company is one of the earliest images of downtown Newport. Harmon Remmel and his brother Augustus came to Jackson County from New York in 1874 and made a fortune in the lumber business, capitalizing on the depressed southern economy and the easy availability of extensive hardwood, which was being cleared to make way for the planting of cotton.

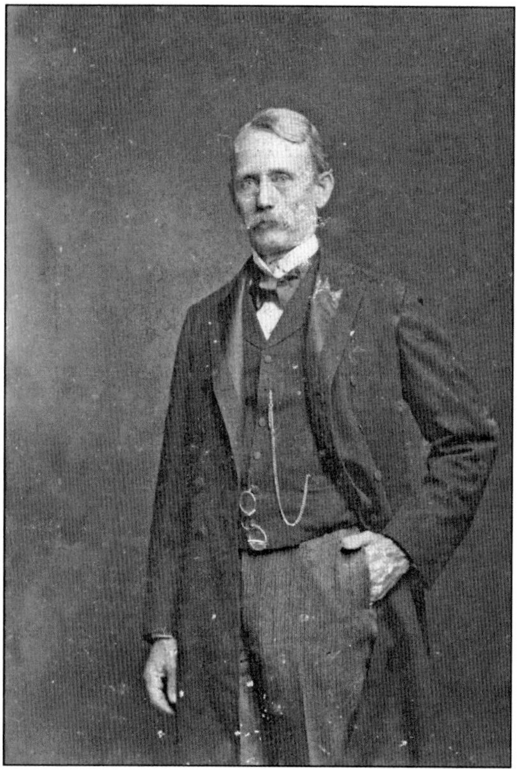

Harmon Liveright Remmel (1859–1927) and his brother Augustus had learned the lumber business in Indiana before moving to Arkansas. In 1896, Harmon left the lumber business and moved to Little Rock, where he quickly became an important force in Republican Party politics, banking, civic affairs, and the state militia. Remmel was 31 at the time of this photograph. (Courtesy of James Logan Morgan Jr. and the Butler Center.)

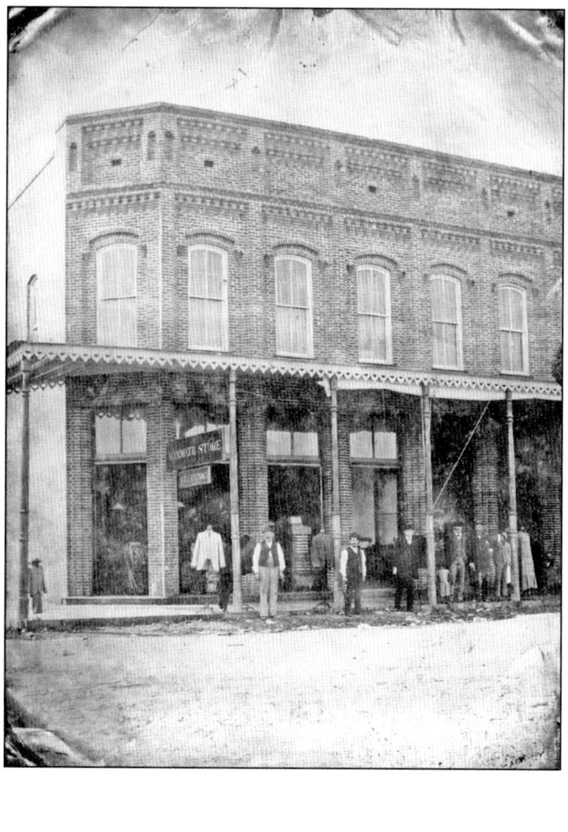

Located on the southwest corner of Front and Hazel Streets, the M.L. Cohn Company became a leading mercantile establishment in early Newport, later occupied by the Sterling Store. M.L. Cohn was closely related to the M.M. Cohn who founded the upscale clothing store in Little Rock. The Cohns were among the many Jewish families who migrated to Newport after the Civil War.

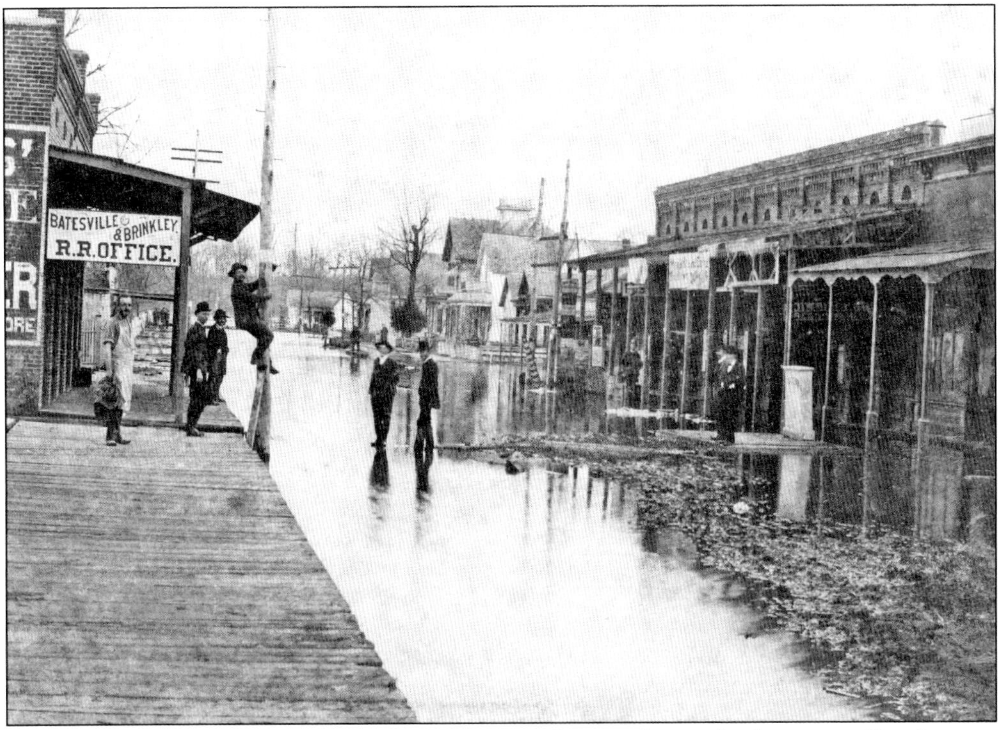

In 1884, the White River rose over its banks, creating this overflow in the downtown. Handwritten on the back of this photograph is this note: "Newport, Ark, Hazel Street, looking from Front Street towards Third Street." In 1885, Newport's town council gave a contract to the Batesville and Brinkley Railroad Company to build a levee around Newport, and work commenced the next year.

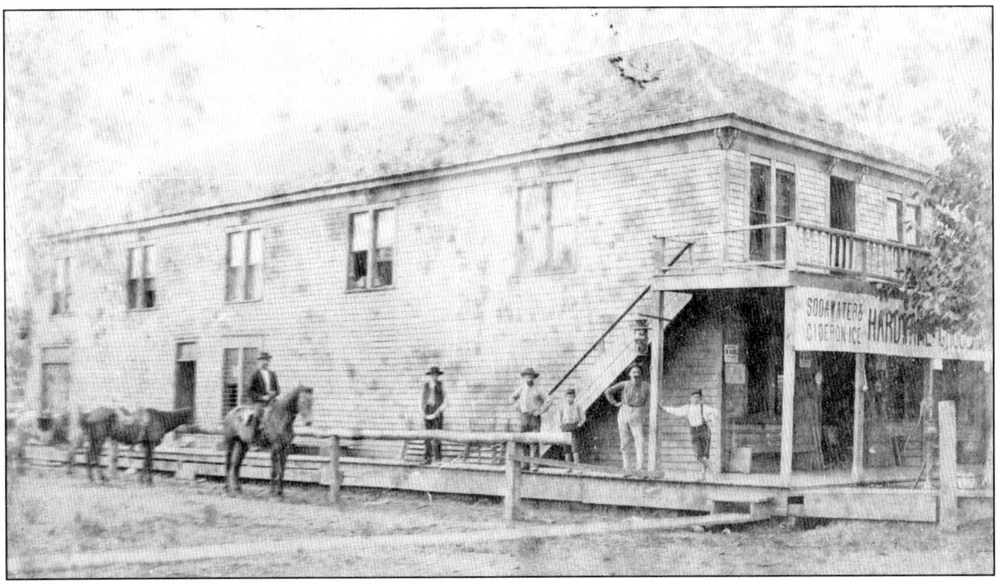

Situated north of Newport on the Iron Mountain Railway line, the little town of Swifton was blessed with fertile land and a thriving economy. Joseph Coffin's store was a leading mercantile establishment in the 1880s.

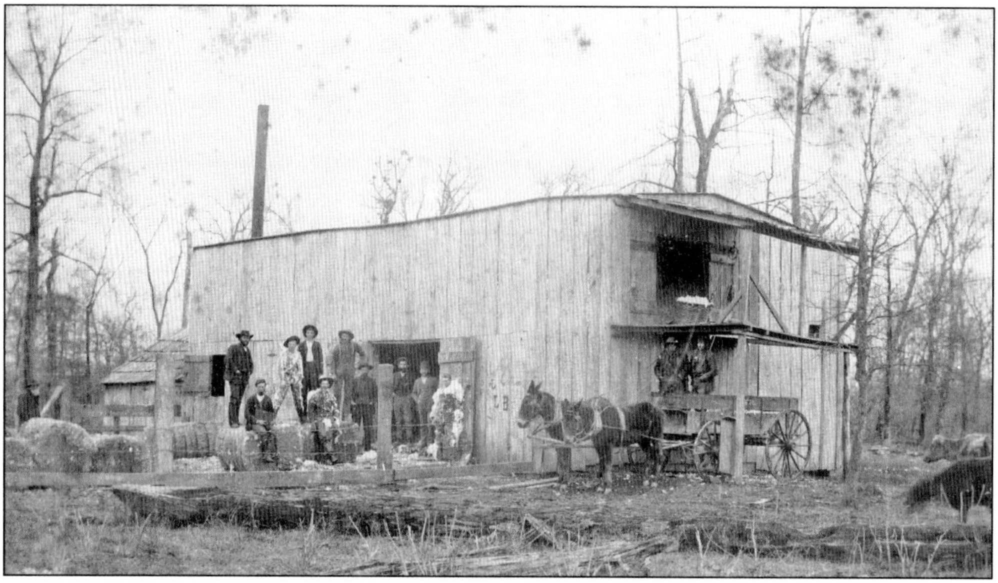

Joseph C. Sharp's cotton gin was another important element in Swifton's economy. This photograph from 1880 shows cotton arriving at the gin on a mule-drawn wagon, where it would be cleaned of trash, the seeds removed, and then compressed into bales. Apparently, some of the workers in the gin emerged from their labors barely distinguishable from the bales they fashioned.

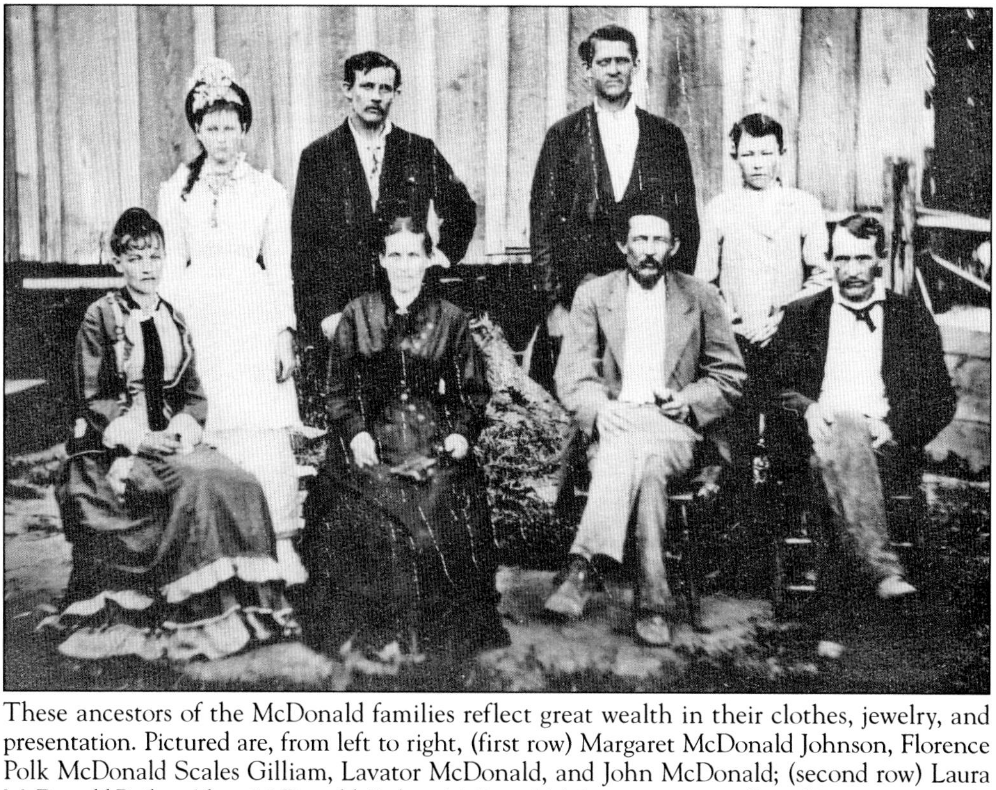

These ancestors of the McDonald families reflect great wealth in their clothes, jewelry, and presentation. Pictured are, from left to right, (first row) Margaret McDonald Johnson, Florence Polk McDonald Scales Gilliam, Lavator McDonald, and John McDonald; (second row) Laura McDonald Bailey, Alvin McDonald, Robert McDonald (who never married), and Forest McDonald (who died young). (Courtesy of C. Phillip McDonald.)

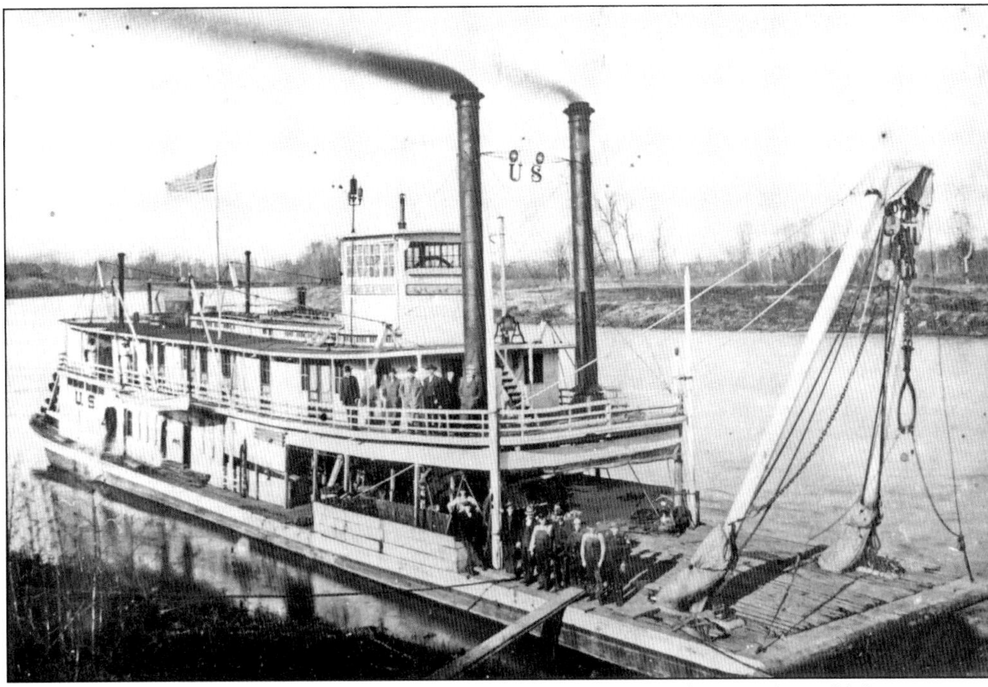

The *Quapaw* was typical of the government snag boats that kept the river free of fallen trees and other debris that could snag or sink a steamboat or a barge. Because the White River ran through heavy forests, snag-boating was very important in the early years of steamboat traffic.

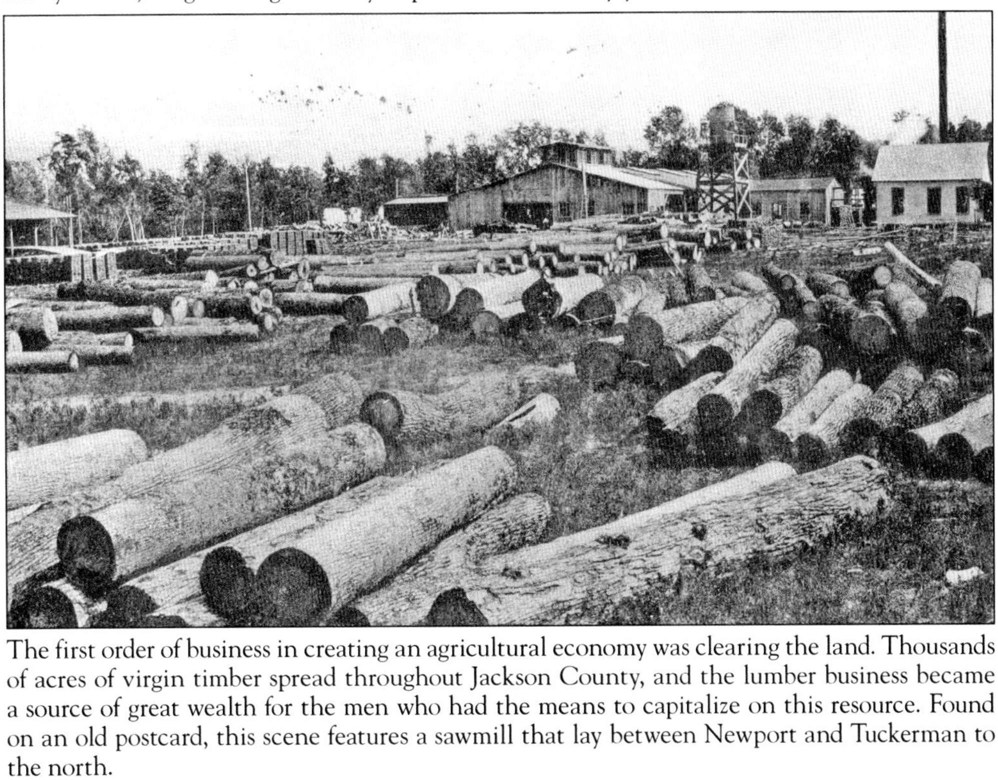

The first order of business in creating an agricultural economy was clearing the land. Thousands of acres of virgin timber spread throughout Jackson County, and the lumber business became a source of great wealth for the men who had the means to capitalize on this resource. Found on an old postcard, this scene features a sawmill that lay between Newport and Tuckerman to the north.

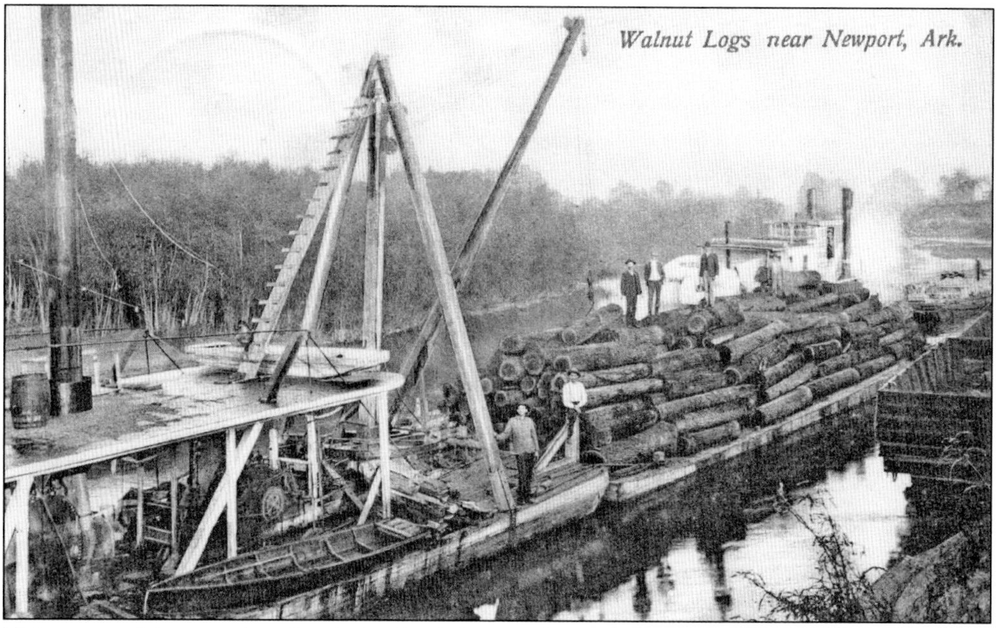

This postcard shows walnut logs being loaded onto a barge somewhere near Newport. They were on their way to a sawmill downriver—perhaps the Empie Lumber Mill in Newport, where they would be cut and planed into boards, studs, or shingles—but they occasionally traveled as far downstream as Memphis on the Mississippi River. Another method of transporting logs to the mill was to chain them together and float them downriver. (Courtesy of Robert Craig.)

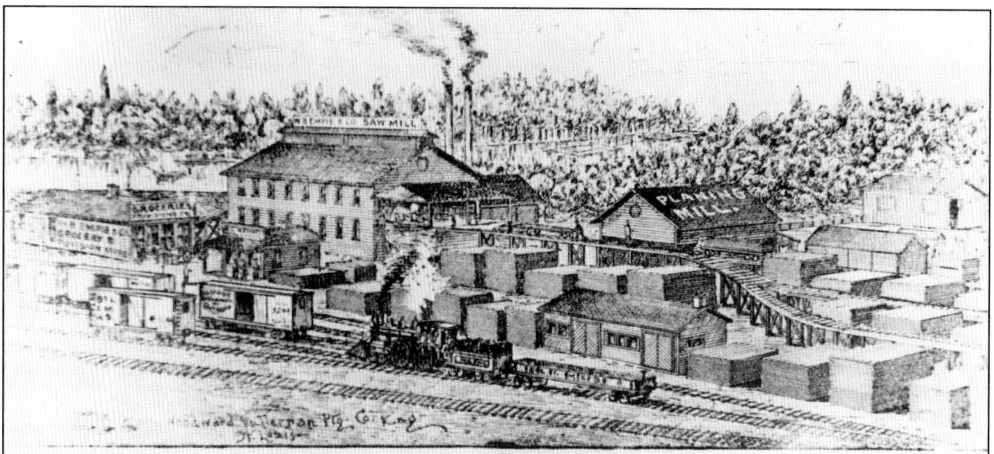

THE GREAT HARDWOOD LUMBER MILL OF W. B. EMPIE & CO., NEWPORT, ARK.

The W.B. Empie lumber mill was one of the largest mills in Jackson County, as is reflected in this drawing. Located between the railroad tracks and the river, as the mills usually were, the Empie operation could transport its product by railcar or steamboat. In this era, most river towns of any size sported at least one lumber mill.

Two

New Opportunities
The 1890s

In 1892, the town of Newport became the sixth seat of Jackson County and as of this writing, its last. Frequent flooding and fires had doomed Jacksonport, with the coup de grâce being the location of the new railroad line through the old ferry landing of New Port, three miles downriver from Jacksonport. By the 1890s, a new steamboat landing was already in operation in Newport, and the rail lines, which had been located on the bluff parallel to the river, made transshipment between rail and river traffic convenient and profitable.

Newport was a bustling center of commercial, financial, social, and religious life by the end of the decade, with new banks, churches, businesses, and schools constructed within the years following the building of the new Jackson County Courthouse in 1892. The population of Newport almost doubled in the decade of the 1890s, indicative of the growing importance of the region. With the new wealth of the city and the county, many beautiful homes sprang up and the town quickly expanded from its original limits.

As historian Marvin Schwartz writes,

> Timber and cotton flourished in a region with some of the richest topsoil in the world. The boom times allowed communities in Jackson County and northeast Arkansas to build conspicuous wealth. Vast stands of virgin hardwood supported the economic growth. As railroad lines were constructed and lumber crews cleared thousands of forest acres, the cut timber was floated down the Black River to sawmills and processing facilities at Newport. Wealthy families celebrated their good fortune, building large, expansive homes with elaborate parquet flooring, railings, and wall panels.

Drawn almost exclusively from other southern states and proud of their Confederate heritage, many of the residents of Jackson County worked to instill in their children a reverence for the "lost cause" of Southern independence and a reverence for the elegance of the Old South. The competing values and tendencies of the frontier and the town made life in Jackson County rich and exciting, and the sky seemed to be the limit for what might be accomplished there.

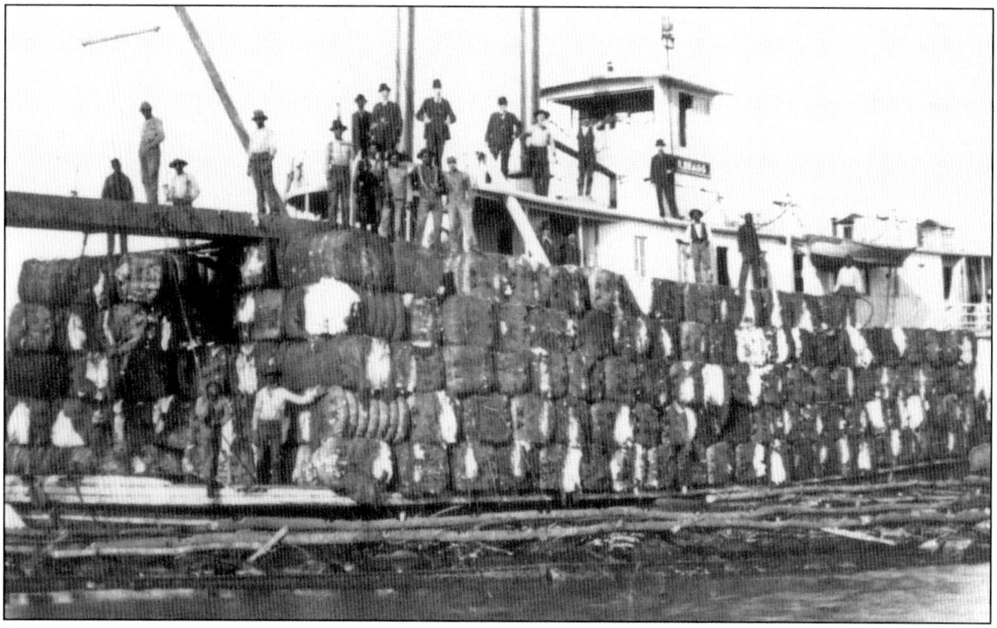

Built at Newport in 1890 by the Morrison-Decker Company, the steamboat *A.R. Bragg* was the largest boat built at Newport, displacing 162 net tons. A packet boat, it was smaller than the standard steamboat and could run farther up the smaller shallower rivers. It ran for years from Newport to Black Rock and made frequent side trips to the upper White River.

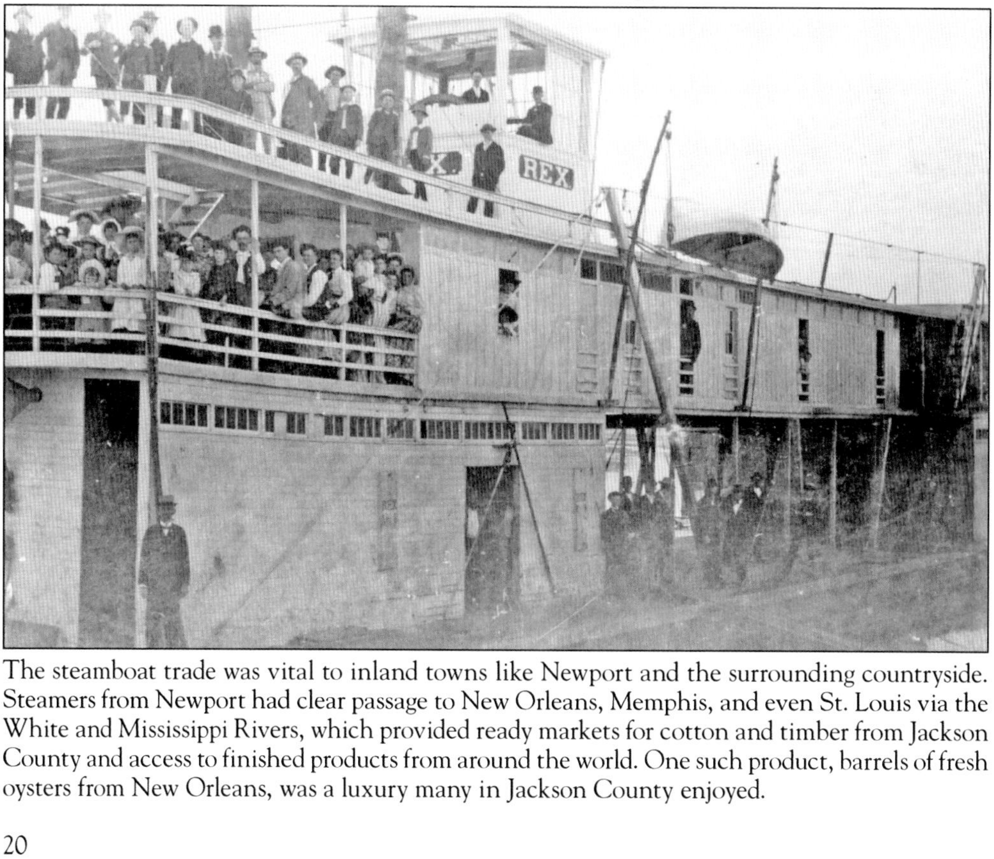

The steamboat trade was vital to inland towns like Newport and the surrounding countryside. Steamers from Newport had clear passage to New Orleans, Memphis, and even St. Louis via the White and Mississippi Rivers, which provided ready markets for cotton and timber from Jackson County and access to finished products from around the world. One such product, barrels of fresh oysters from New Orleans, was a luxury many in Jackson County enjoyed.

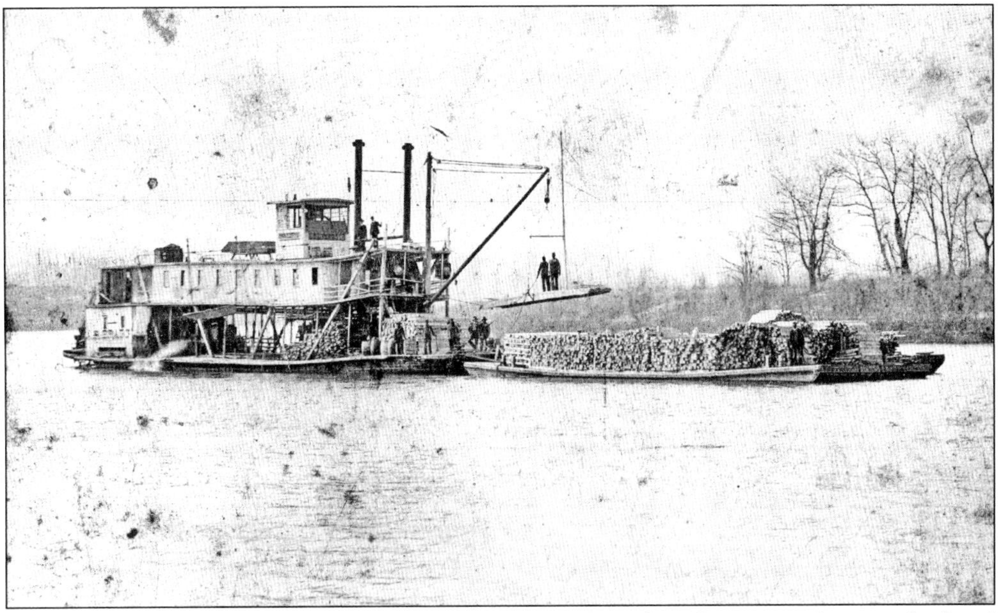

This unidentified steamer pushing a lumber barge on the White River was photographed and the image printed by W.D. Ross, who produced many of the photographs in Jackson County in the 1880s and 1890s. These boards have been milled and are ready for delivery to Memphis, New Orleans, or beyond.

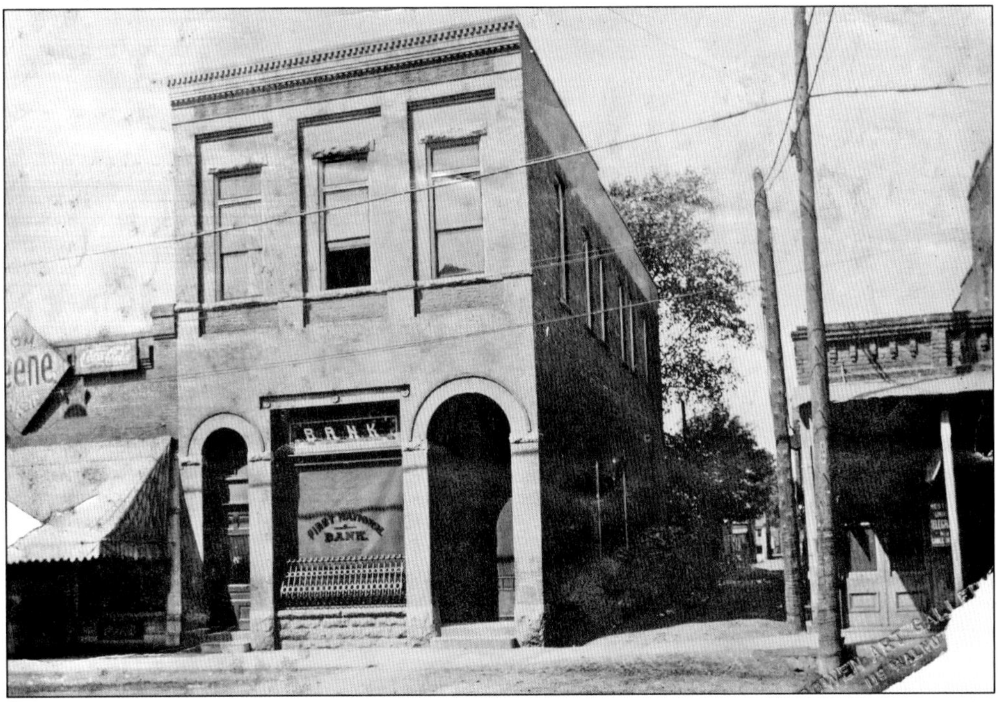

This building originated in 1896 as the Jackson County Savings Bank and later became the First National Bank. The Newport Club occupied the second floor, and an *N* is discernable in this photograph on the entrance at the left of the bank window. The bank stood at 113–115 Hazel Street.

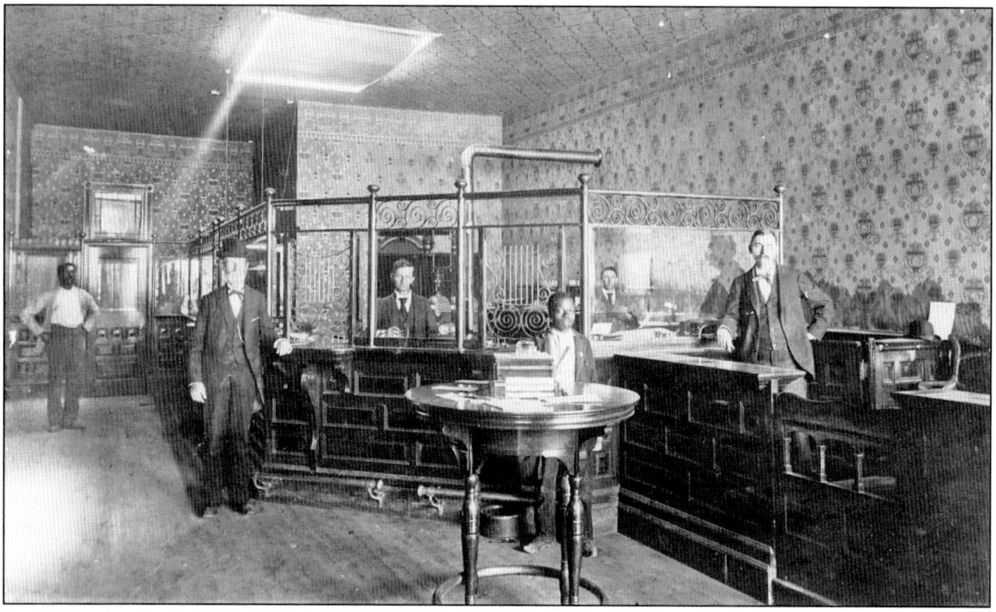

In 1890, the Safe Deposit Bank, a private entity, was reorganized as the Bank of Newport to provide more banking services. Pictured here are E.L. Watson, founder and president (wearing hat) and T.D. Kinman (cashier at right); all others are unidentified. (Courtesy of James Logan Morgan Jr. and the Butler Center.)

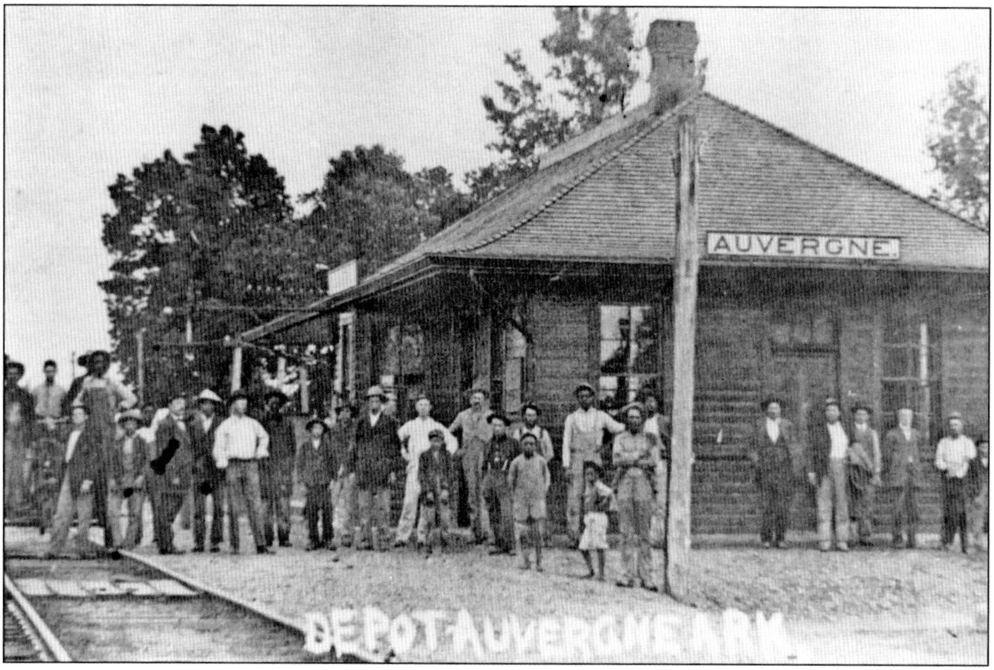

The Batesville and Brinkley depot at Auvergne was built in 1884 but blew away in the tornado of 1892. The tracks of the B&B, which were laid from Brinkley north, reached Newport around 1890. Because of opposition from the Iron Mountain Railway, the B&B never reached Batesville. The Chicago, Rock Island, and Pacific Railroad Company leased the tracks in 1904, and it came to be called the Rock Island Line. (Courtesy of James Logan Morgan Jr. and the Butler Center.)

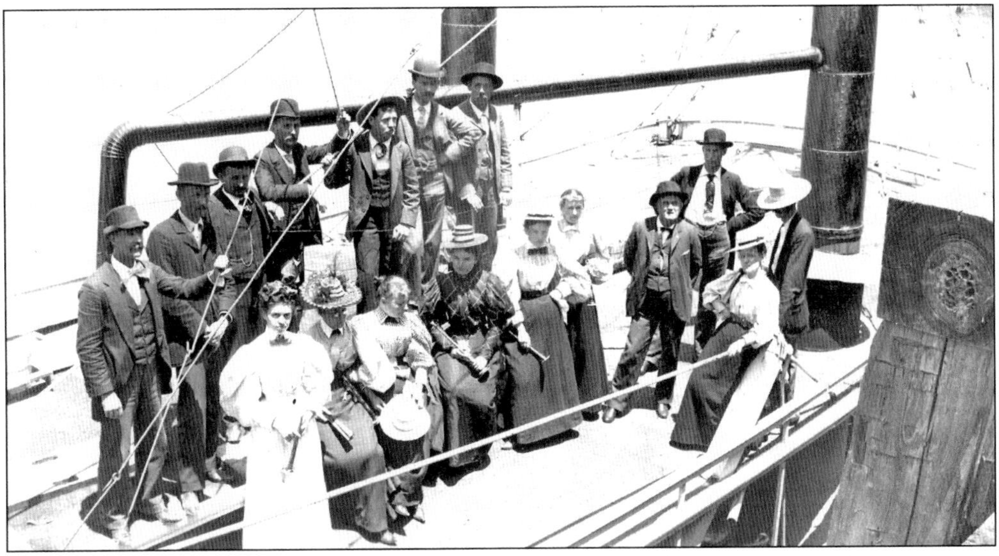

In what seems to have been a fairly typical afternoon outing, this boating party made an excursion up the White River in 1895. Lou Minor, the only one identified in this picture, is seated on the far right. One can only speculate about why some of the women are carrying musical instruments.

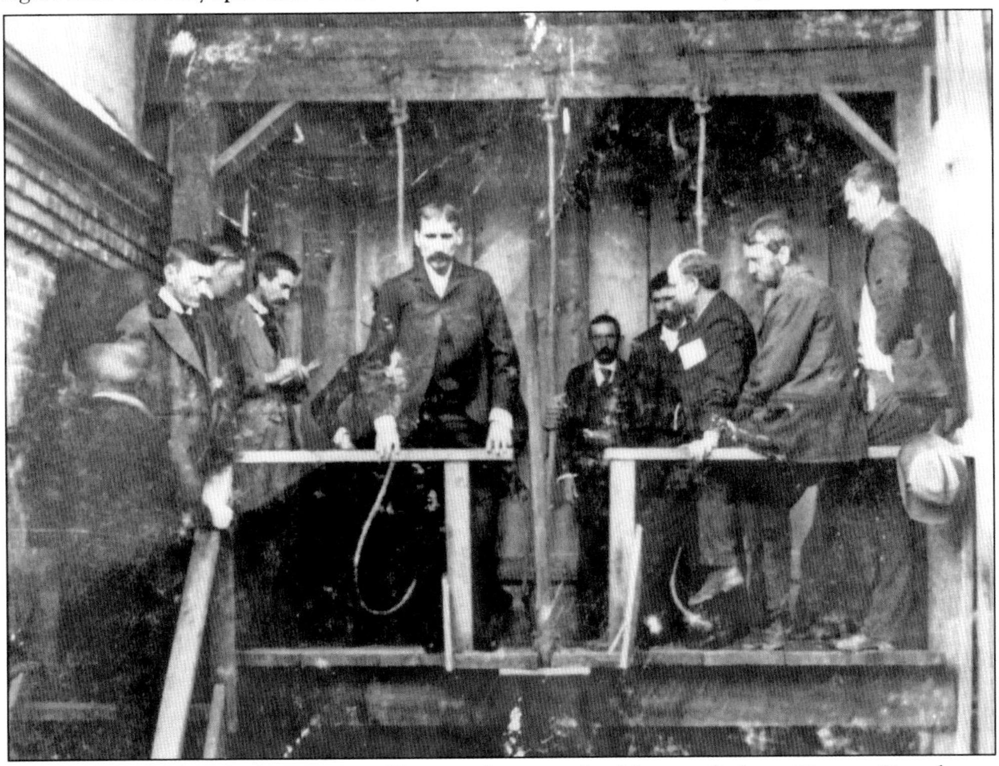

The hanging of the Olyphant train robbers on the grounds of the new Jackson County Courthouse was one of the most exciting events in Newport in 1894. This photograph shows one of the robbers speaking his last words before being hooded and hanged. The local photographer made a tidy sum selling photographs of the robbers all over the county. The bandits included James L. Wyrick, Tom Brady, George W. Padgett, and Albert Mansker.

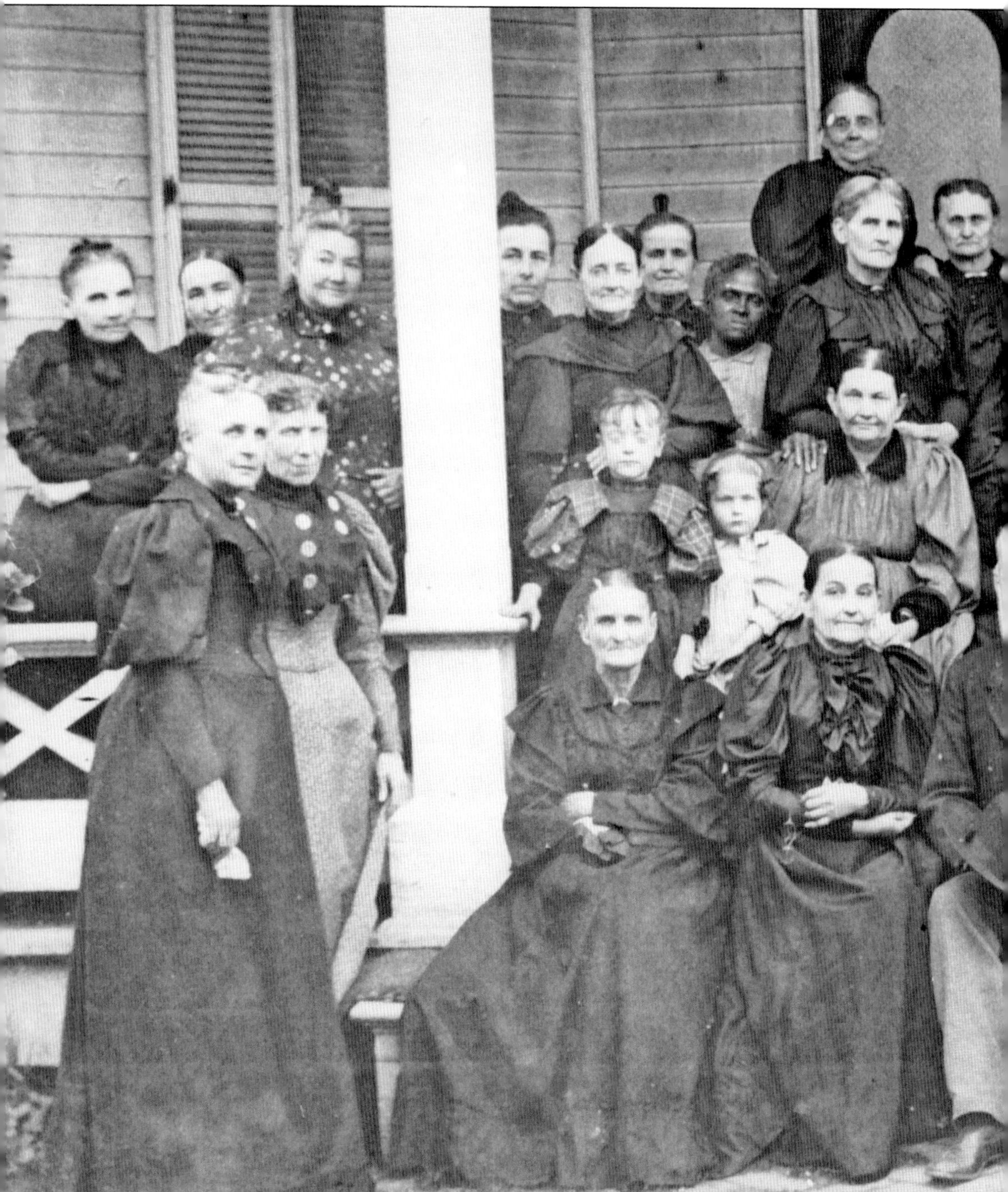

The home of Mr. and Mrs. E.L. Watson at Second and Main Streets was the scene every year for many years of an All Day Dinner. According to family lore, on the day that Lavator McDonald died, his wife sent a note to the Watsons, saying, "Lab's dead, but I'm comin!" And she did! The attendees in 1896 are identified on the back of the photograph as, from left to right, (first row) Aunt Mary Daughtery, Mrs. Hal Dyer, E.L. Watson, Martha Huddleston, Aunt Tant Foushee, and Mrs. Guy Smith; (second row) Aunt Jo Brown, Laura Dills, Minnie Lee Jago, Madie Stephens,

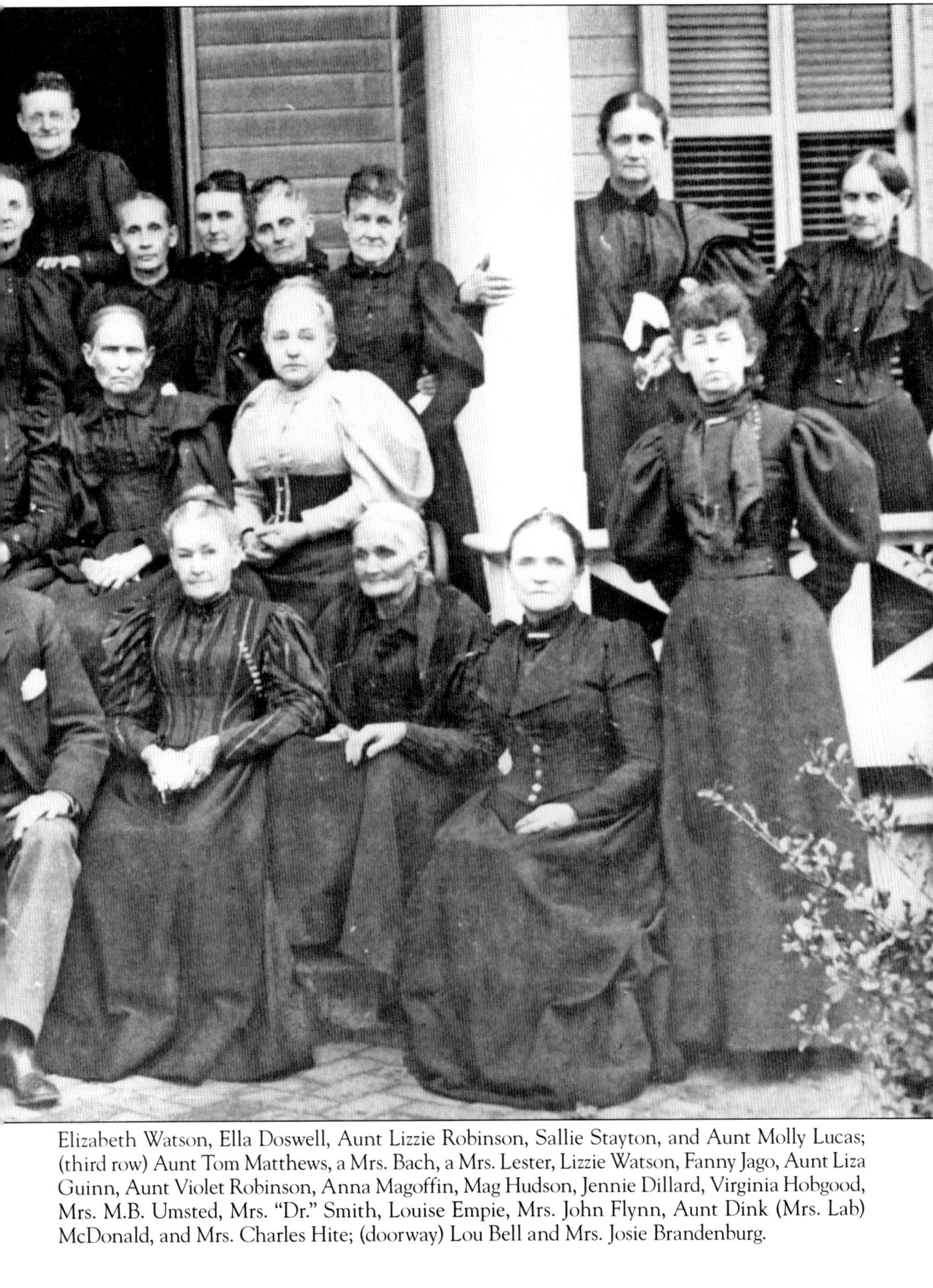

Elizabeth Watson, Ella Doswell, Aunt Lizzie Robinson, Sallie Stayton, and Aunt Molly Lucas; (third row) Aunt Tom Matthews, a Mrs. Bach, a Mrs. Lester, Lizzie Watson, Fanny Jago, Aunt Liza Guinn, Aunt Violet Robinson, Anna Magoffin, Mag Hudson, Jennie Dillard, Virginia Hobgood, Mrs. M.B. Umsted, Mrs. "Dr." Smith, Louise Empie, Mrs. John Flynn, Aunt Dink (Mrs. Lab) McDonald, and Mrs. Charles Hite; (doorway) Lou Bell and Mrs. Josie Brandenburg.

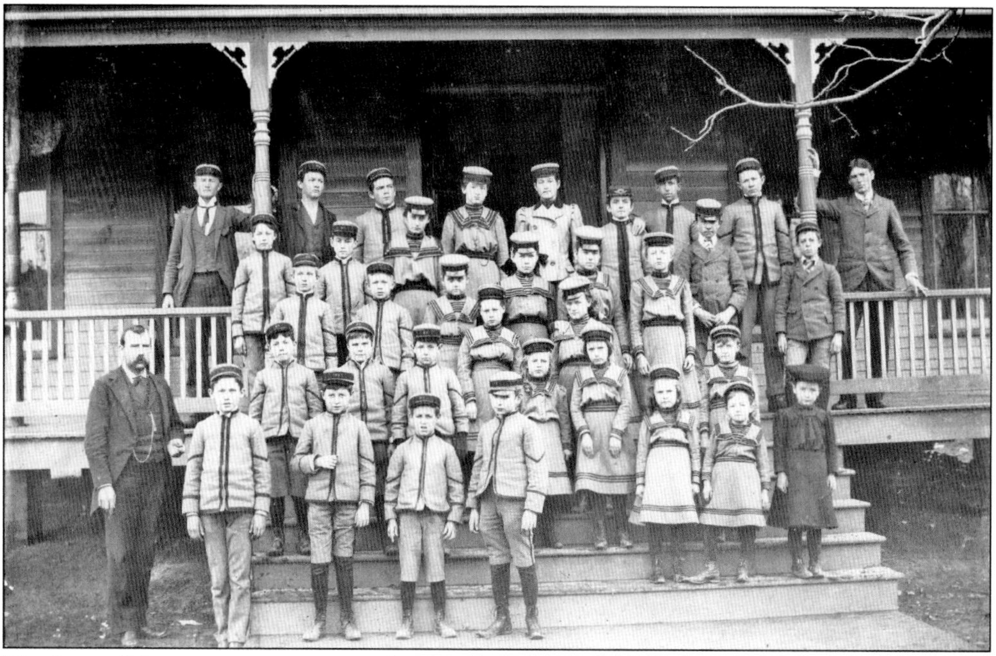

The Doswell Institute was a private school in Auvergne established in 1896 by Franklin Doswell, who was prominent in leading education efforts in Jackson County. Although the students paid tuition, the school was not successful and closed in 1906, perhaps because by that time public schools had become countywide.

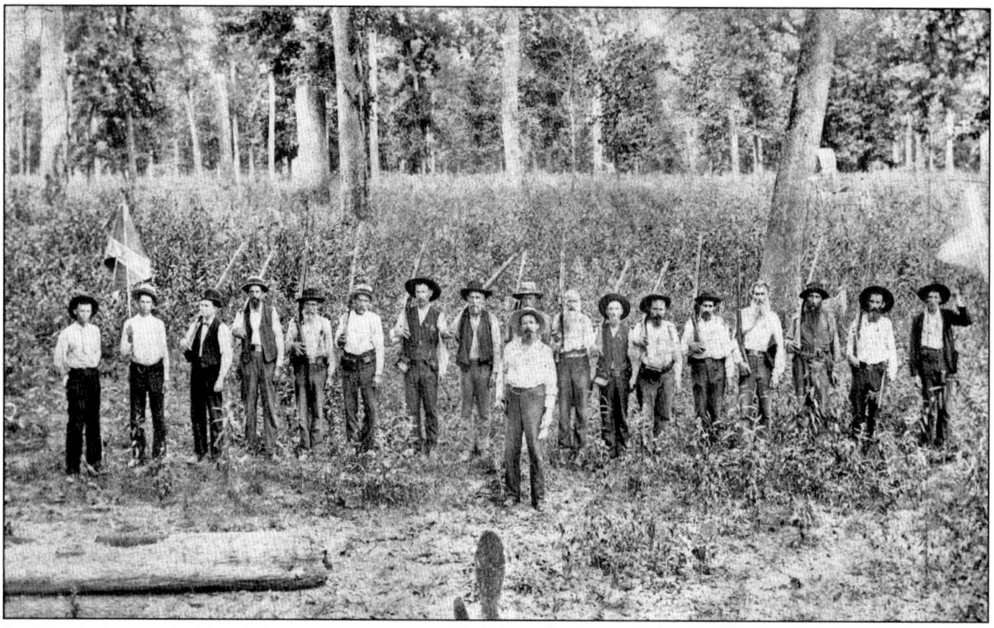

In 1898, the sixth Confederate reunion was held at the site of the old town of Elizabeth, which had been a thriving river port on the White River and the seat of Jackson County in the 1840s. The reunions were held at Camp Pat Cleburne, named for the Confederate general from Arkansas. Most of the old soldiers present were veterans of the Jackson Guards, a Confederate company raised in Jacksonport in May 1861.

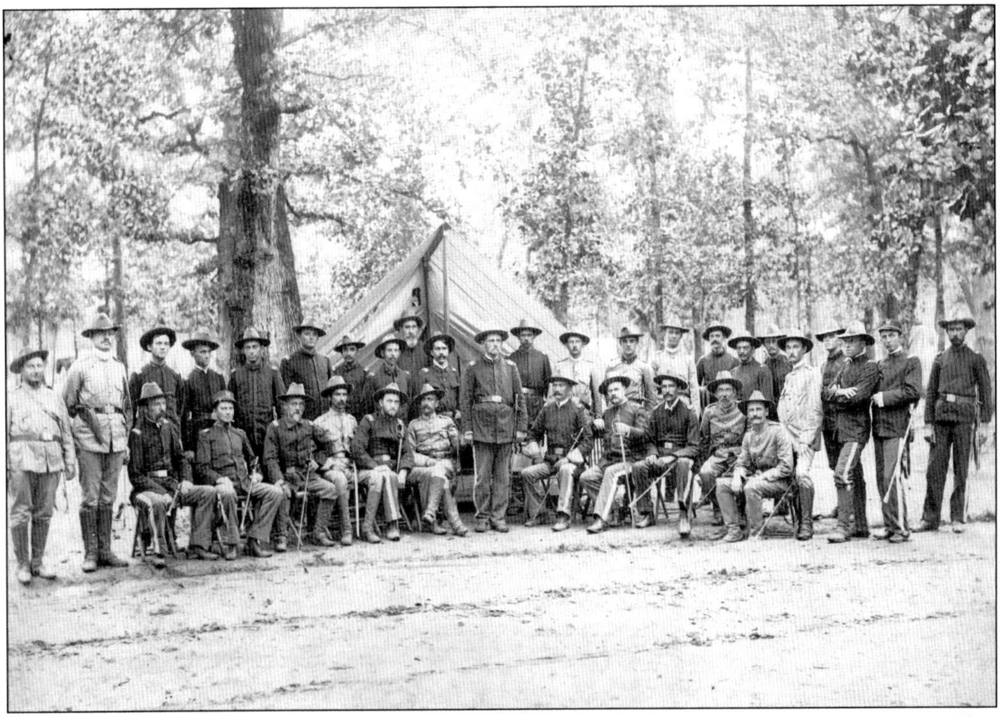

Company F, the 2nd Arkansas Volunteers, fought in the Spanish-American War in 1898. This photograph was taken at Camp Chickamauga.

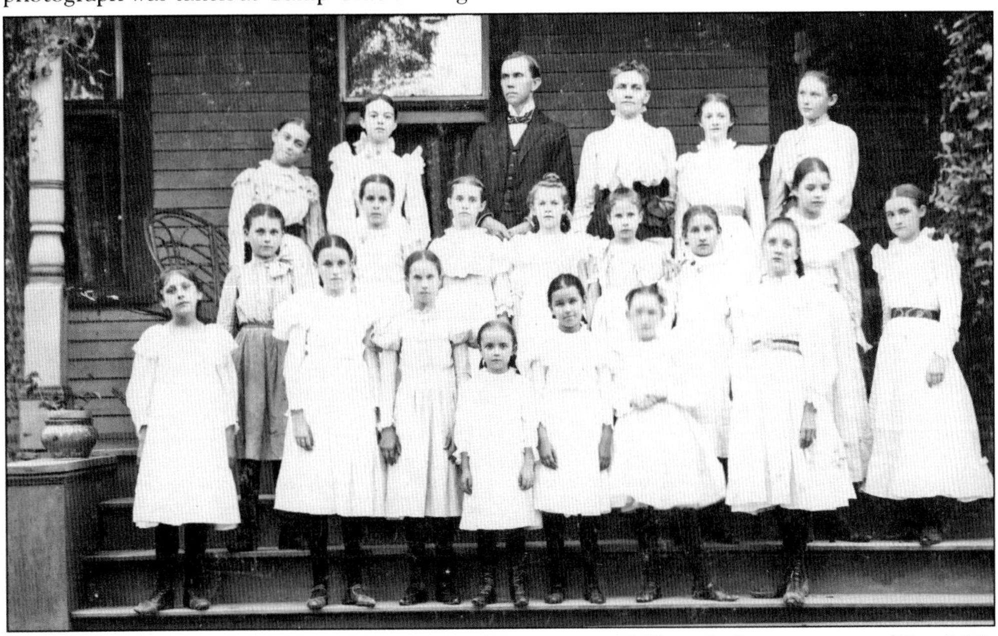

Ada E. Remmel organized the Junior League of Newport in 1898, with the assistance of Rev. N.B. Ricks, pastor of the Methodist Episcopal Church, South. Among the girls are Misses Phillips, Erwin, Lindsey, Ross, Ross, Irby, Maud Richardson, Birdie Bains (or Barns), Lizzie Irby, Lulu Wolff, May Whittaker, Mabel Stayton, Neill Bandy, Pearl Alexander, Rinn Price, Annie Belle Bridges, Louise Irby, Katie Price, and Gene Bandy. (Courtesy of the Butler Center.)

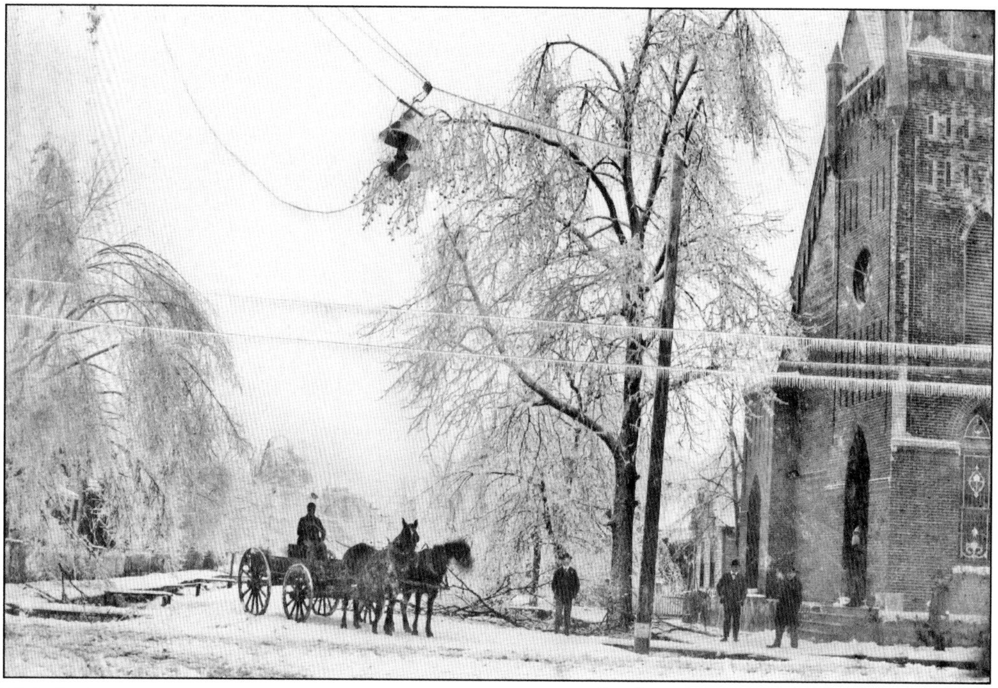

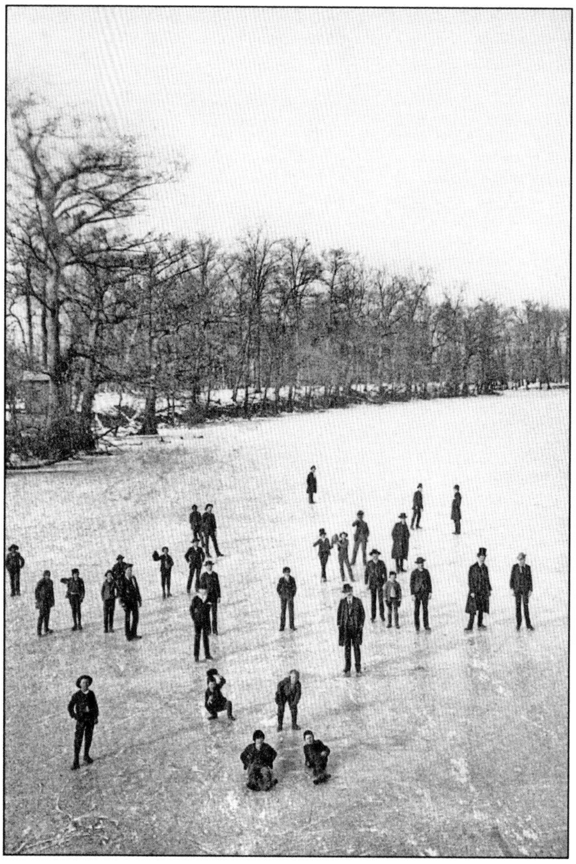

In the severe ice storm of 1898, the Methodist Episcopal Church, South, at the corner of Laurel and Second Streets is shown on a very cold day. This weather was unusual enough in the southern latitudes of Newport that the men had not purchased heavy overcoats.

In the same 1898 ice storm, Newport Lake froze solid, and men and boys had a fine time challenging Mother Nature. The banks of Newport Lake had been the site of many Indian encampments before the coming of the white settlers. The lake was a source of both pleasure and fish for early Newport residents.

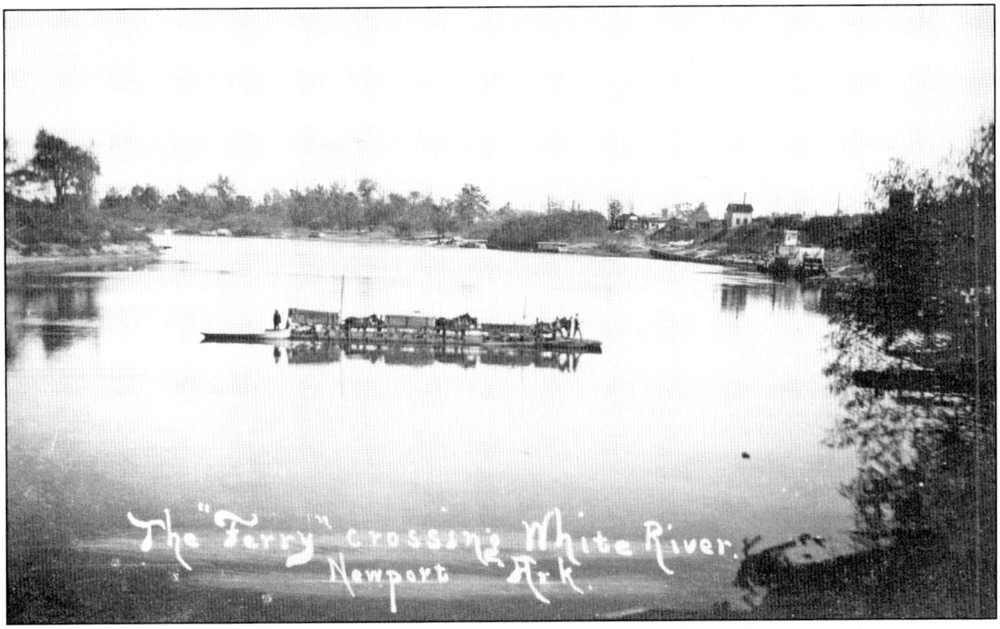

In the days before a bridge crossed the White River, ferries were the only means of transporting mules and wagons, with their loads of goods and people, from one side to the other. This postcard, with the signature white ink of photographer Parker, made its way to many points beyond Jackson County. (Courtesy of Ray Hanley.)

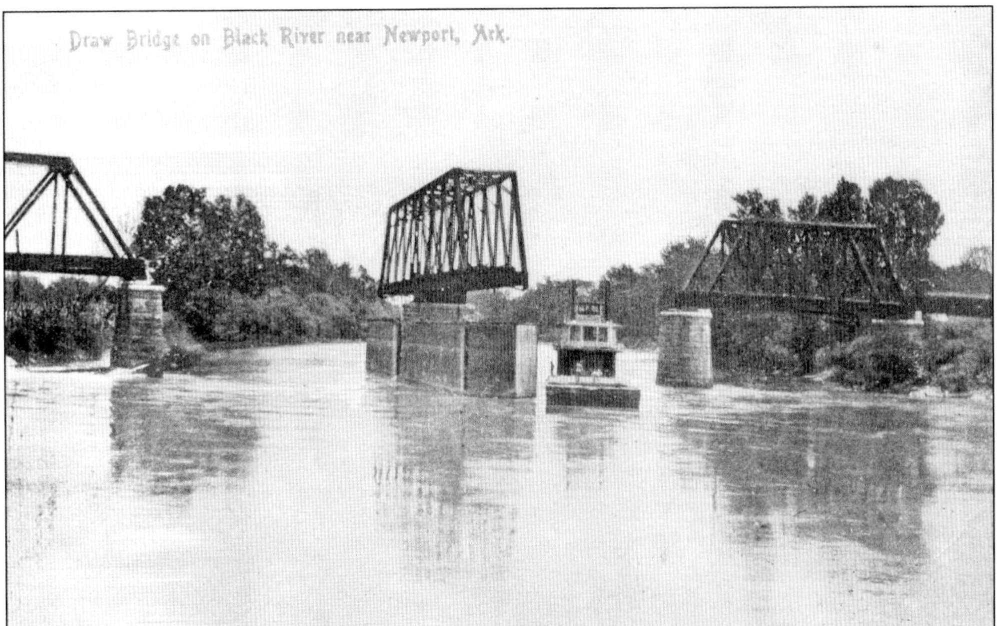

The railroad bridge over the Black River had a swinging section in order to let the tall steamboats pass through, as did most railroad bridges of this era. The St. Louis, Iron Mountain, and Southern Railway Company built a branch line at the little town of Diaz that led from the main line between St. Louis and Newport northwesterly to Batesville and on to Springfield, Missouri. (Courtesy of Ray Hanley.)

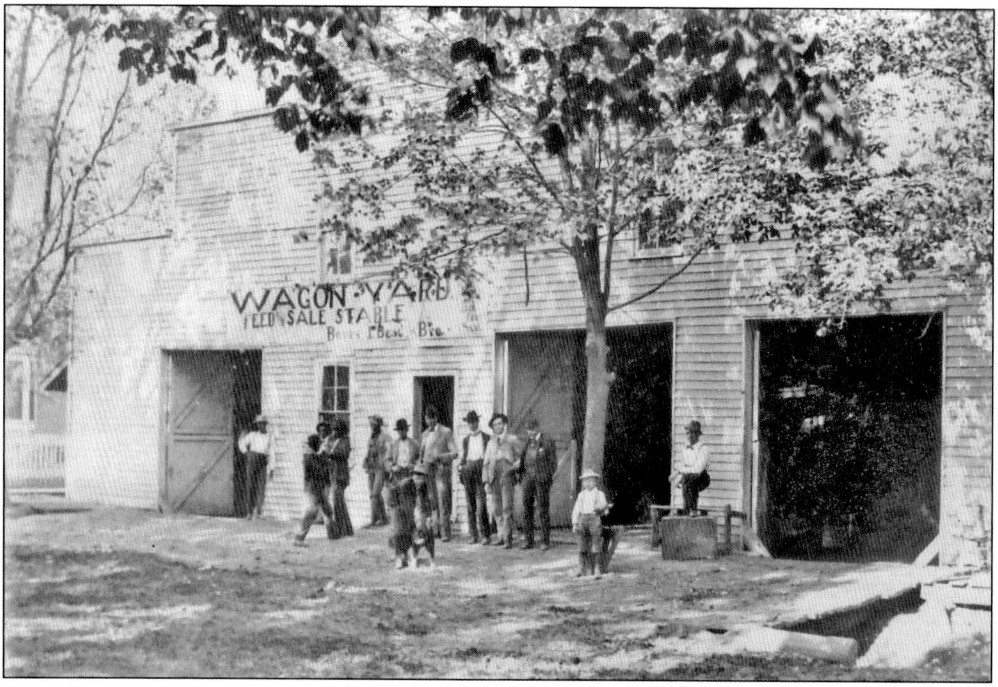

Berry J. Best ran a thriving wagon yard and livery stable at the turn of the 20th century. Here, he bought and sold horses and mules, built and repaired wagons, and sold feed for livestock, which were crucial to one of the major forms of transportation at that time.

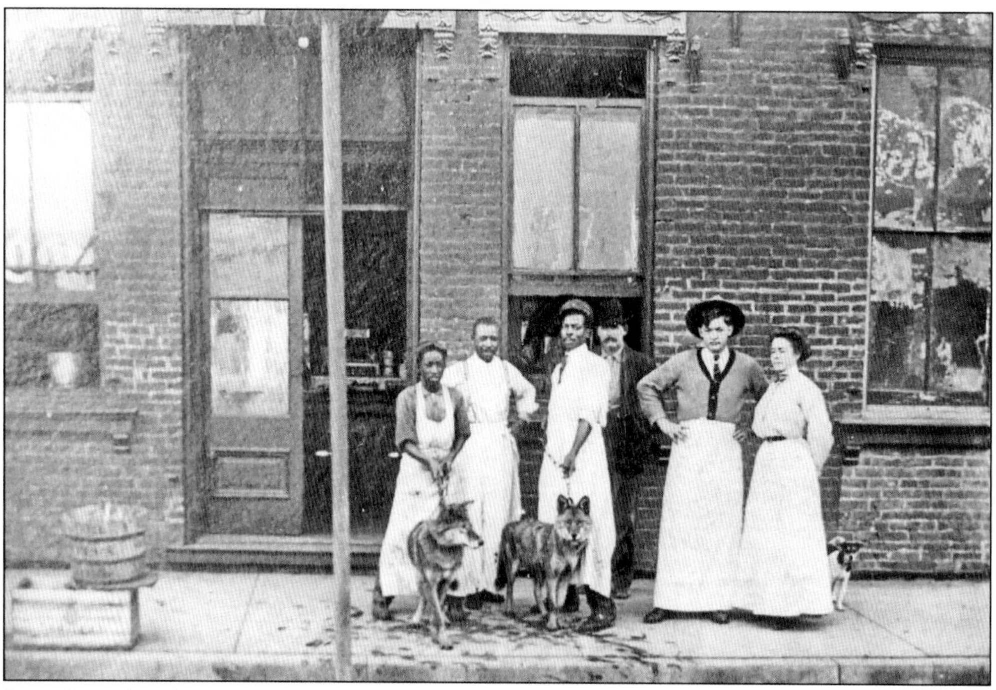

Berry Best's brother and sister-in-law Ira and Jewel Best owned a popular restaurant and saloon at the corner of Walnut and Front Streets. The kitchen help is pictured here standing outside with Ira's domesticated wolves. The man in the dark hat in the middle may be Ira.

Three

New Growth
The 1900s

Jackson County continued its steady growth during the first decade of the 20th century. New businesses and schools emerged all around the county at this time, providing shopping and education for the burgeoning population. The past was not forgotten, however, as reunions of former Confederate soldiers were held every few years, the most prominent among them being the reunions of the Jackson Guards, a company raised in Jacksonport in May 1861. These reunions gathered on the site of the old town of Elizabeth, which had been the third county seat.

The towns of Tuckerman and Swifton became thriving centers of local agriculture. Both were railroad towns, having developed on the pathway of the Iron Mountain Railway through the county. The little farming settlement of Grubbs developed on the eastern edge of the county. The towns of Auvergne, Shoffner, Weldon, and Tupelo were farming communities and sported their own railroad, the B&B (later the White and Black River Valley Railroad, and finally, the Chicago, Rock Island and Pacific).

Busy residents cleared virgin forests and put new rich soil into farming, with cotton the king, all over the county. With increasing populations came increasing lawlessness, and Newport built a new Jackson County Jail next to the county courthouse. A stone Gothic Revival building, the new jail was the site of several hangings in its tower.

Former resident Neill Phillips wrote that in 1900 Newport had its sidewalks "thronged not only with townspeople, but also with a sizeable transient population: gamblers, drummers, cotton buyers, and people brought in by trade and pearl fishing on the river, by traveling shows, and by the fact that the town was a railroad center." In the Front Street business district, the curbs were "blocked solidly with teams and wagons, the wagons packed with cotton bales if it were the fall, buyers moving among them . . . all the stores and sidewalks jammed with country people, white and black, doing their marketing and enjoying a dash of town life."

The county's economy was strong in this Edwardian decade, and local citizens enjoyed life in the many new amusements available, as well as the old standby, a day on the river. Life was good in Jackson County for almost all its citizens, and the American Dream of upward mobility seemed to have found a hearty form of expression.

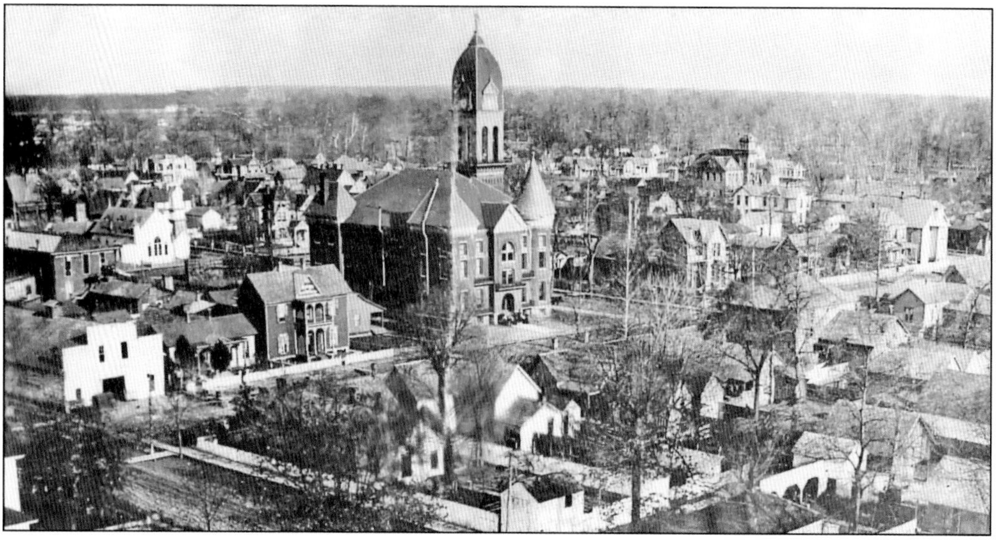

The newly constructed Jackson County Courthouse (with bell tower and cupola) stands at the corner of Third and Main Streets. The First Christian Church is the white building to the upper left of the photograph. The large building to the upper right is the Newport Free (or public) School. The road traversing the lower part of the picture is Second Street, and the business district lies one block closer to the viewer.

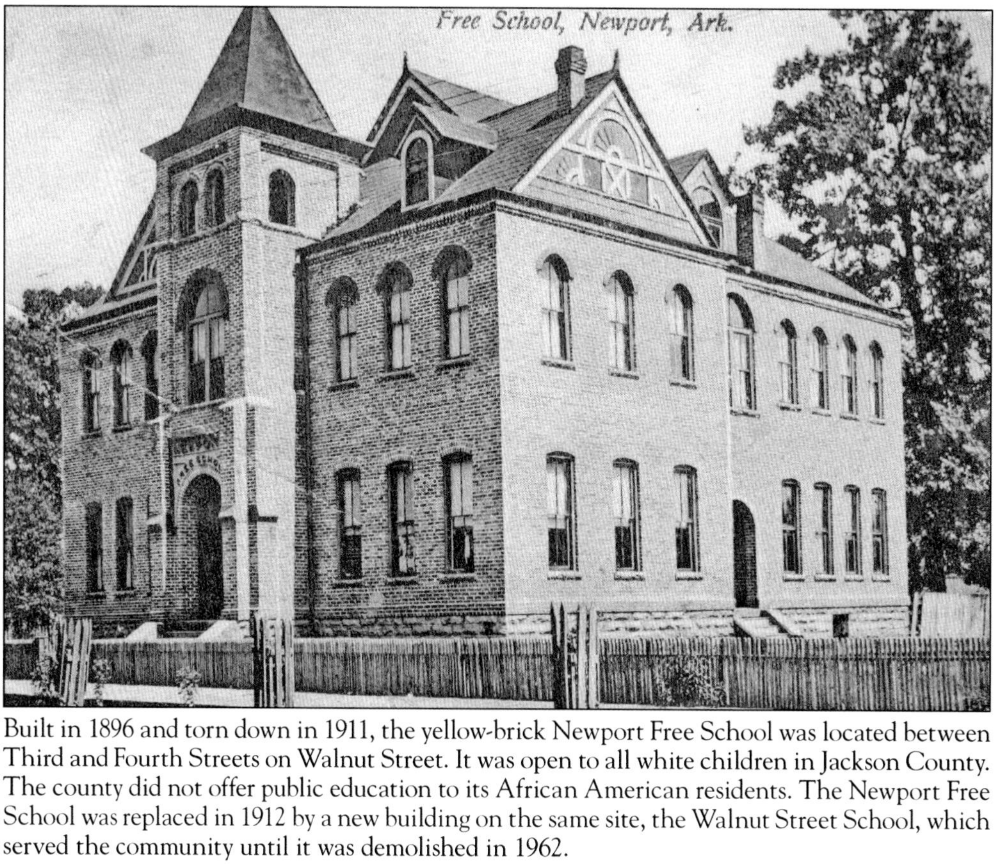

Built in 1896 and torn down in 1911, the yellow-brick Newport Free School was located between Third and Fourth Streets on Walnut Street. It was open to all white children in Jackson County. The county did not offer public education to its African American residents. The Newport Free School was replaced in 1912 by a new building on the same site, the Walnut Street School, which served the community until it was demolished in 1962.

The tennis club was a favorite diversion for some of the young ladies of Newport. Pictured here are, from left to right, (first row) Lucy Watson and Lottie Dill; (second row) Elizabeth "Lib" Brandenburg; (third row) Narcissa "Narcie" Phillips and Ellen Watson. (Courtesy of Tim Watson Sr.)

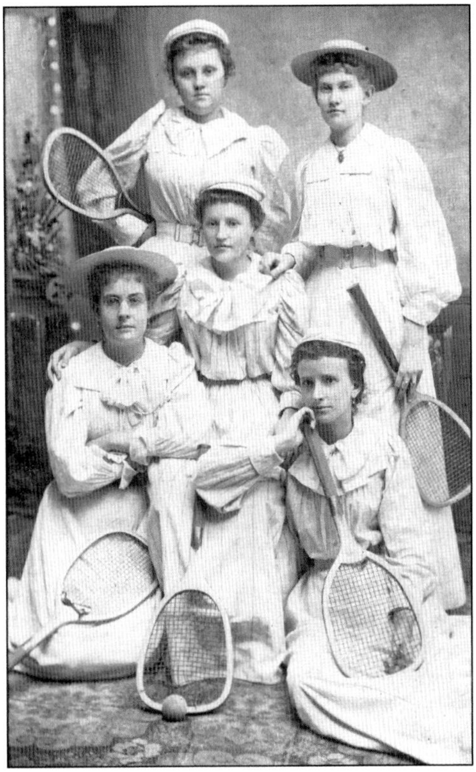

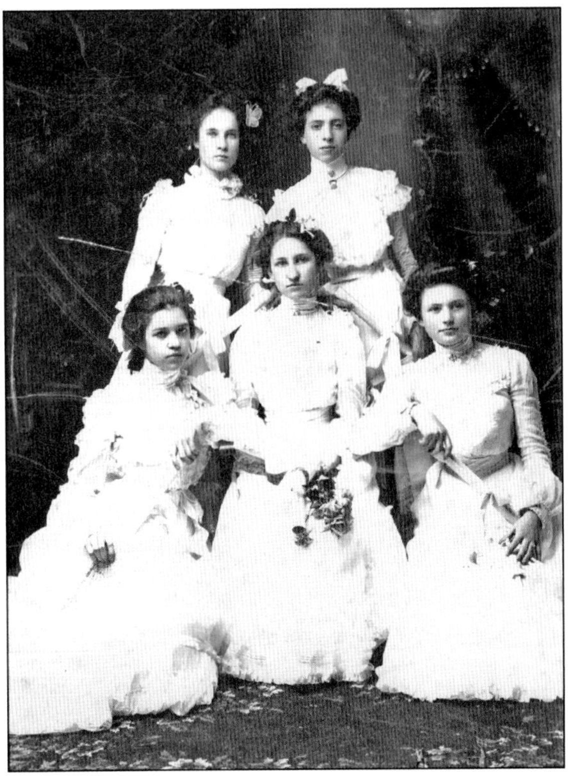

The first class graduated from Newport High School in 1901. The commencement was held in the elegant and ornate Newport Opera House at Second and Laurel Streets. The five graduates are, from left to right, (first row) May Whittaker, Lula Wolff (later Stevens), and Minne Ross; (second row) Louise Irby (later Stephens) and Janie Stephens (later White). The boys may have left school already to work in the fields or attend boarding school.

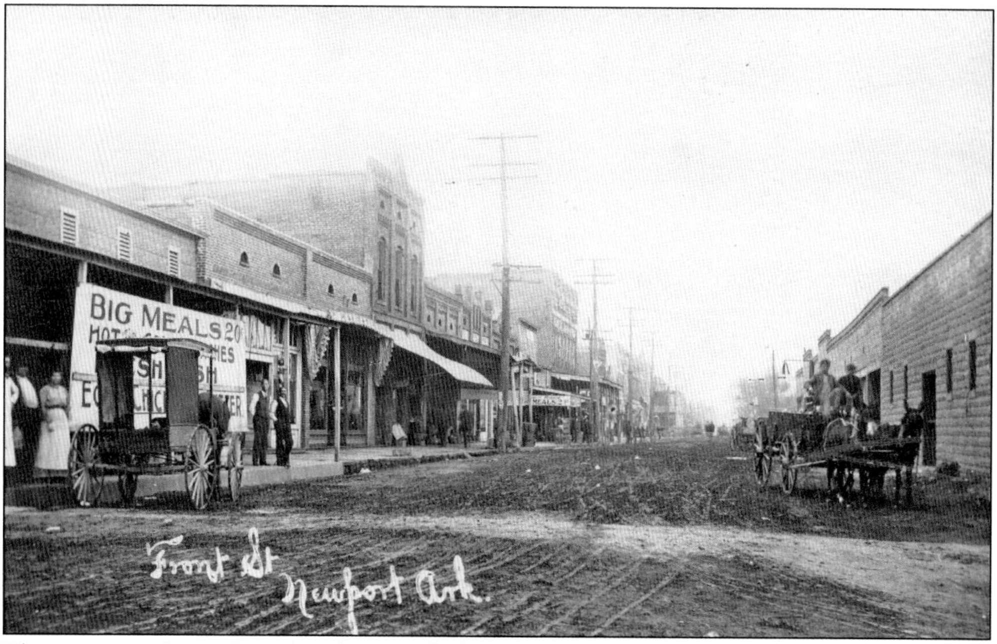

The signature white ink on this photograph shows that it was taken by local photographer Parker. It features the east end of Front Street in 1907. Two establishments in the same block offer hot meals for 20¢.

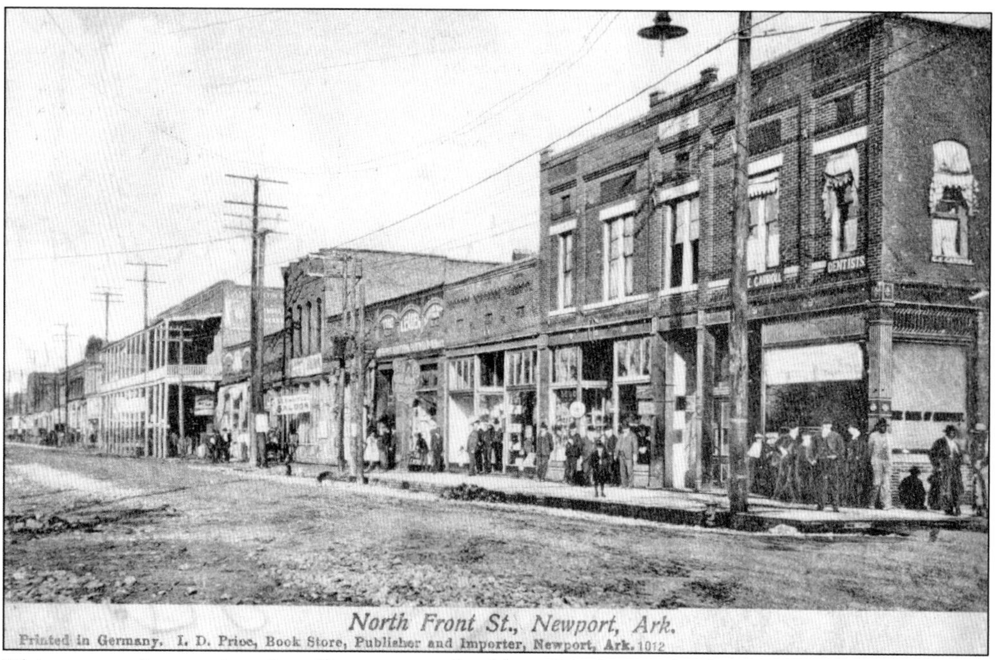

This postcard was printed in Germany and sold in I.D. Price's bookstore on Newport's Front Street in 1907. It features a view of the west end of the street, facing the railroad and the river. The city fathers were already using mussel shells, abundant in the river, to pave the muddy streets. (Courtesy of Ray Hanley.)

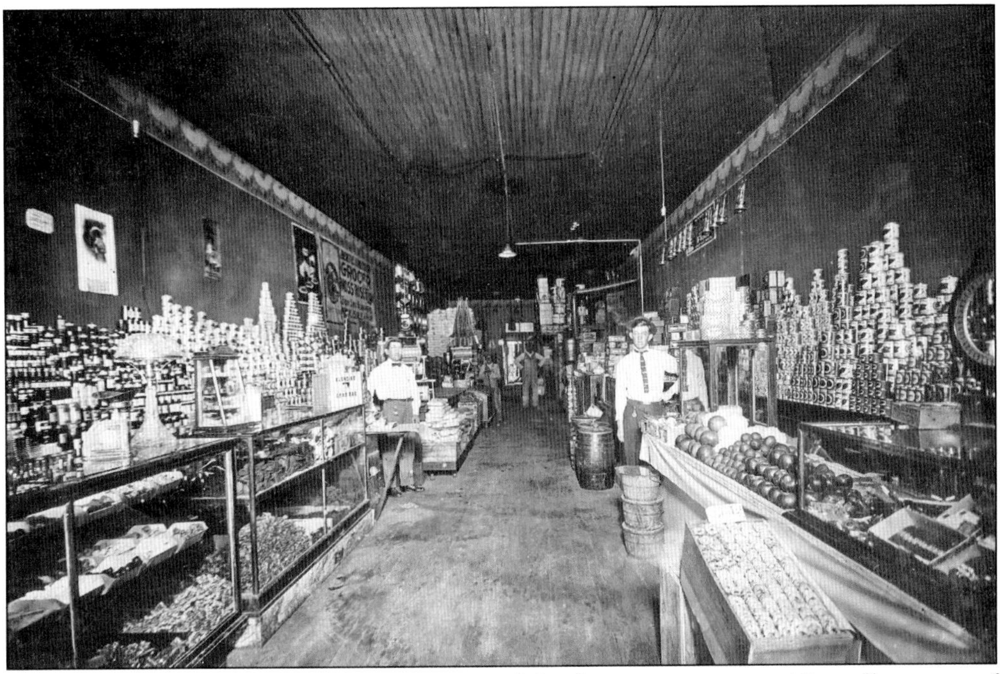

Snetzer's Grocery Store in Newport was one of the finest in town, providing all manner of "fancy groceries" as well as the usual stock. Bert Snetzer's store on Front Street was a constant in Newport's economy for 51 years. Bert is on the left in this photograph, and his nephew Charles is on the right, with two unidentified helpers in the background. Dried apple rings in the foreground tempted shoppers as they walked in the door.

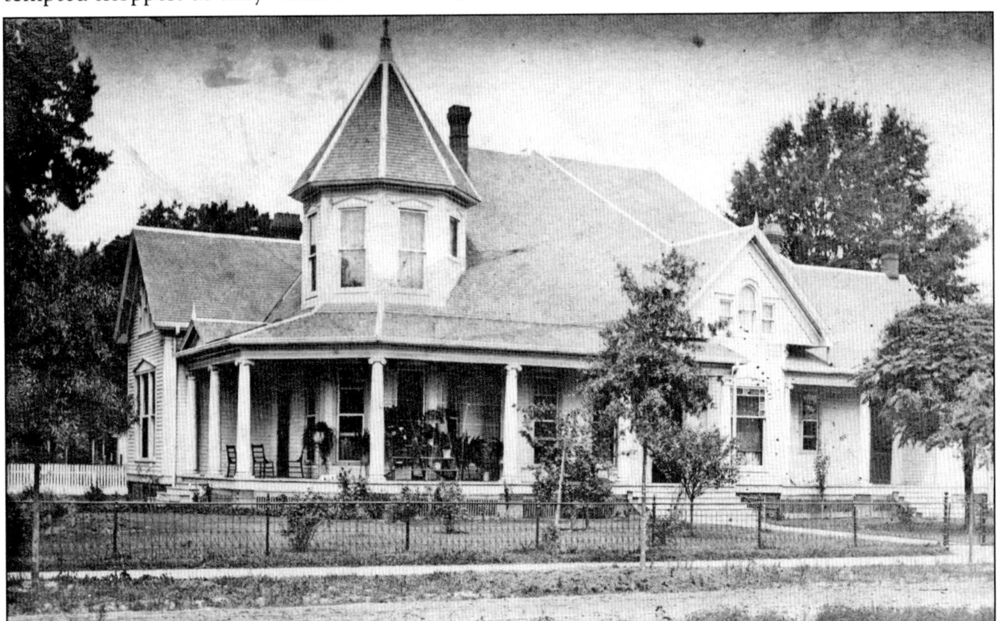

This is thought to be T.D. Snetzer's home, and it is typical of the Victorian architecture that was common in this period throughout Newport and the South. Note the Ionic columns, the octagonal tower, and the large porch.

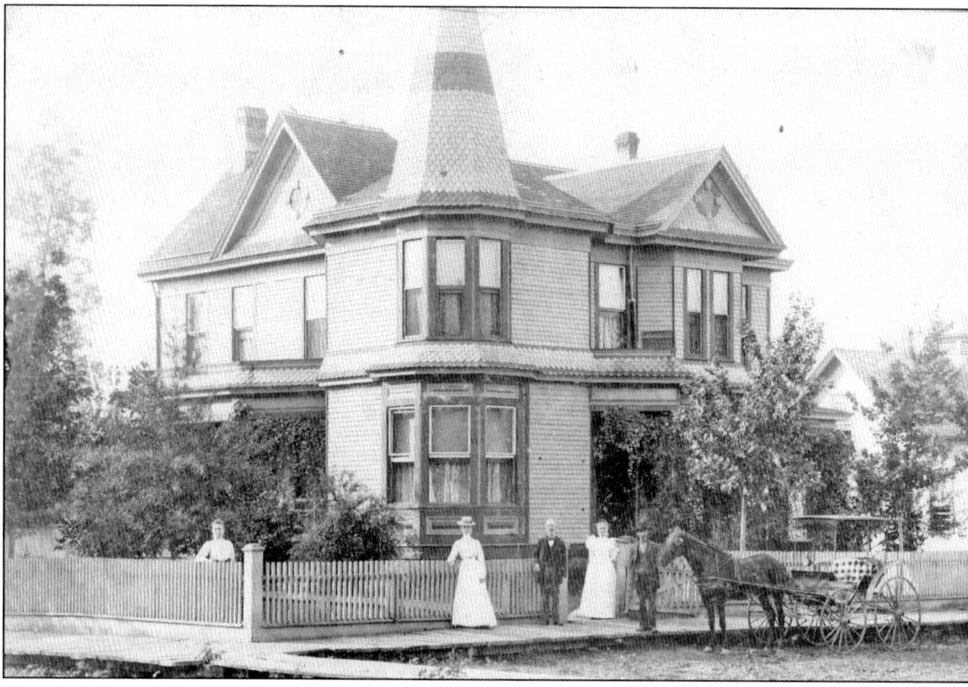

W.B. Empie built a fine Queen Anne home at the corner of Fourth and Laurel Streets that later became known as the Van Dyke House when Empie's daughter Lula married Percy Van Dyke. Members of the Van Dyke family lived in the home for over 80 years. Pictured here are, from left to right, Ada Remmel, Lula Empie, W.B. Empie, Louise Empie, coachman Patrick ?, and Madge the horse.

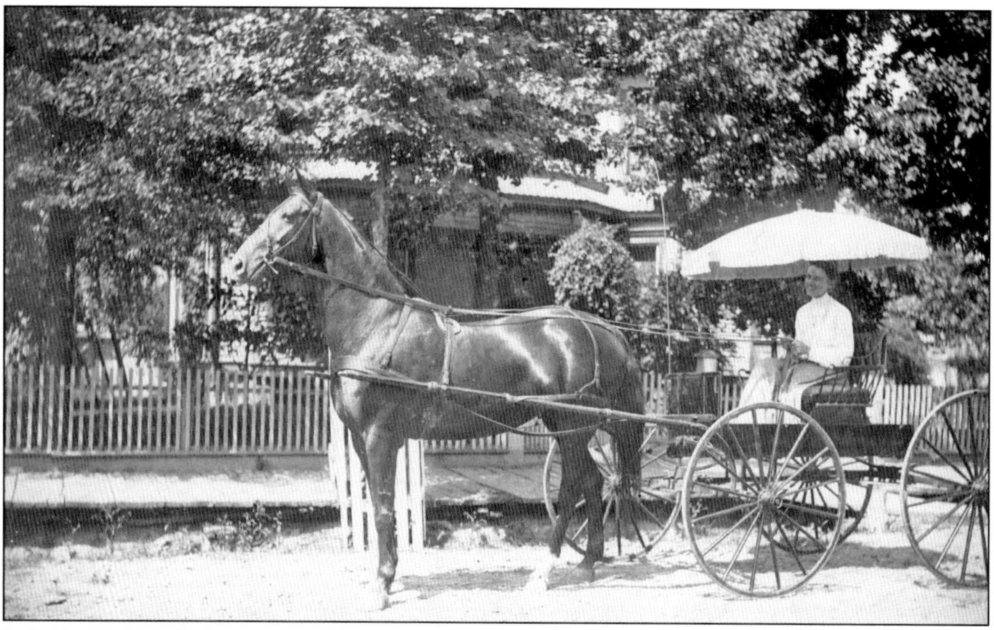

Lula Empie Van Dyke is pictured here seated in the family buggy. The carriage horse, Nellie, is harnessed. This is a typical scene in Newport before the automobile age. Many ladies had their own light buggies as well as a family surrey. They were good horsewomen as well.

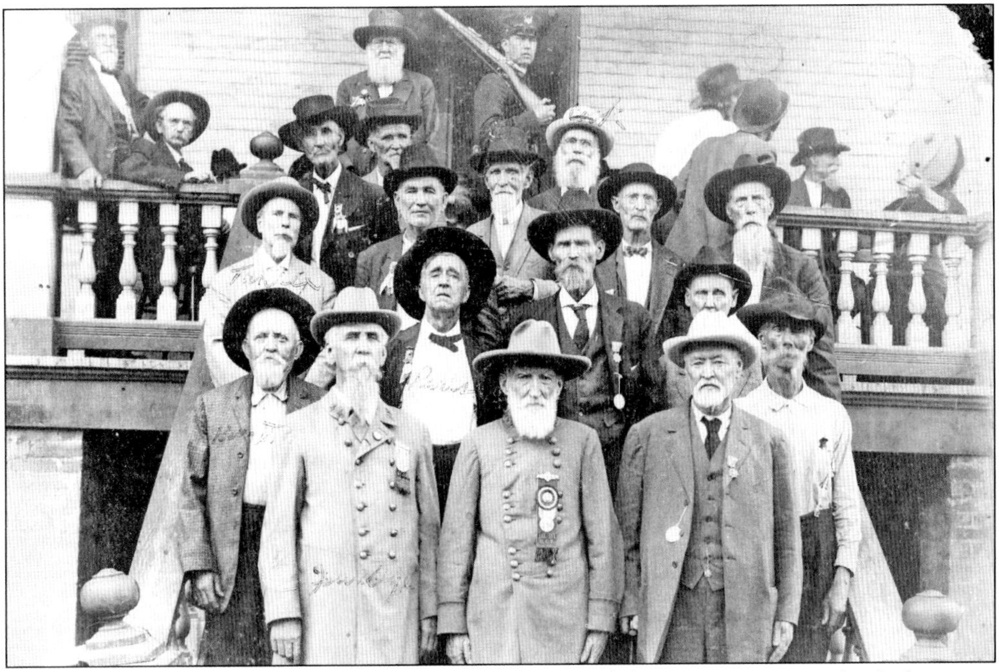

These old soldiers are veterans of the Jackson Guards, a Confederate company raised in Jacksonport in May 1861 that served in the Virginia theater as Company G of the 1st Arkansas Infantry Regiment, CSA. The date they left was the day before the state of Arkansas seceded from the Union. Two of the leaders of the group are Robert Shaver (front center) and William Bevens (front right).

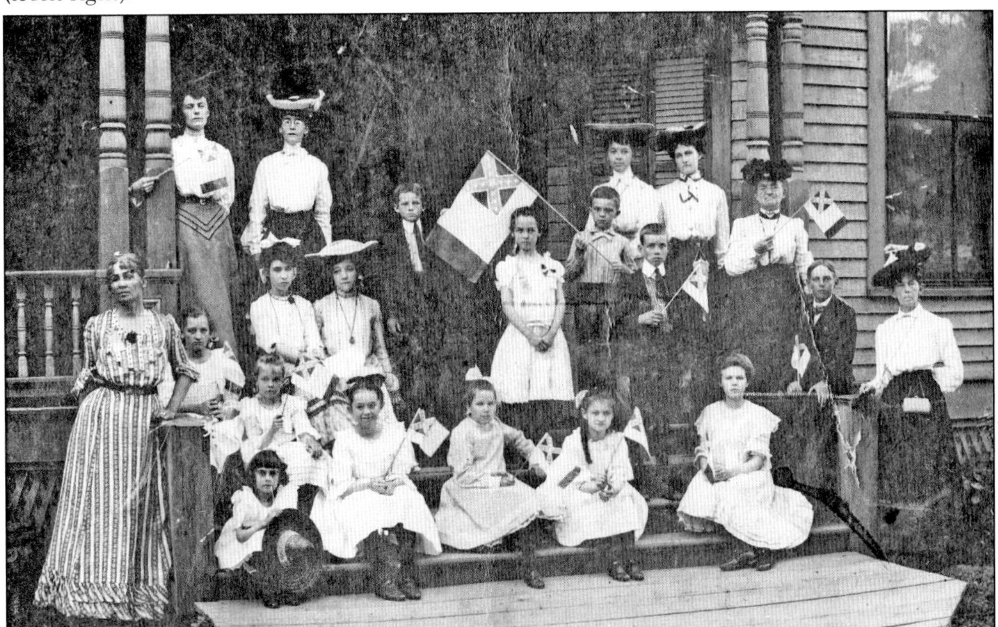

Founded by Miss Jim Watson (top left), the daughter of Confederate general James Fleming Fagan, the Junior Chapter of the Southern Memorial Association (United Daughters of the Confederacy) poses in 1903 on the porch of the Watson home at Second and Elm Streets in Newport.

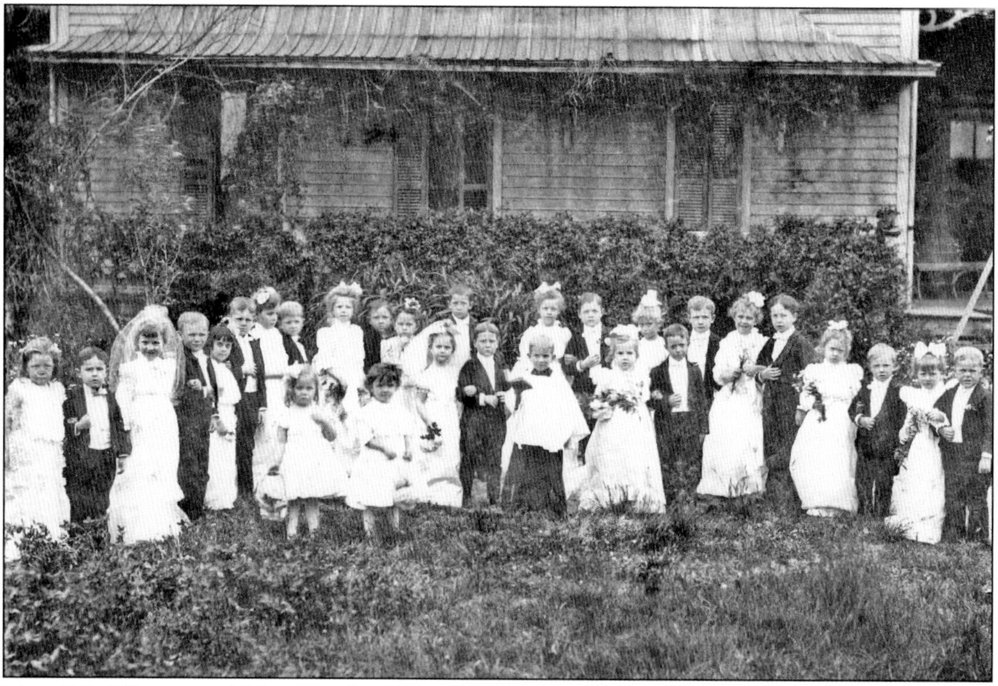

Mrs. O.D. Watson and Mrs. Charles Wilmans sponsored this Tom Thumb wedding as a benefit for the United Daughters of the Confederacy. The performance was in the Newport Opera House. This photograph was taken in front of the Brandenburg house on the southwest corner of Third and Vine Streets.

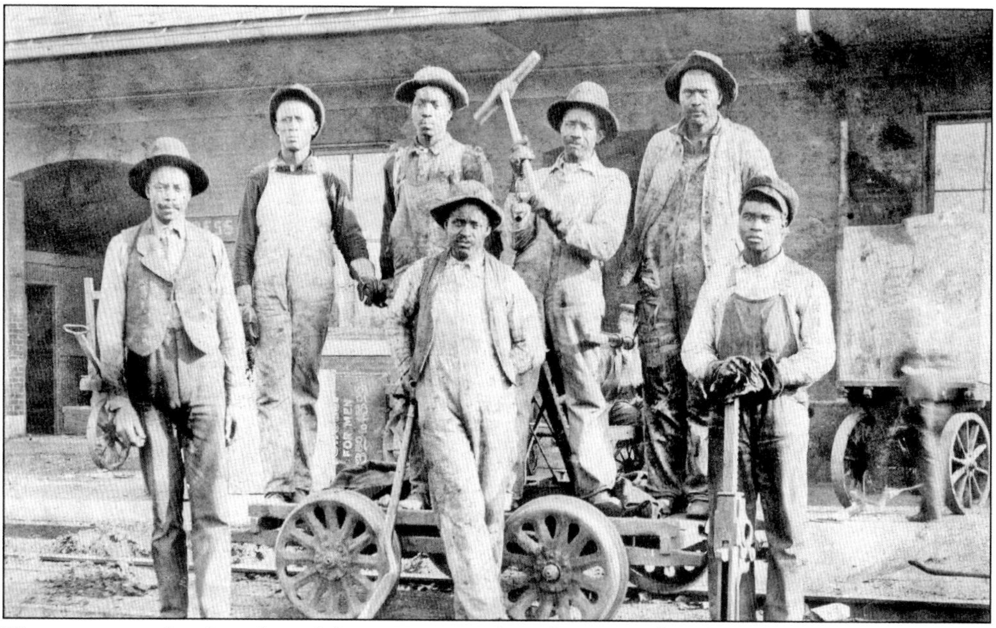

These unnamed rail workers did not get invited to the Tom Thumb wedding, and they would not have wanted to support the work of the UDC. Their faces and clothes show that they had hard lives. They worked up and down the rails repairing ties, replacing spikes, and clearing the tracks of debris.

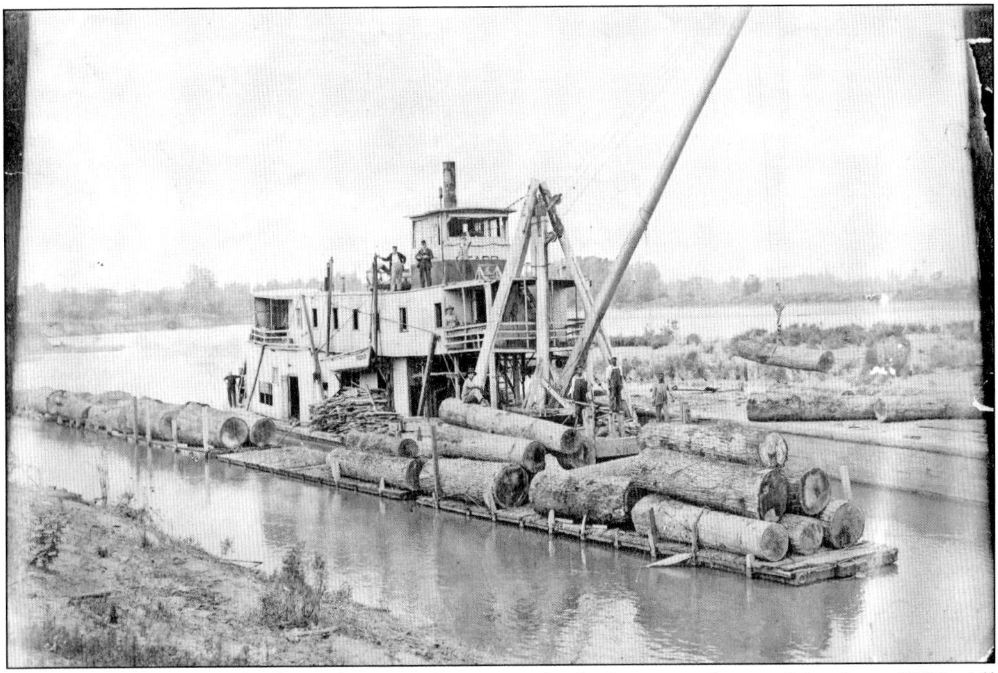

The paddleboat *Sears* loads timber onto barges at the Jacksonport log yard in about 1900. All types of lumber—including cottonwood, gum, hickory, elm, oak, maple, ash, and cedar—were brought down from the Black, Current, and upper White Rivers to Jacksonport for shipment. The White River Cooperage Company operated there at that time. The Riddell Barge Line made regular trips to Jacksonport bringing timber from upriver.

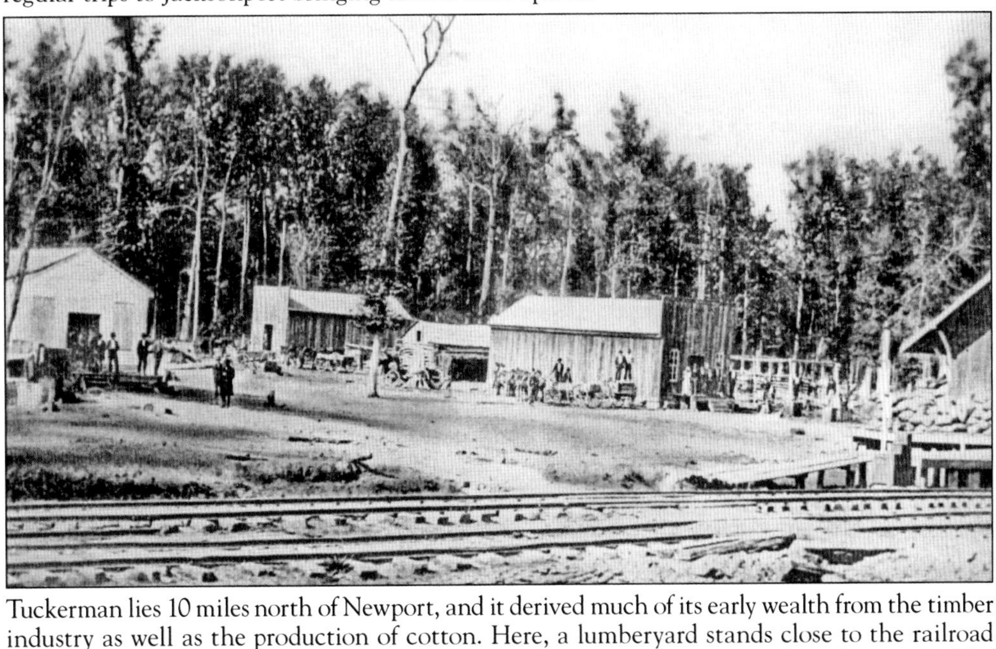

Tuckerman lies 10 miles north of Newport, and it derived much of its early wealth from the timber industry as well as the production of cotton. Here, a lumberyard stands close to the railroad tracks, since Tuckerman is not situated on the river. This photograph was taken about 1900. The railroad is the St. Louis, Iron Mountain, and Southern, to become the Missouri Pacific in 1917 and later the Union Pacific.

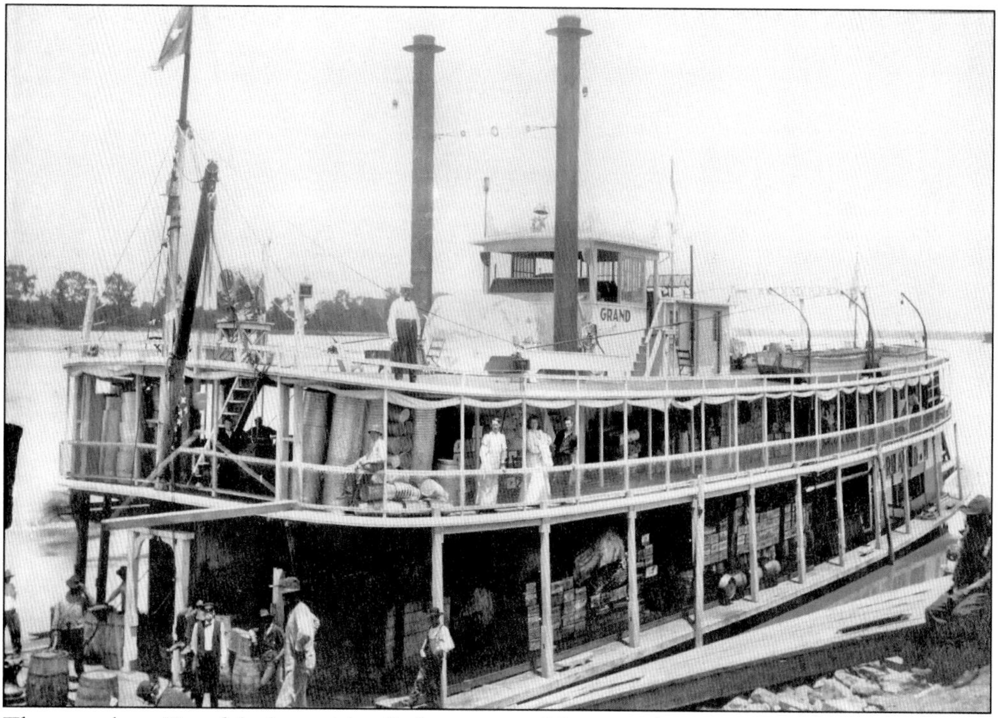

The steamboat *Grand* docks at either Jacksonport or Newport about 1903. It seems to be coming upriver since the deck is loaded with boxes and buckets instead of bales of cotton. The containers are most likely filled with salt, sugar, coffee, and even oysters, and the decks of the boat will be covered with cotton bales when it turns downstream.

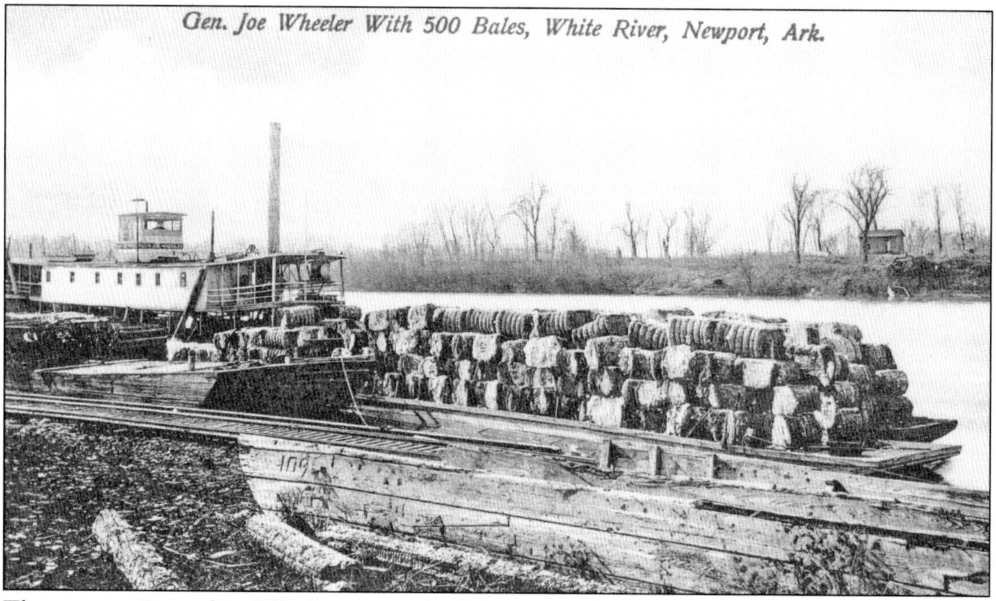

The steamer *General Joe Wheeler* ran on the White and Black Rivers and is shown at Newport in 1904, loaded with 500 bales of cotton. Built in 1899, the boat was owned by Capt. W.A. "Billy" Joyce and Capt. Tom Stallings of Newport when this photograph was made. A big rise tore the boat loose from its moorings in January 1906, and its was wrecked about half a mile below Newport.

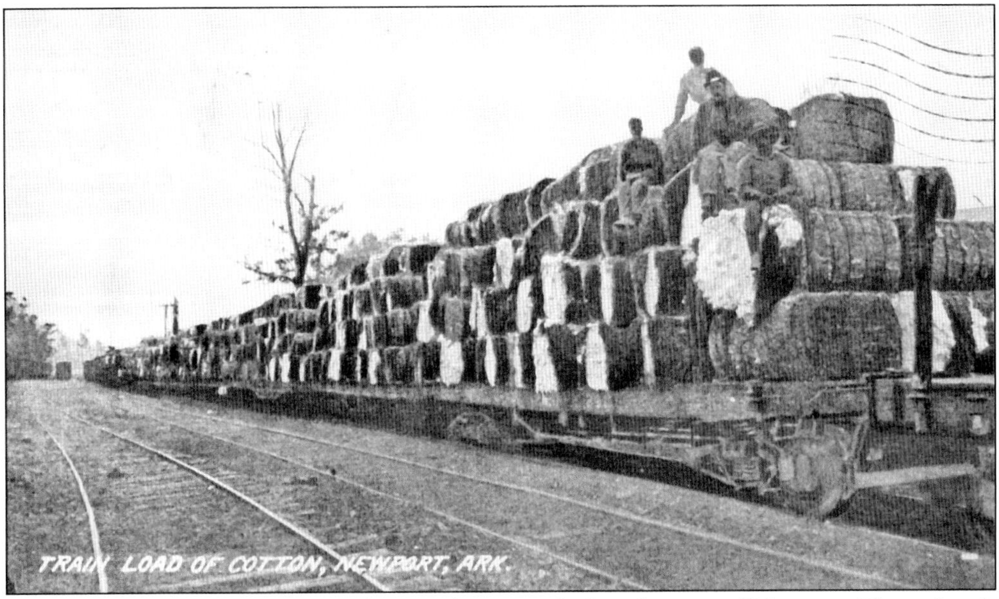

This postcard shows a trainload of cotton being readied to ship out of Newport. The railroads would soon surpass the steamboats as carriers of the area's farm crops, and the age of the steamboat on the South's inland waterways would be gone with the wind. (Courtesy of Robert Craig.)

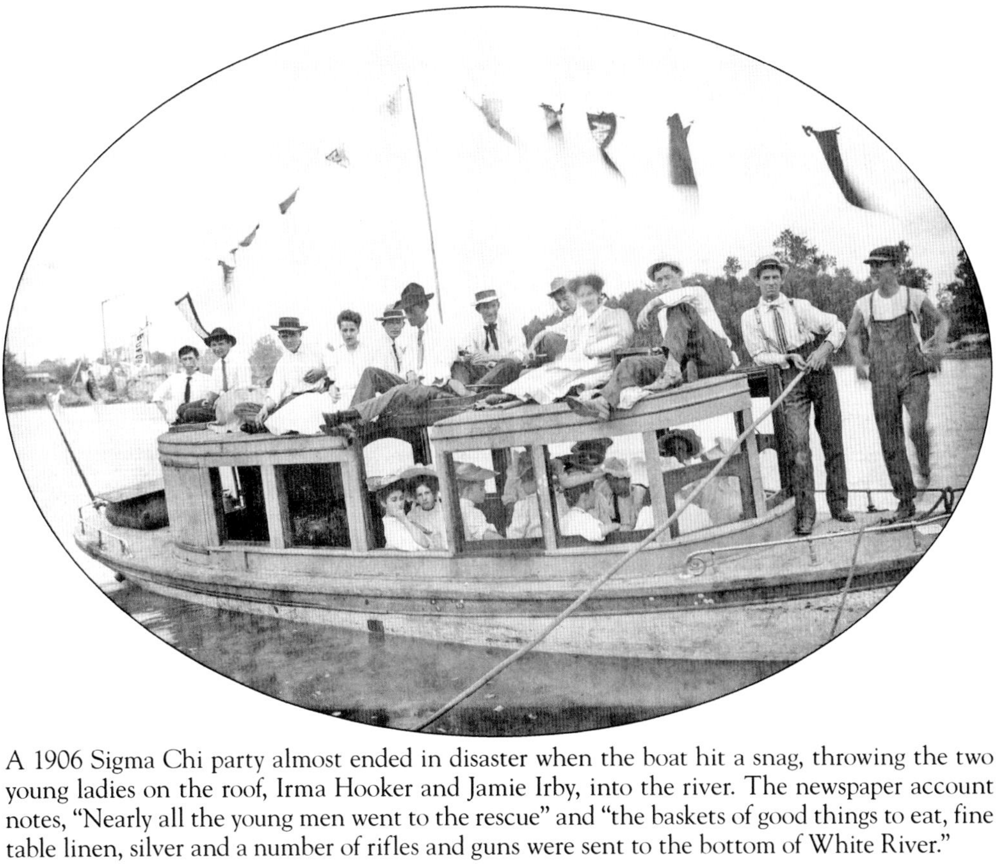

A 1906 Sigma Chi party almost ended in disaster when the boat hit a snag, throwing the two young ladies on the roof, Irma Hooker and Jamie Irby, into the river. The newspaper account notes, "Nearly all the young men went to the rescue" and "the baskets of good things to eat, fine table linen, silver and a number of rifles and guns were sent to the bottom of White River."

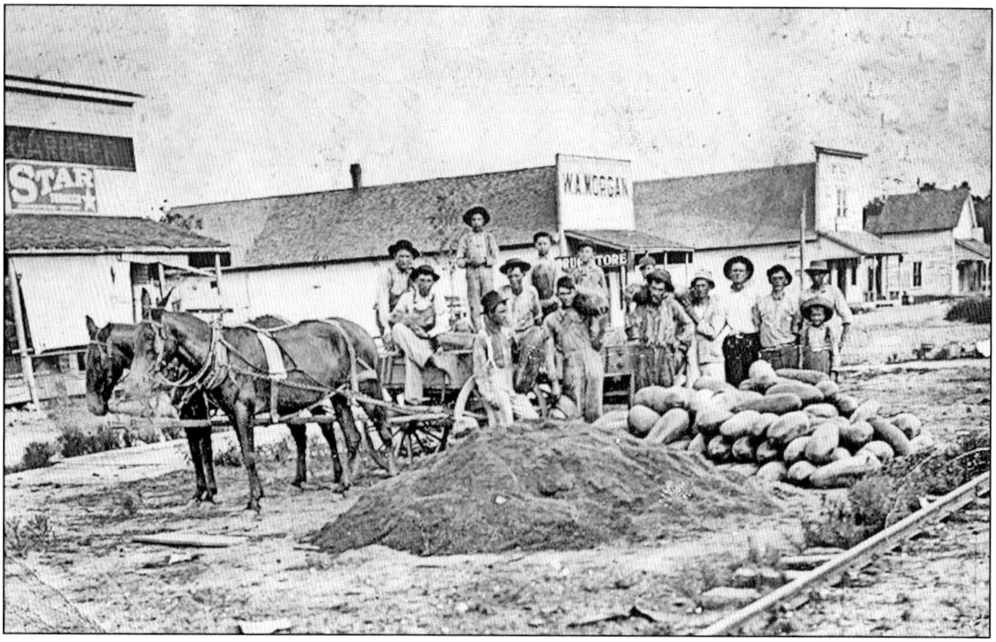

These men and boys are pictured here on Main Street in Tupelo, in southern Jackson County, next to an unloaded a wagon that carried watermelons. Stacked next to the railroad tracks, the melons were obviously intended for shipment to market. The notation on the back explains, "Ed Wallace raised watermelons. Edd Taylor hauled watermelons." Undoubtedly, a few of the melons escaped shipment and ended up in picnic baskets.

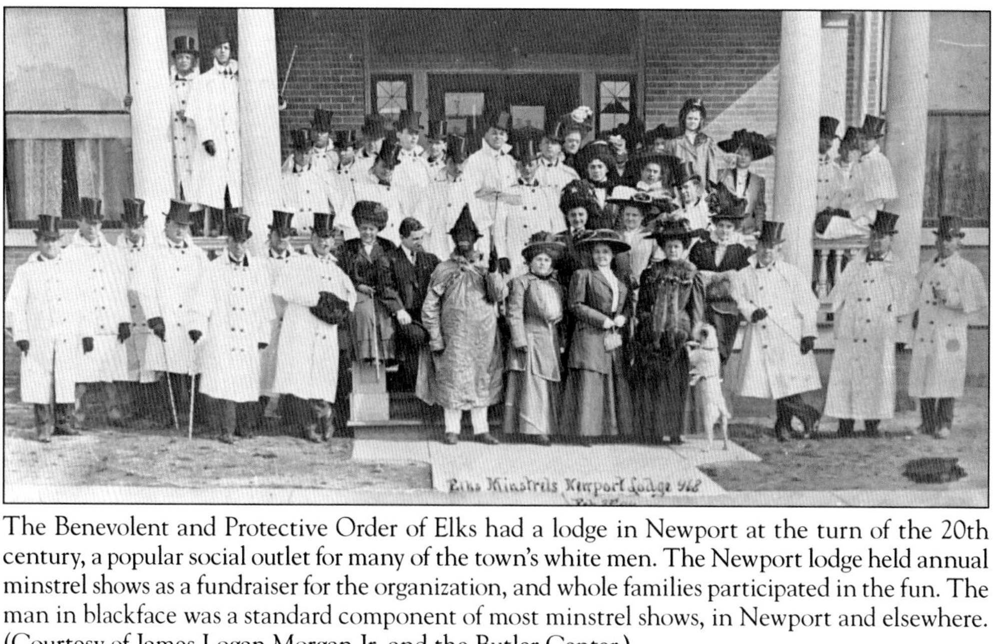

The Benevolent and Protective Order of Elks had a lodge in Newport at the turn of the 20th century, a popular social outlet for many of the town's white men. The Newport lodge held annual minstrel shows as a fundraiser for the organization, and whole families participated in the fun. The man in blackface was a standard component of most minstrel shows, in Newport and elsewhere. (Courtesy of James Logan Morgan Jr. and the Butler Center.)

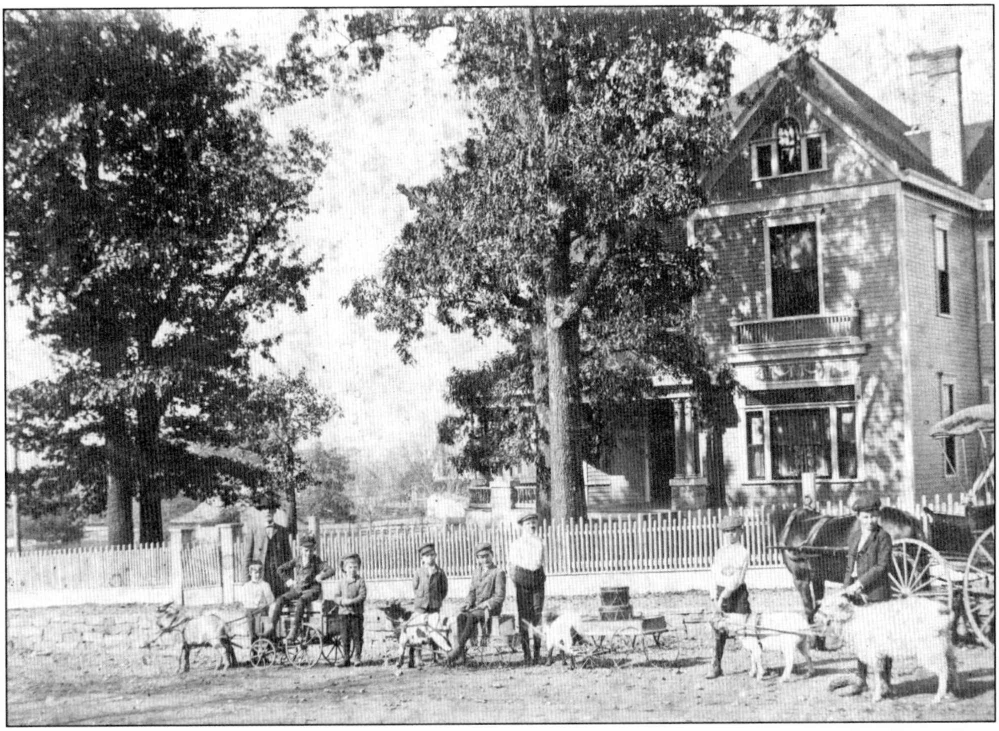

The Shoffners were wealthy landowners in the southern Jackson County town that bore their name. Here, the patriarch seems to be supervising a goat-cart race among his sons or grandsons. The lovely two-story home with much attention to architectural detail shows refinement and taste, as do the clothes of all of the children. (Courtesy of James Logan Morgan Jr. and the Butler Center.)

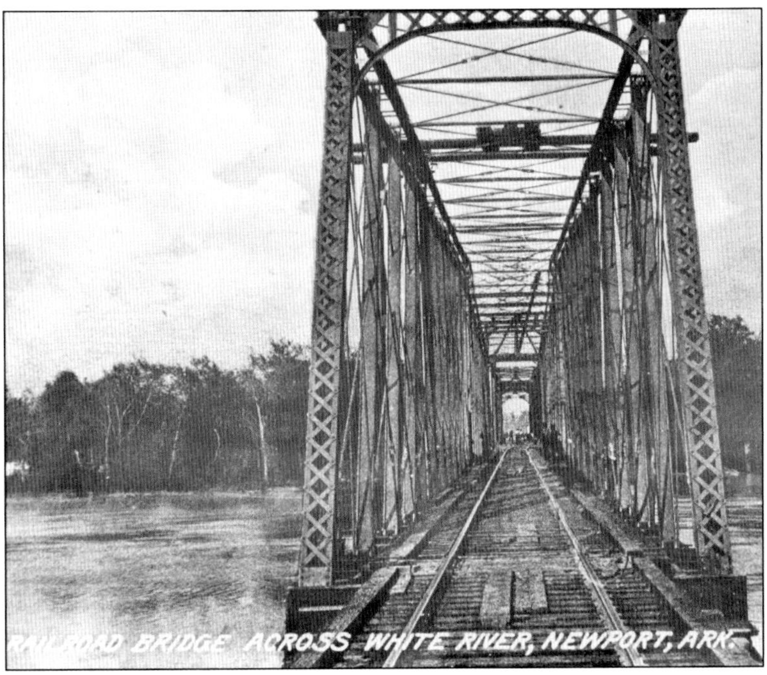

This postcard shows the St. Louis, Iron Mountain, and Southern Railway bridge over the White River, three miles downstream from Newport. The tracks then proceeded through town along the bluff side of the river, protecting the rails from the frequent overflows in the spring and fall. (Courtesy of James Logan Morgan Jr. and the Butler Center.)

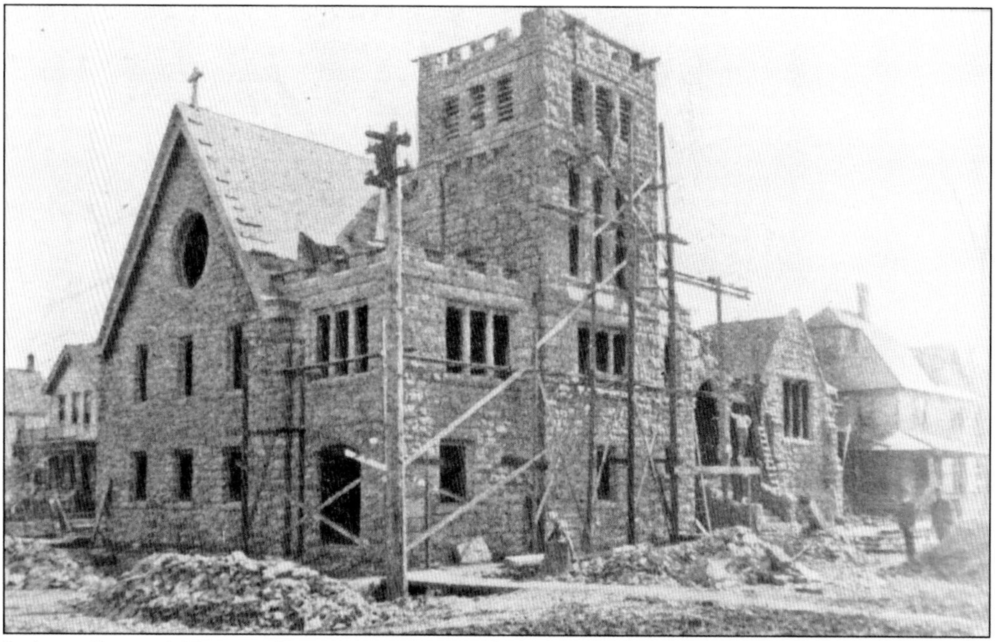

Jackson County's Episcopal congregation moved into Newport in 1879, changing its name from Grace Church to St. Paul's Episcopal Church and building a small wooden structure at the corner of Third and Hazel Streets. In 1904, St. Paul's built a fine new church on the same lot in the style of an English country stone church. (Courtesy of James Logan Morgan Jr. and the Butler Center.)

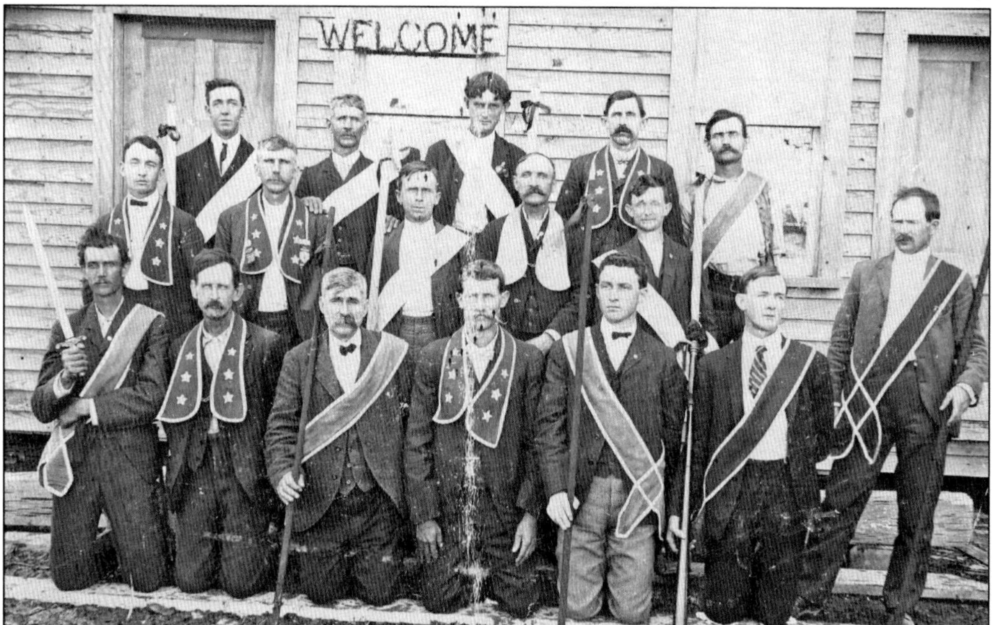

The Independent Order of Odd Fellows had a chapter in the town of Grubbs, east of Newport. Among those pictured here in 1908 are, in no particular order, Jim W. Ivy, Perry P. Stegall, Alonzo Moseley, John E. Williams, Jacob M. Kinard, M.S. "Pony" Littleton, Mem Blansett, John McEllrath, Nathan Jay Goss, Milzie Stegall, and Dock Camp. (Courtesy of James Logan Morgan Jr. and the Butler Center.)

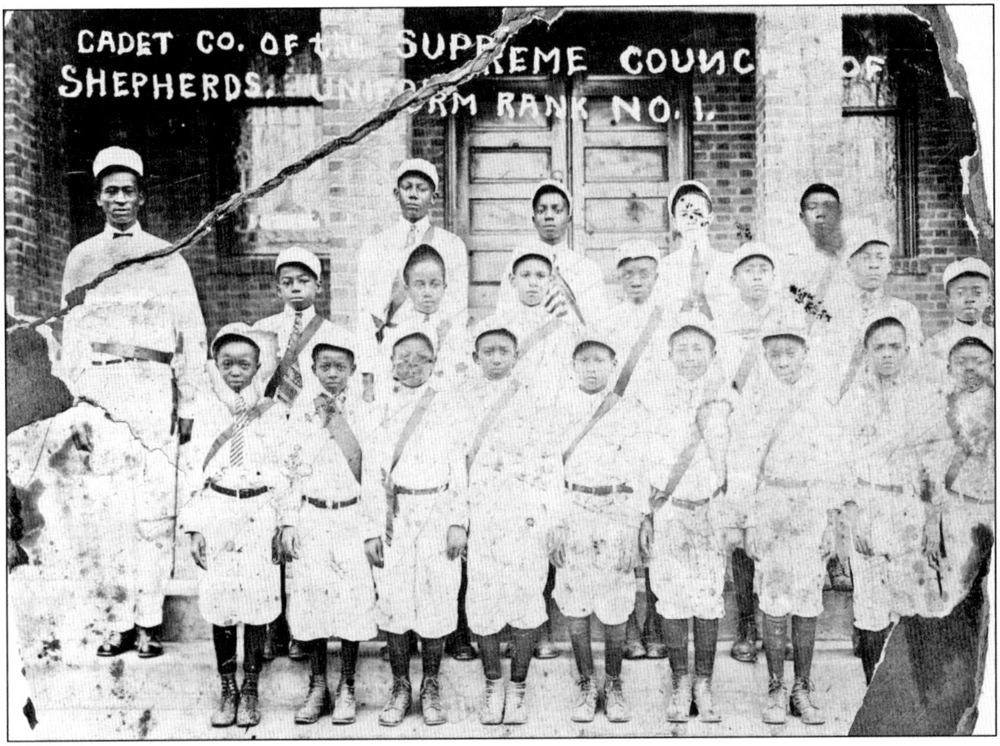

The cadet company of the Supreme Council of Shepherds, Uniform Rank No. 1 was an organization for the benefit of African American youngsters, apparently in Newport. This photograph from the early 1900s captures the pride that these young men felt in their recognition, uniforms, and achievement. (Courtesy of James Logan Morgan Jr. and the Butler Center.)

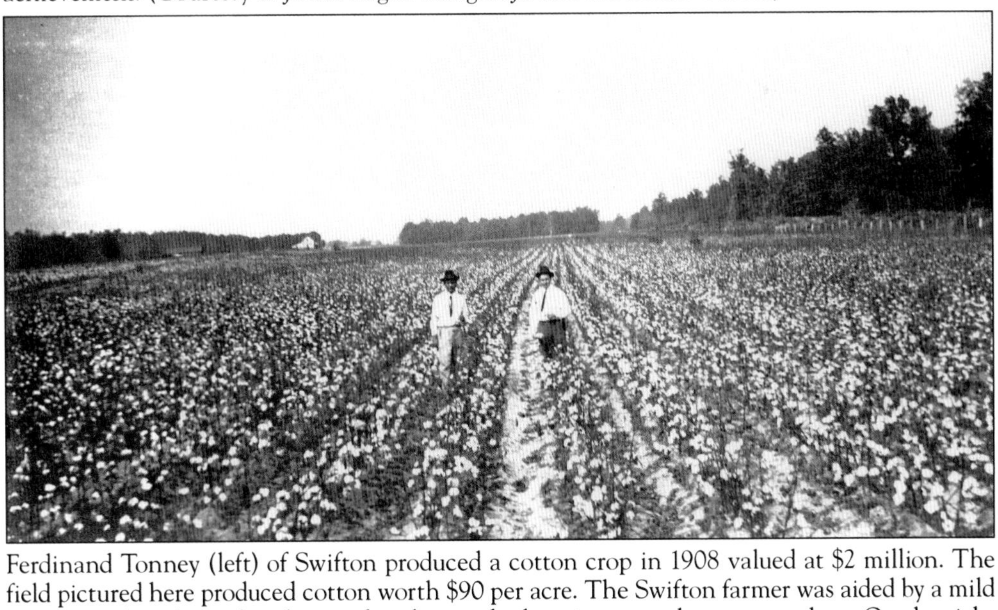

Ferdinand Tonney (left) of Swifton produced a cotton crop in 1908 valued at $2 million. The field pictured here produced cotton worth $90 per acre. The Swifton farmer was aided by a mild climate, rich soil, an abundance of timber, and a location near the great markets. On the right is W.D. Morgan, who was president of the local bank. In 1910, Tonney produced the first rice grown in Jackson County. (Courtesy of J.W. Hulen.)

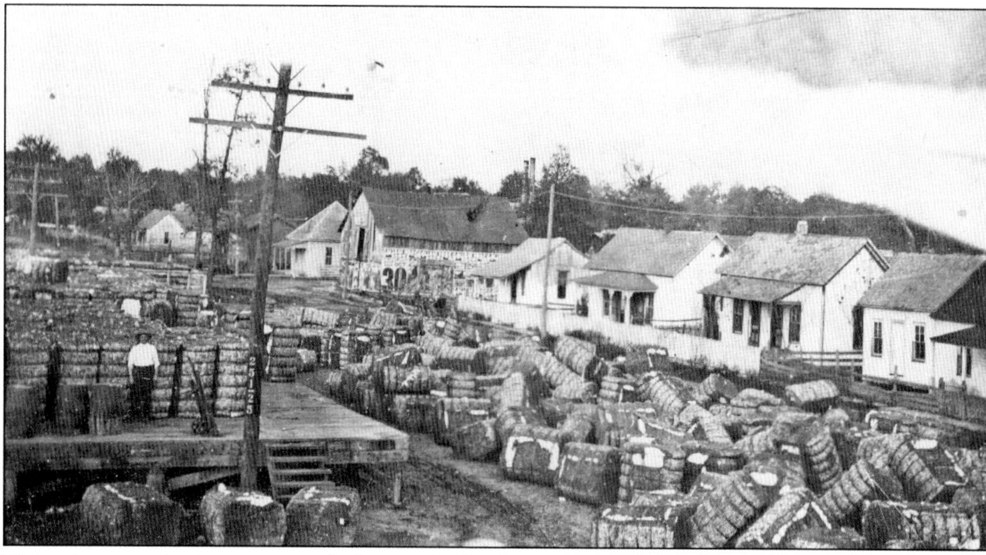

This photograph shows cotton bales at the Tuckerman gin. From here, they would have been loaded onto railroad cars and shipped to cotton mills in the North. (Courtesy of Jean Boyce.)

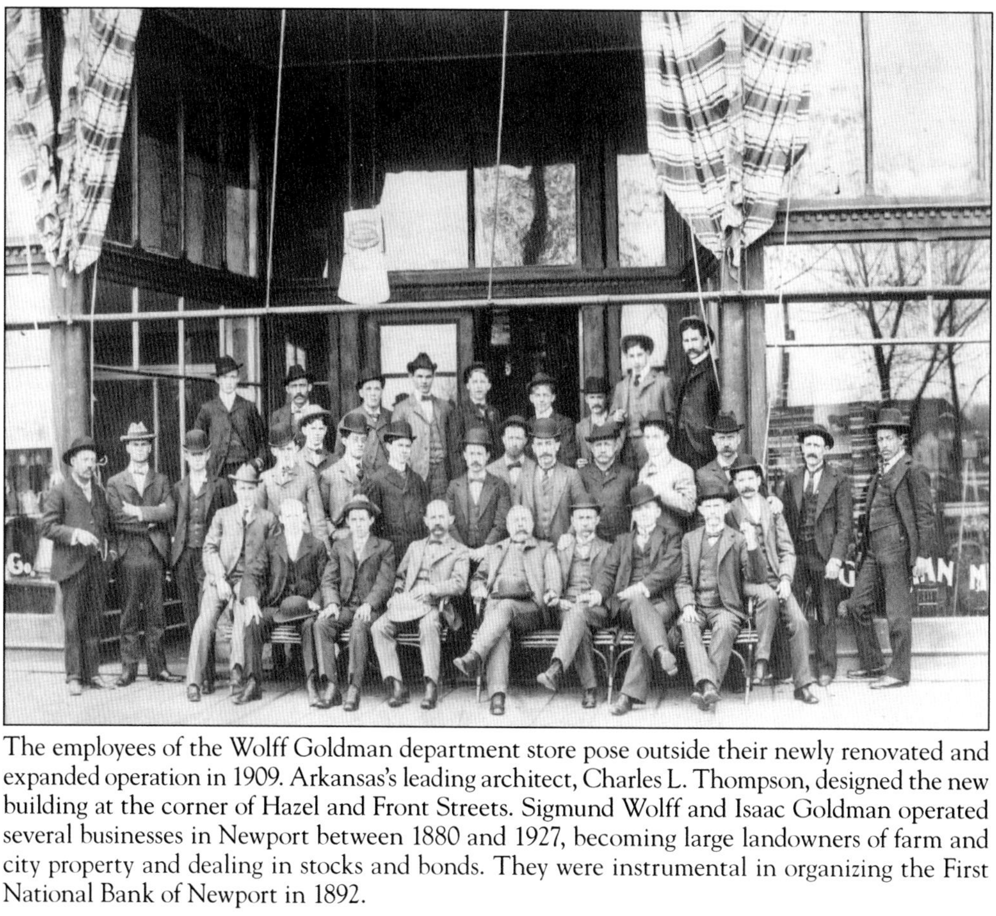

The employees of the Wolff Goldman department store pose outside their newly renovated and expanded operation in 1909. Arkansas's leading architect, Charles L. Thompson, designed the new building at the corner of Hazel and Front Streets. Sigmund Wolff and Isaac Goldman operated several businesses in Newport between 1880 and 1927, becoming large landowners of farm and city property and dealing in stocks and bonds. They were instrumental in organizing the First National Bank of Newport in 1892.

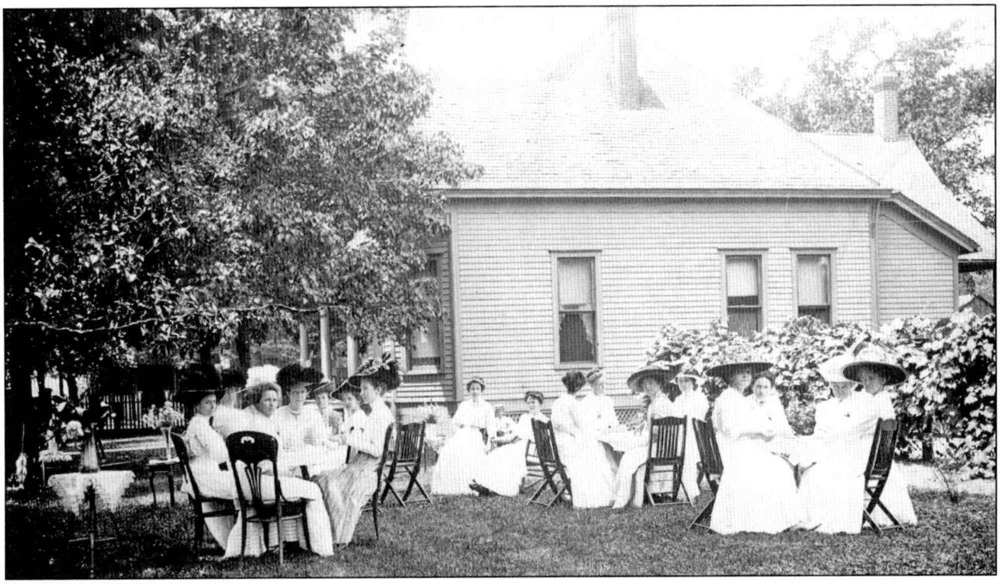

An afternoon card party at the home of O.D. Watson offered a pleasant outing for a few Newport ladies. Pictured here are, from left to right, Mrs. Gus Jones, Kate Watson Bennett, Mrs. Bob Harder, Nette Bond, Sweet Minor, two unidentified ladies, Bessie Watson, O.D. Watson, Jim Watson, Stevie Fagan (sister of Jim), Josie Bailey, Anna Wilmans, Ethel Stainback, Lady Bridgeman (sister of Jim), Lib Maris, Mannie Hooker, and unidentified.

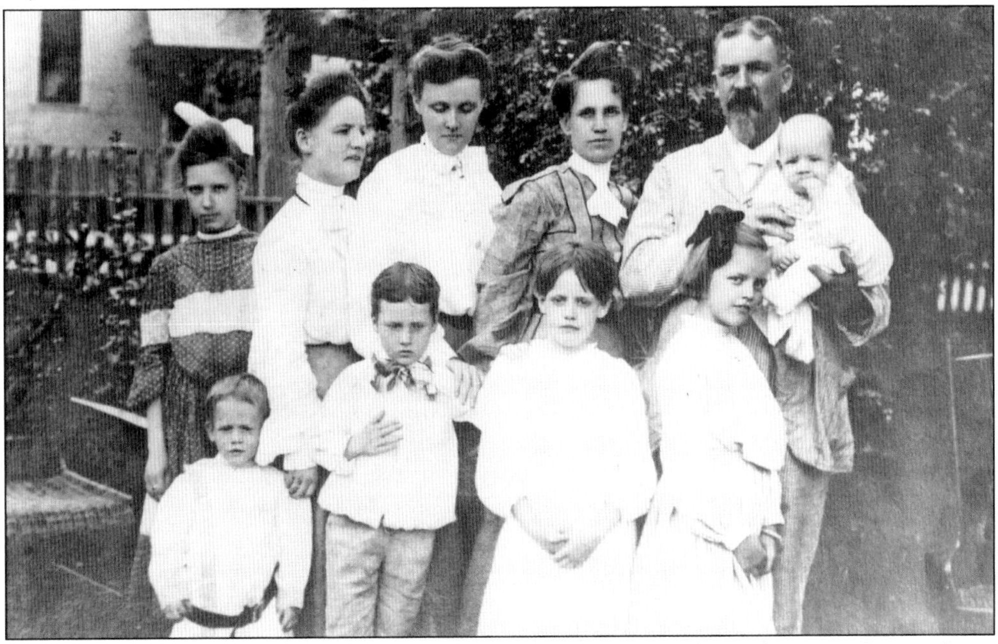

The family of Col. Lancelot Minor poses outside their home in the early 1900s. Pictured are, from left to right, (first row) Alcorn F. Minor, Charles L. Minor II, Willie Overton Minor (later Forsyth), and Mildred Minor (who drowned in her teens); (second row) Minerva Minor (later Cast, then Baatz), Louisa Noland "Sis Ty" Minor, Narcissa Phillips Minor (later Mack), Theo Ferguson "Sweet" Minor, Colonel Minor, and Lancelot Cabell Minor. (Courtesy of Jackson County Historical Society, Mildred Minor Gregory Collection.)

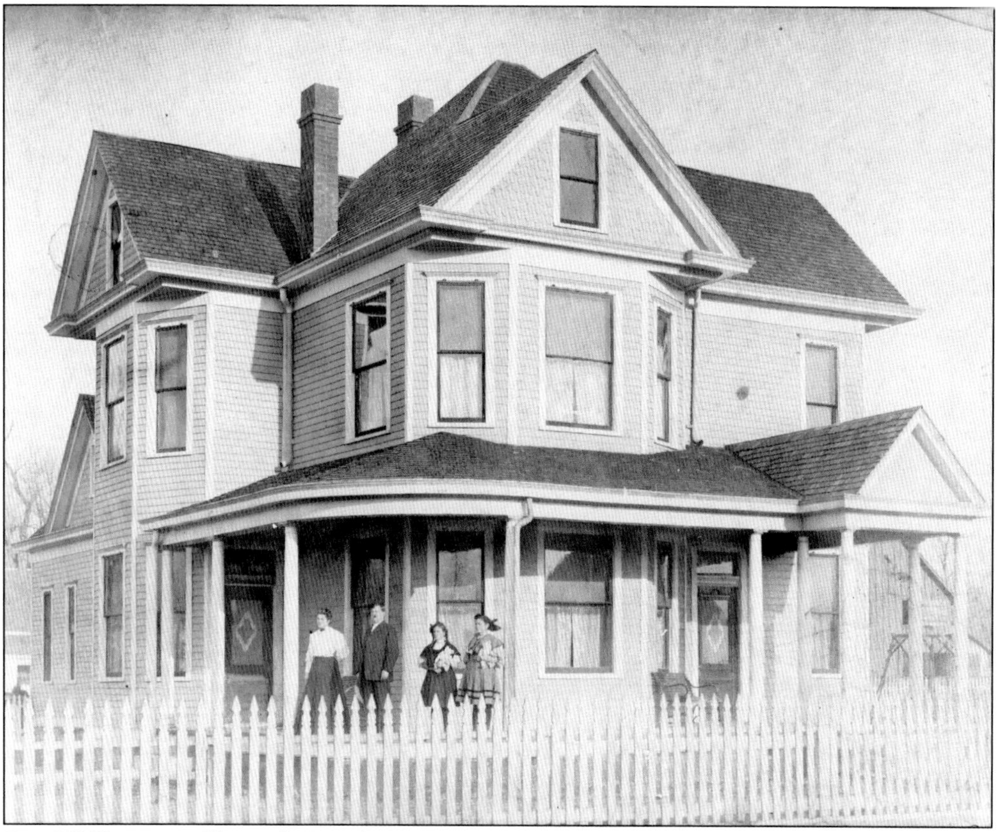

Sam W. Harvey and his wife, Maud Harrison Harvey, and daughters Sylla (left) and Clara stand outside their new home in Tuckerman in 1905. Harvey was a prominent merchant, planter, and ginner. Sylla married Edward Wayne Boyce Sr., who was a ginner, and she later became a longtime school teacher in Newport and Tuckerman. Clara married Taylor G. Dowell and taught in Tuckerman and Swifton.

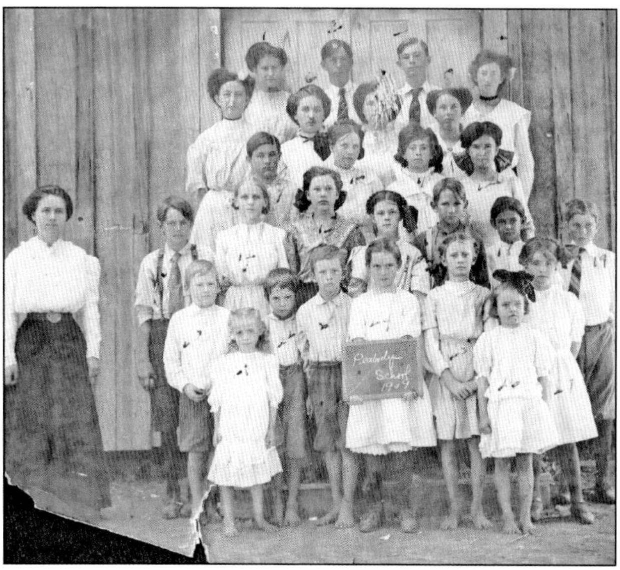

These students from the Peabody School in Tupelo, a farming town south of Newport, stand with their teacher, Ruby Harris, who taught all grades. A note on the back of the photograph identifies the students by last names as, from left to right, (first row) Taylor, Hallis, Ferguson, Taylor, Bolton, Hite, Simmons, and Johnson; (second row) Simmons, Patrick, Taylor, Taylor, Patrick, Simmons, and Taylor; (third row) Taylor, unidentified, Hallis, and Johnson; (fourth row) Simmons, Taylor, Lemons, and Marlow; (fifth row) Patrick, Simmons, Taylor, and Sprayberry.

Four

New Directions
The 1910s

Newport and Jackson County continued to grow and thrive during the 1910s, barely noticing the war in Europe, although many Jackson County men marched off to "fight the Huns." Business was good, thousands of acres of prime farmland were added each year following the cutting of the virgin timber, and most communities around the county shared Newport's prosperity.

The old nemesis, flooding from the White River, came twice in the decade, each time creating lakes of water in the streets of Newport and surrounding towns. Most buildings in Newport were prepared for this onslaught, however, with raised first floors five to six feet higher than the surrounding yards. The first Newport High School building was constructed with such a plan and opened for students in 1912. The Newport Greyhound football team took the gridiron for the first time the following year.

The 1915 flood covered the railroad tracks with 12 feet of water. A newspaper story from the Associated Press carries this headline: "Newport Ark. Is Still Completely Isolated. 4,000 Refugees from that Place Are Crowded into Hotels at Little Rock." Another flood the next year persuaded Newport's citizens to build a tax-funded $500,000 levee around the town.

Improvements in roads and bridges throughout the county made the delivery of farm products to the rail centers of Newport, Tuckerman, and Swifton much easier and safer, although the Iron Mountain and Rock Island railroads still carried the bulk of farm products to northern markets. America's entry into World War I in 1917 caused cotton prices to soar, and farmers in the county took full advantage, devoting more and more acres to cotton and creating even larger traffic jams of cotton wagons on the main streets of Newport and Tuckerman. The county continued to prosper until the farm crash of the late 1910s.

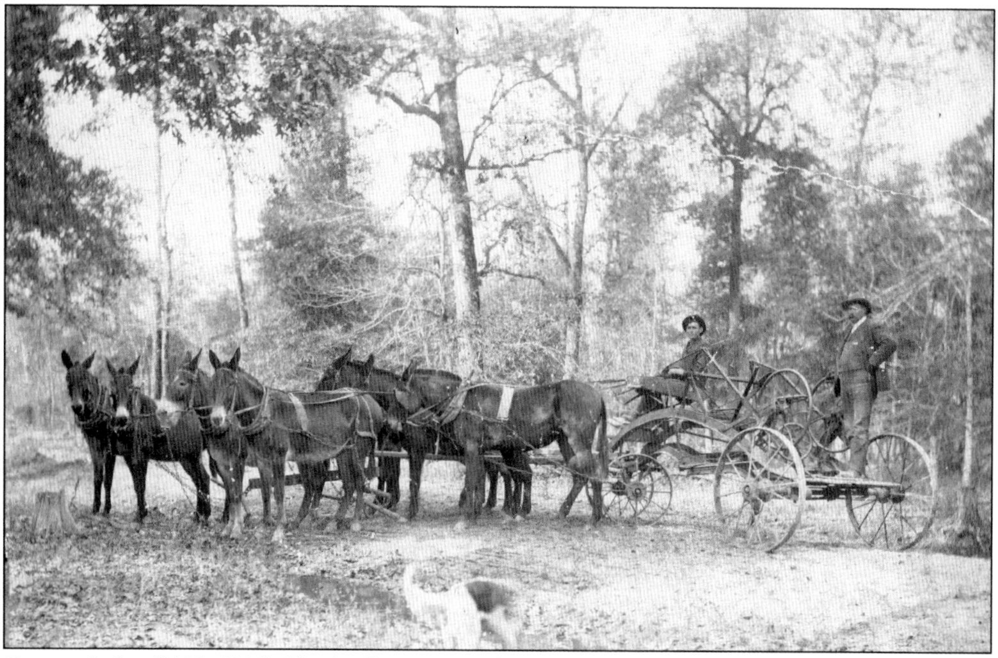

County Judge (1910–1914) Charles B. Coe stands on an early road grader his employees used to improve the roads of Jackson County. Driving the mules is his son J. Herbert Coe. Judge Coe made it his business to improve the roads, bridges, and highways of Jackson County, which, according to one reporter, "won him the respect of nearly all the county's inhabitants." (Courtesy of Jackson County Historical Society, Mildred Minor Gregory Collection.)

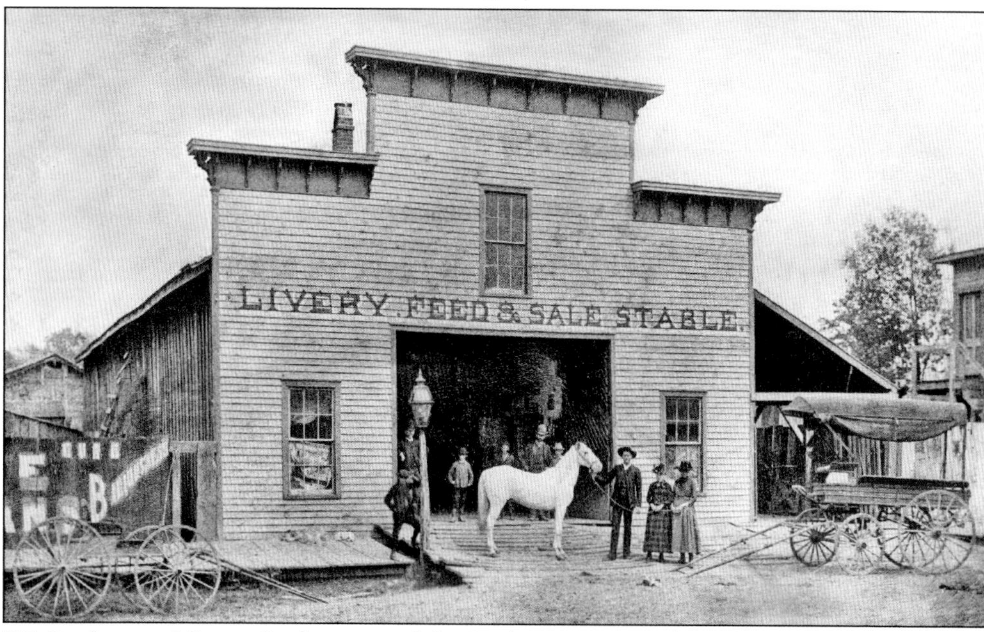

T.S. Stephens and George Stephens started the Stephens Livery, Feed & Sale Stable in Jacksonport in the 1870s. In the 1890s, they moved their business to Newport, where, in addition to other services, they offered three round-trips each day between Newport and Jacksonport in the hack pictured at the right. A note on the back of the photograph reads "Harry Stephens Livery Stable."

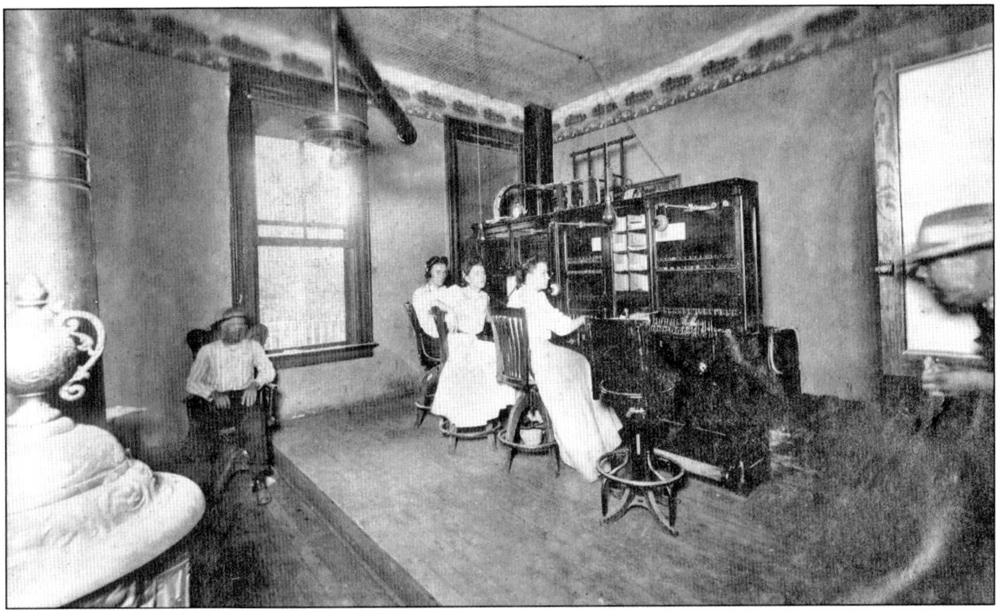

Pictured here in 1910 is the office of the Southwestern Telephone and Telegraph Company at 404 ½ Front Street in Newport. The operator was Maude Dunham. The first Newport telephone company started in 1885 as the White River Telephone Company with C.R. Hite as manager, and the exchange was located in the office of Lancelot Minor on Walnut Street.

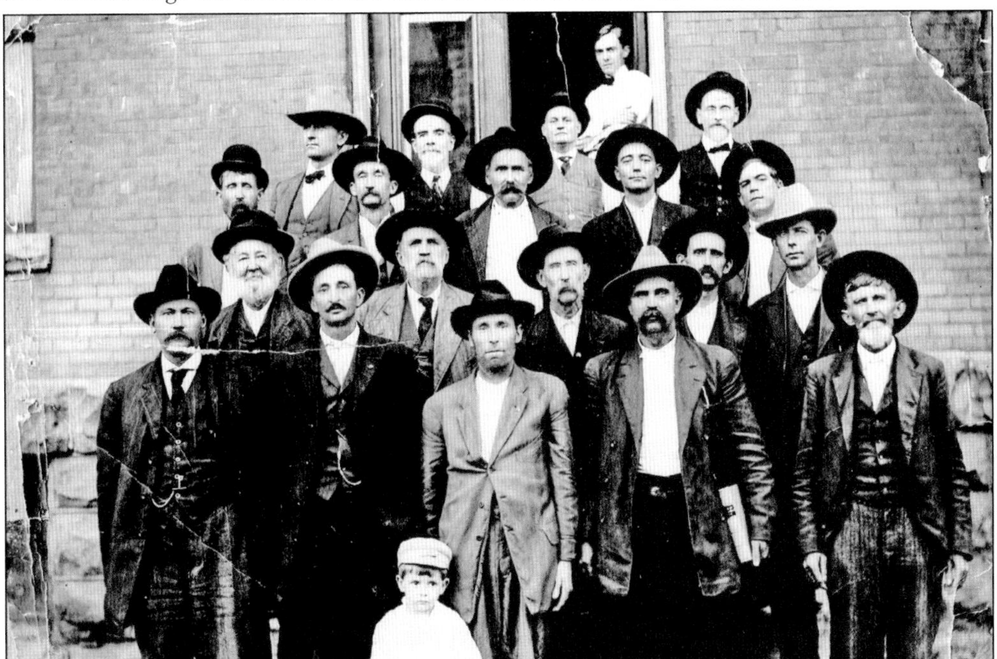

Jackson County judge Charles Coe's levying court for 1912 includes (first row) Fred ?, Judge Coe, R.F. Tyro, B.F. Johnson, unidentified, and A.B. Collier; (second row) John R. Loftin, H.C. Nuckolls, two unidentified men, and John F. Smith; (third row) W.G. Hogan, W.T. Atway, A.M. Keeton, Jake Ivy, and Charles Balch; (fourth row) Sheriff John McCuistion, county clerk Alex Lockard, Milton Stuckey, and Jim F. Jones; (doorway) unidentified.

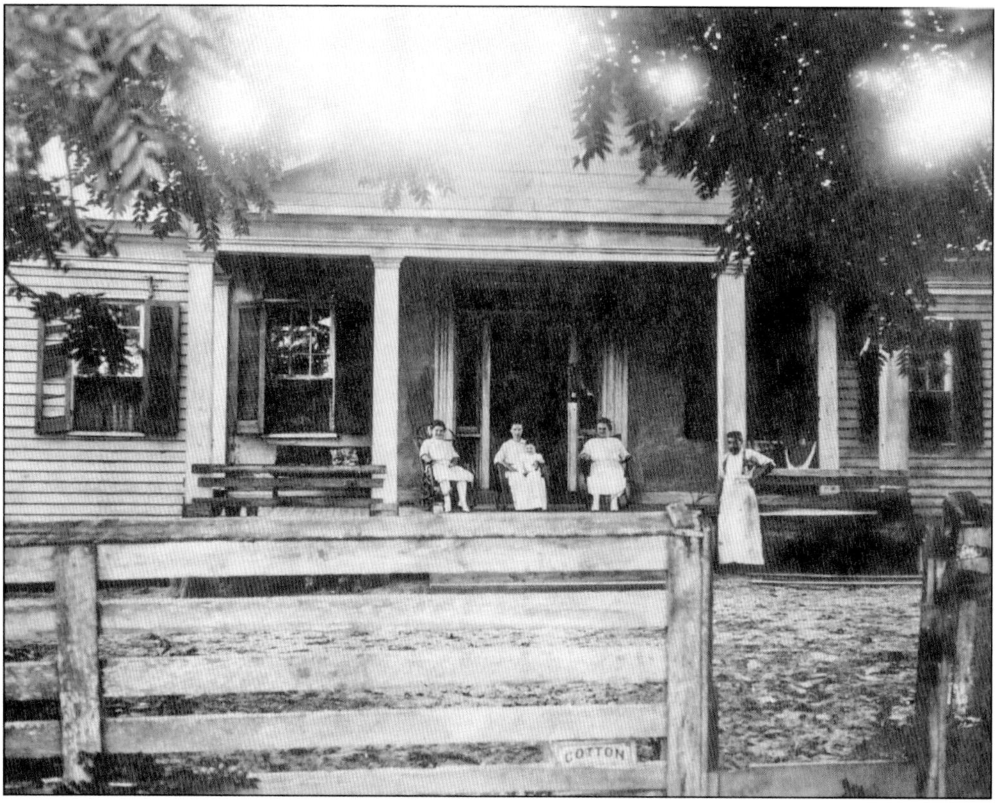

The Williams-Harper House was built in 1835 with slave labor, and as of this writing it is the oldest extant structure in Jackson County. Located several miles north of the later town of Jacksonport, it was the seat of the Williams Plantation. The Harper family later bought this home, and the baby in this photograph (captured in 1912 or 1913) could be Reuben Harper, father of the later county judge Reuben "Buzz" Harper.

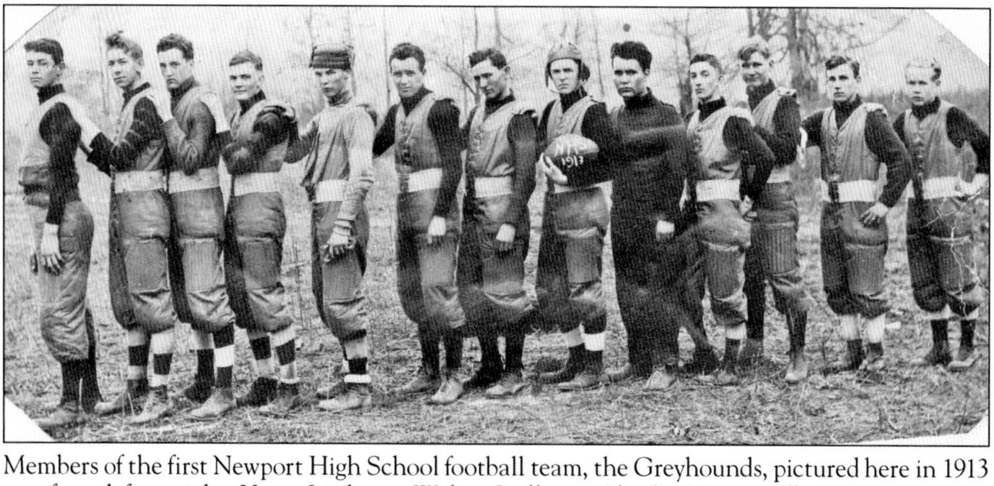

Members of the first Newport High School football team, the Greyhounds, pictured here in 1913 are, from left to right, Harry Littleton, Walter Stallings, Charles Minor, Albert Bevens, W. L. Childers, Elmer Patton, Burley Cox, Willey McMinn (captain), Vernon Singles (coach), Carl Hirsch, Gus Rankin, Herbert Wise, and Virgil Umsted. That season the Greyhounds played McCrory, Batesville, Augusta, and Searcy. (Courtesy of the Butler Center.)

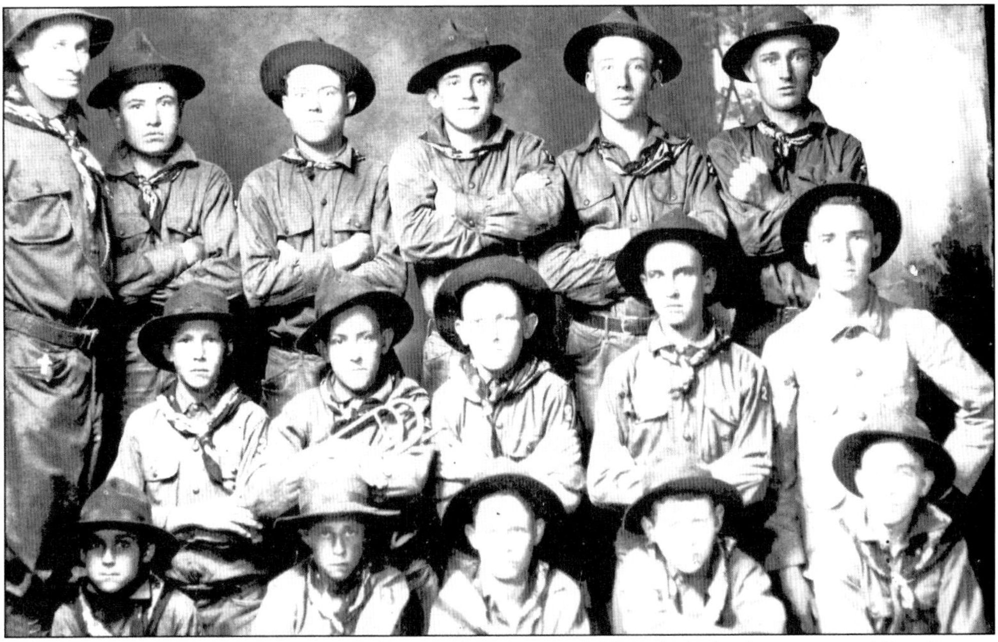

The Reverend Lee Heaton, rector of St. Paul's Episcopal Church, led a fine group of Boy Scouts in 1914. According to the note on the back of the photograph, this was one of the first Boy Scout troops registered west of the Mississippi.

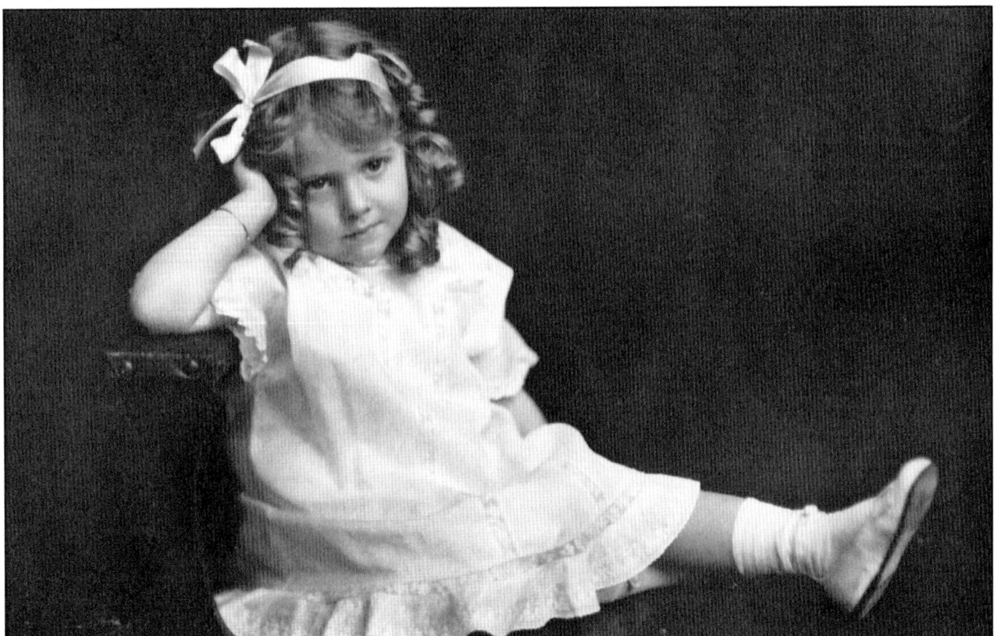

Three-year-old Lady Elizabeth Watson, named for her aunt Lady Fagan Bridgeman, poses for a portrait shortly before she cut off her own curls. Her grandfather Confederate general James Fagan was the first colonel of the Jackson Guards, and young Lady was supposed to help unveil the new Confederate monument on the courthouse grounds. Her distraught mother sewed the curls onto a velvet ribbon and went on with the show.

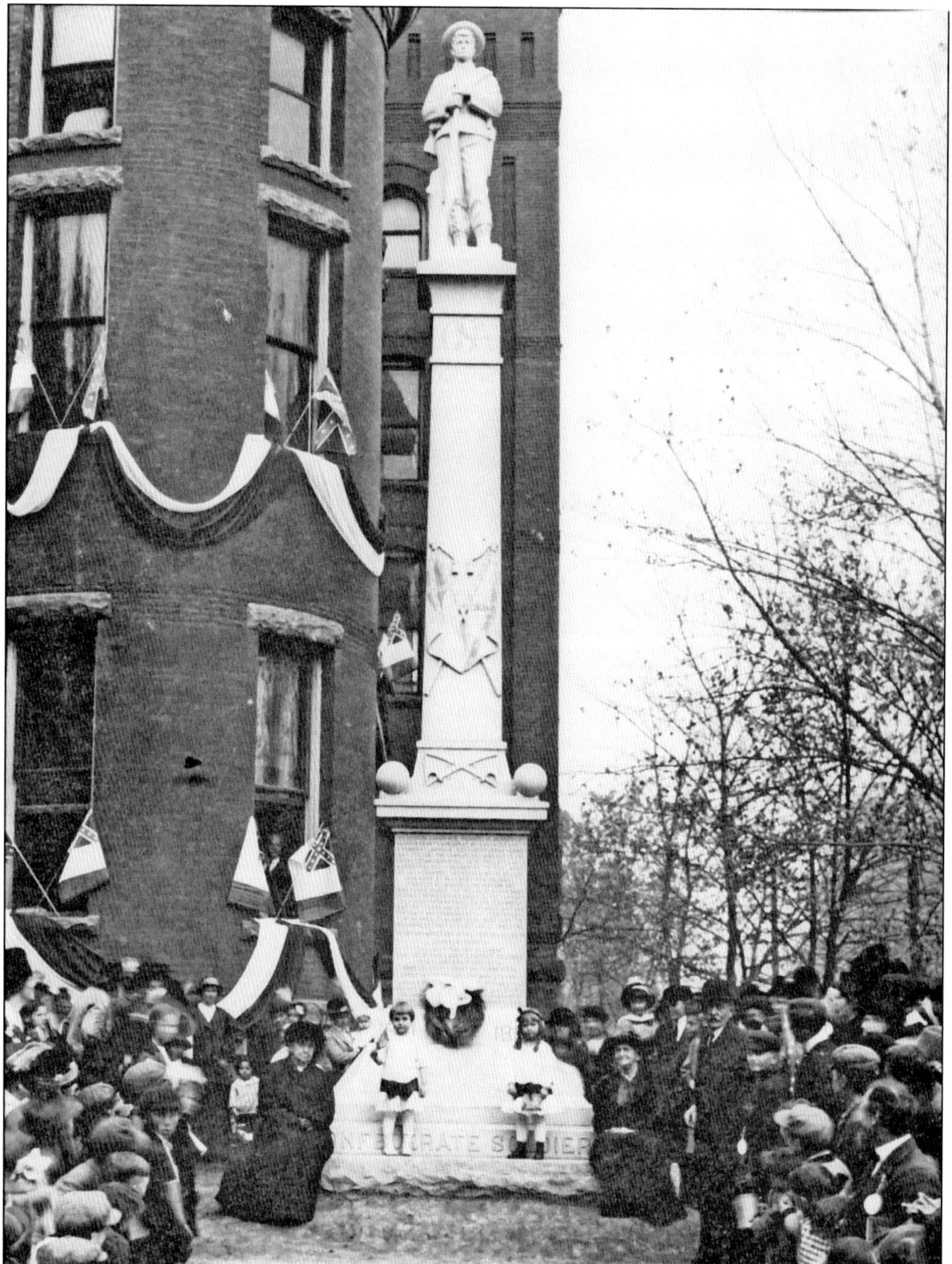

In February 1914, Lady Elizabeth Watson and her best friend, Clare Phillips, unveil the Confederate memorial on the grounds of the Jackson County Courthouse in Newport. Lady's grandmother, Gen. James Fagan's widow, sits to the right of the column. The United Daughters of the Confederacy had raised much of the money for this monument with the help of William E. Bevens, who wrote *Reminiscences of a Private* to help with the fundraising. In the 1970s, the memorial toppled in a storm and broke apart, and in 1976 the restored memorial was moved to Jacksonport State Park, assuming a place of honor in a courtyard down the mall from the courthouse.

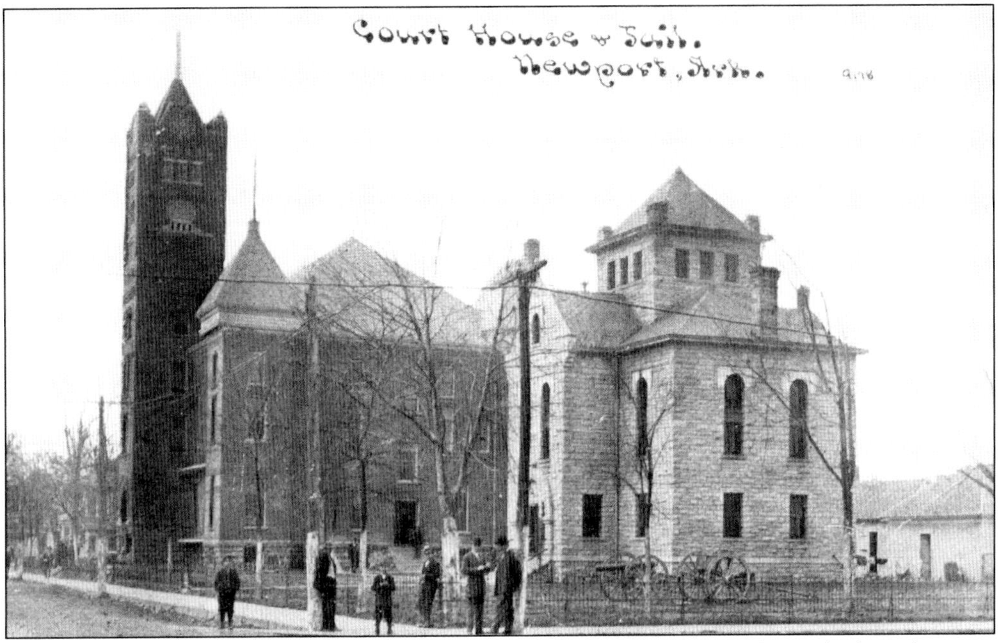

This postcard shows the back side of the courthouse and the adjacent jail. Inside the jail was an apparatus for hanging convicted criminals, though the Olyphant train robbers had been hanged on a makeshift gallows outside. The Civil War cannons that sat on the grounds beside the jail were moved to Jacksonport in the 1960s when the old courthouse was restored, as was the Civil War monument. (Courtesy of Robert Craig.)

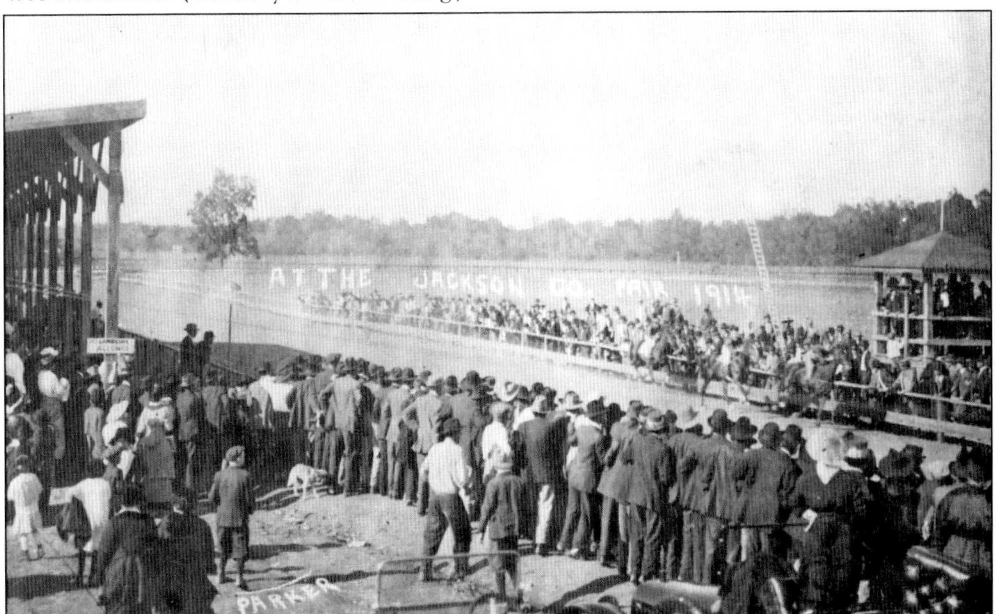

The horse races at the Jackson County Fairgrounds seemed to create as much excitement as the Kentucky Derby. This race in 1914 was no exception, and one has to wonder if anyone paid attention to the sign posted to the left, which reads, "No Gambling Allowed." The fairgrounds were on the Jacksonport Road just beyond the Newport levee.

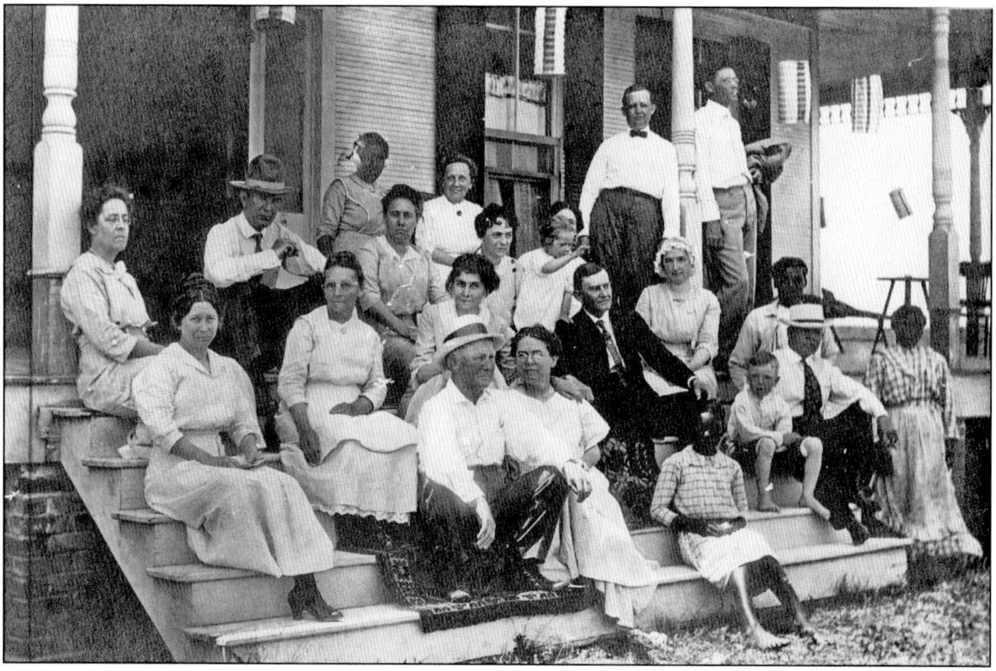

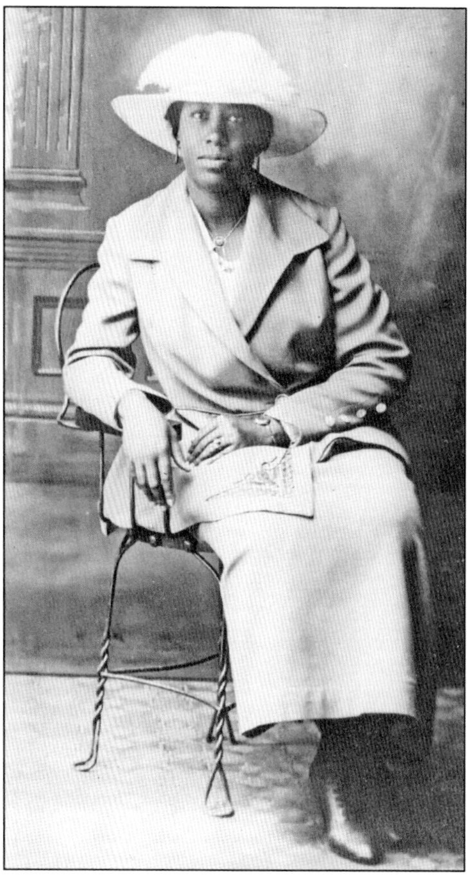

In May 1914, Cap and Ella Wilmans hosted a house party at their plantation in Louisiana. Among the attendees are Newport residents Mr. and Mrs. Wilmans, Charles Wilmans, Ed Wilmans, Mart Lewis (butler), Eliza (cook), Lula and Charlie (maids), Mrs. George Farrat, Mrs. T. Sprigg, Lily Billingsley, O.D. Watson, Anna Laird Wilmans, Lucy Watson Gregg, Tom Gregg, Susie Walker, Mildred Dorsey, Jim Watson, Lady Elizabeth Watson, Dr. Owen Walker, and W.A. Billingsley.

Described only as "Minnie," this beautifully dressed woman was Lady Elizabeth Watson's nursemaid. All wealthy white Newport families hired African American nurses for their small children, and they liked to think they treated their maids as a part of the family. Clearly, Minnie enjoyed many luxuries denied to most others of her race, as is attested to by her fine clothes, hat, and jewelry and her invitation to sit for a portrait. (Courtesy of Tim Watson Sr.)

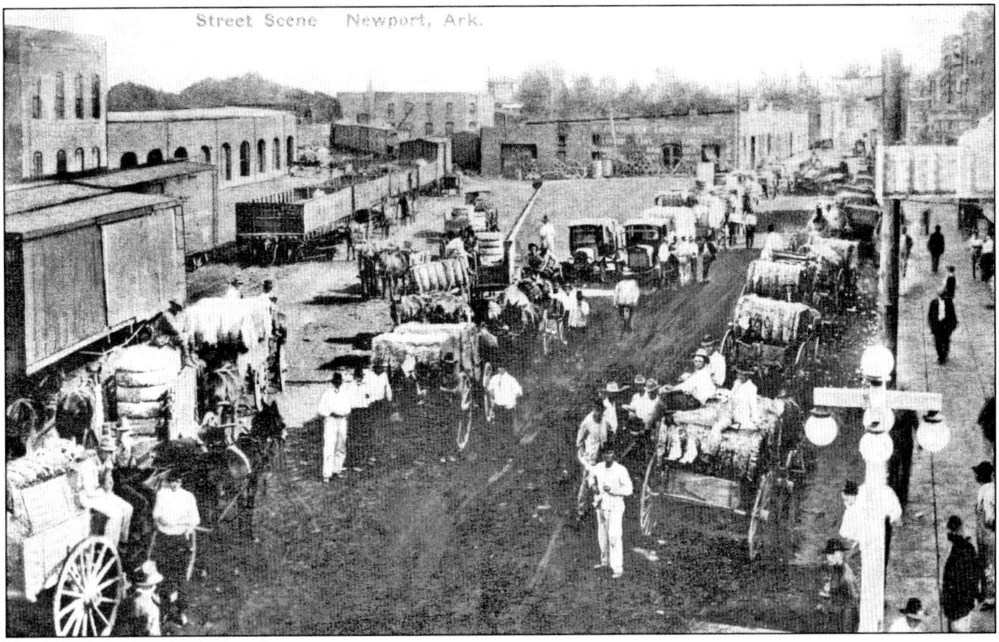

The cotton wagons on Front Street wait while the cotton buyers move among them grading the fiber and deciding which bales to buy for their employers in northern mills. To the left is the old train depot where the buyers could have their newly purchased bales loaded up for shipment to the North. This was the era when cotton was king, and by 1920 Jackson County was one of the 20 wealthiest counties in the United States. (Courtesy of Robert Craig.)

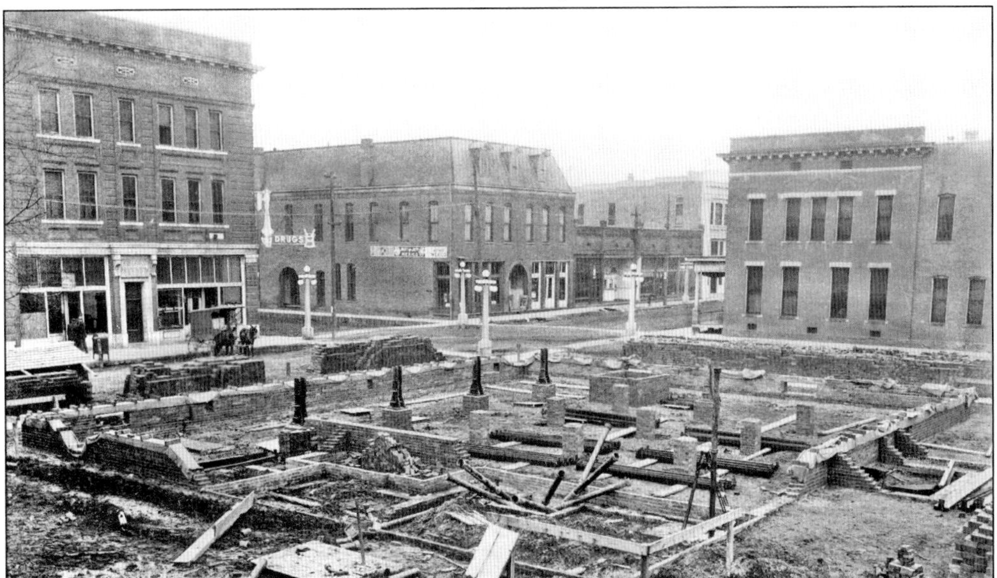

A picture of the new post office under construction also includes one of the few views of the Newport Opera House. Built in 1892, it was considered to be the most elegantly furnished opera house north of Little Rock. On the right across Second Street is the first Hazel Hotel, also built in 1892. On the left across Hazel Street is the McLain Hotel, later called the Hazel Hotel after the first one burned.

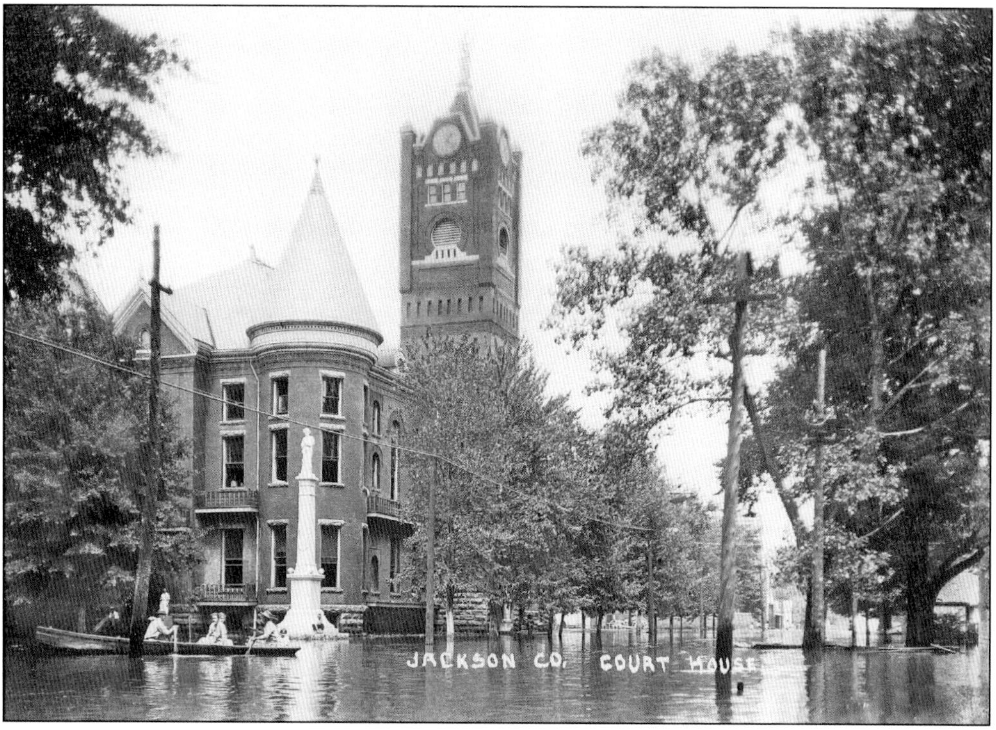

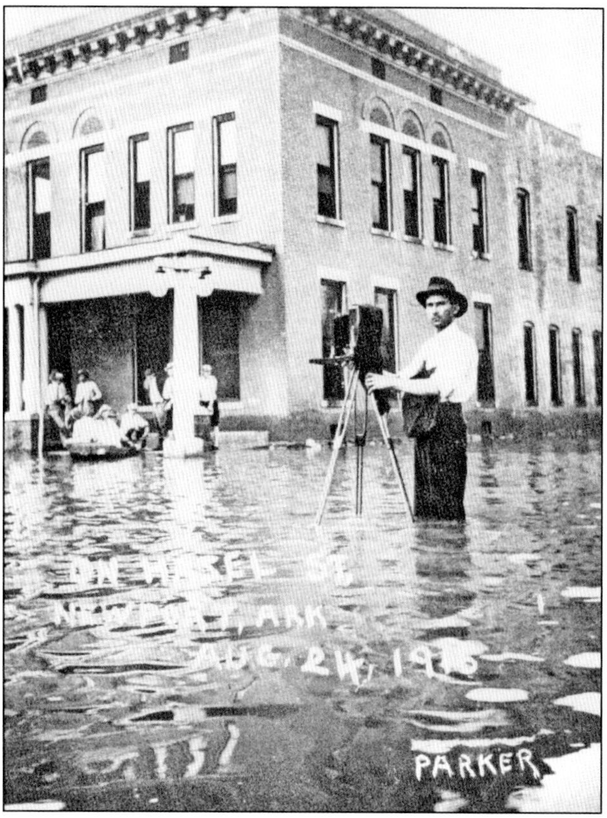

In August 1915, the White River overflowed its banks and flooded Newport in one of the worst floods since the 1880s. Whole families took their boats out for a spin around the town. Four-year-old Lady Elizabeth Watson had chicken pox, so she sadly watched out the window while her friends sped by in their new water chariots.

Here is a rare photograph of the man behind the camera, Parker the photographer, standing at the confluence of Hazel and Second Streets. Parker captured many images of his townsfolk frolicking in the unaccustomed circumstances. (Courtesy of Jackson County Historical Society, Mildred Minor Gregory Collection.)

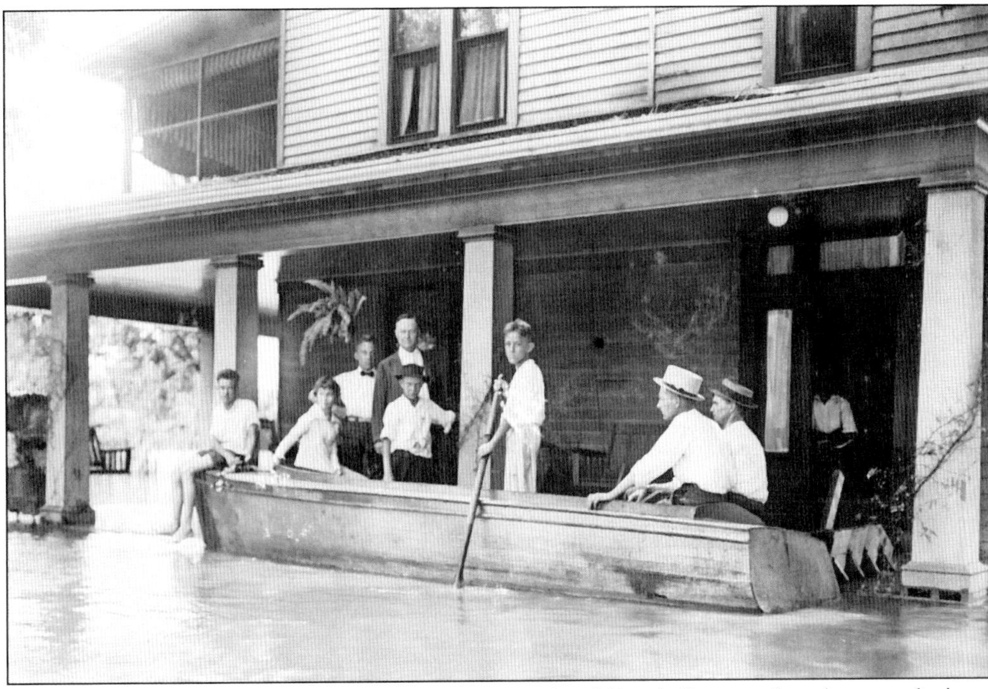

Taken in front of the Gustave Jones home at Second and Beech Streets, this photograph shows boaters enjoying the novelty of the flood. Standing on the porch are Jones (right) and an unidentified man. Jones's daughter, Leah Hones Hurt, sits in the bow of the boat, while Jernigan Reamey and Jeff Avera sit in the stern. The boys are unidentified.

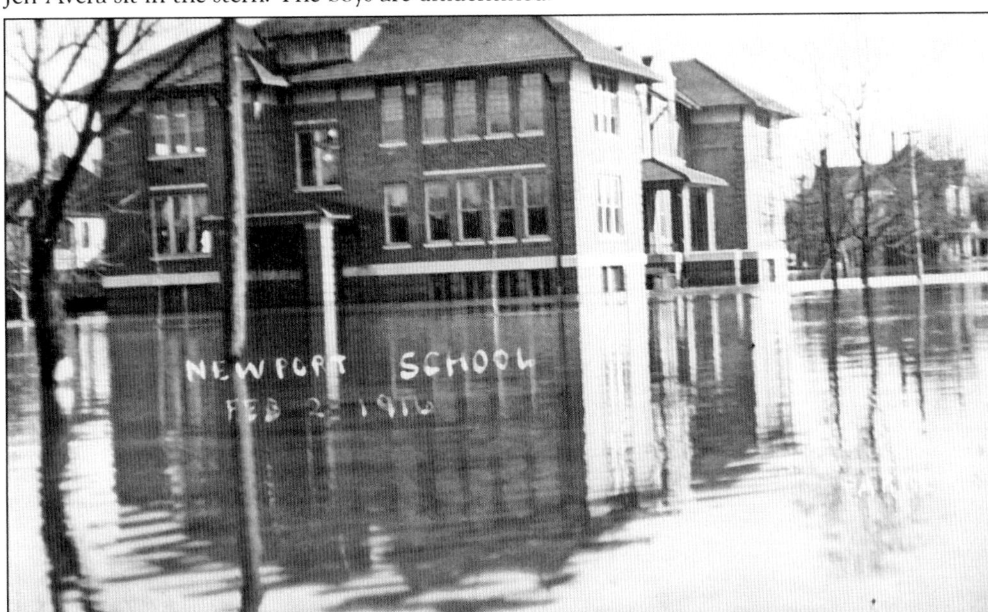

The river flooded again in February 1916, emptying the new Walnut Street School, undoubtedly to the delight of the children. Within a year, the City of Newport began in earnest to raise the existing low levees. But it was not until the late 1930s, after two more such endeavors, that the flooding of Newport was stopped—at least as of this writing. (Courtesy of C. Phillip McDonald.)

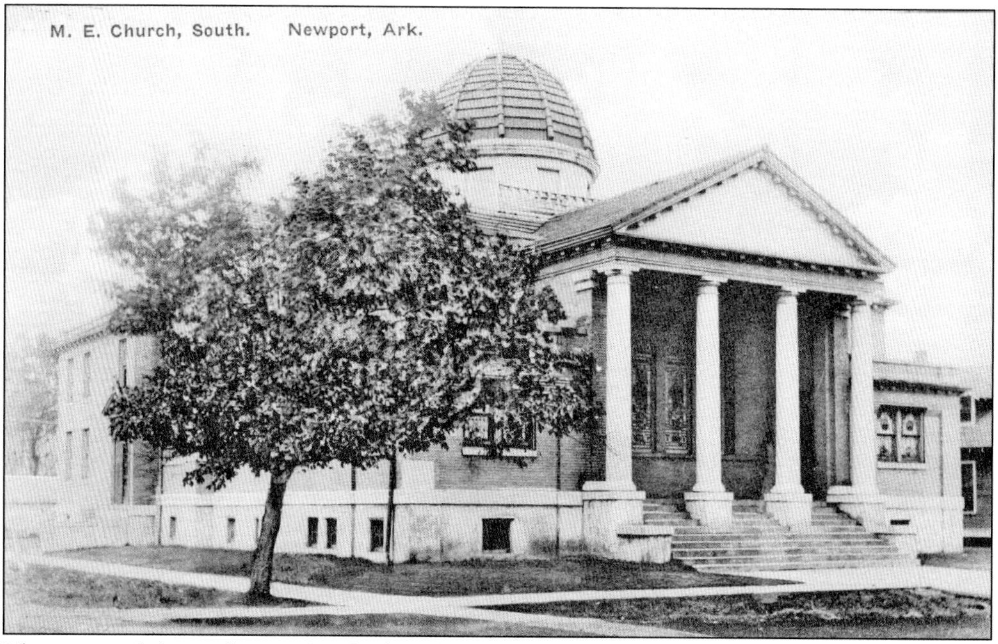

This postcard shows the new Methodist church at the corner of Third and Beech Streets. Built in a Greco-Roman style (note the Doric columns supporting the pediment and the domed roof), this building still serves the local United Methodist congregation. (Courtesy of Robert Craig.)

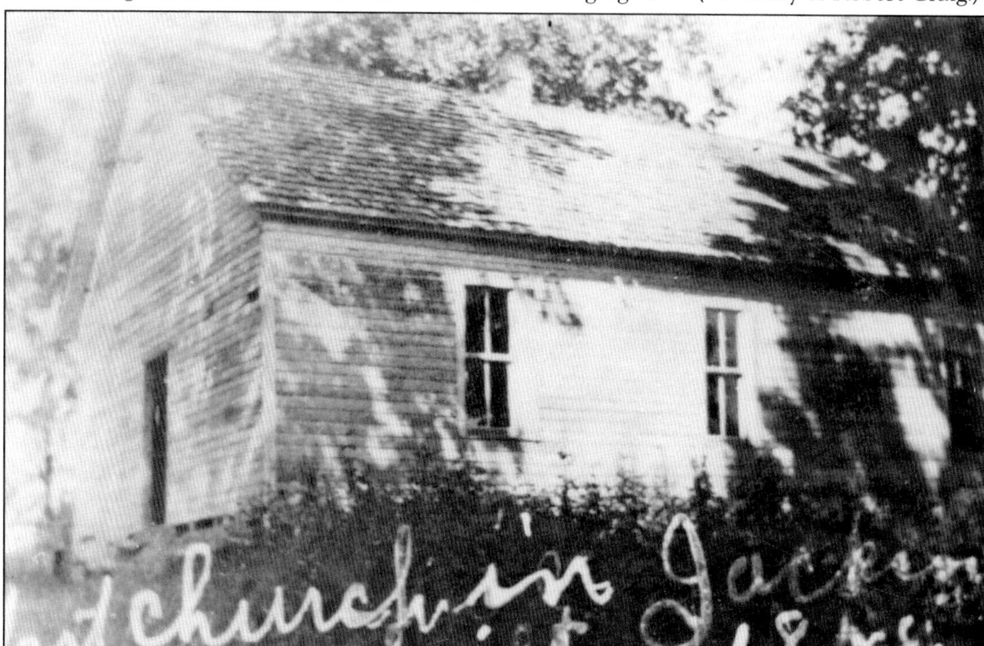

The Surrounded Hill Church of Christ, west of Newport and pictured here in 1915, was thought to be the oldest church in Jackson County, having been built in the 1850s. There are many "surrounded hills" in the Arkansas Delta, which are low, wind-created sand hills that provided haven for the frequent flooding in the area. (Courtesy of James Logan Morgan Jr. and the Butler Center.)

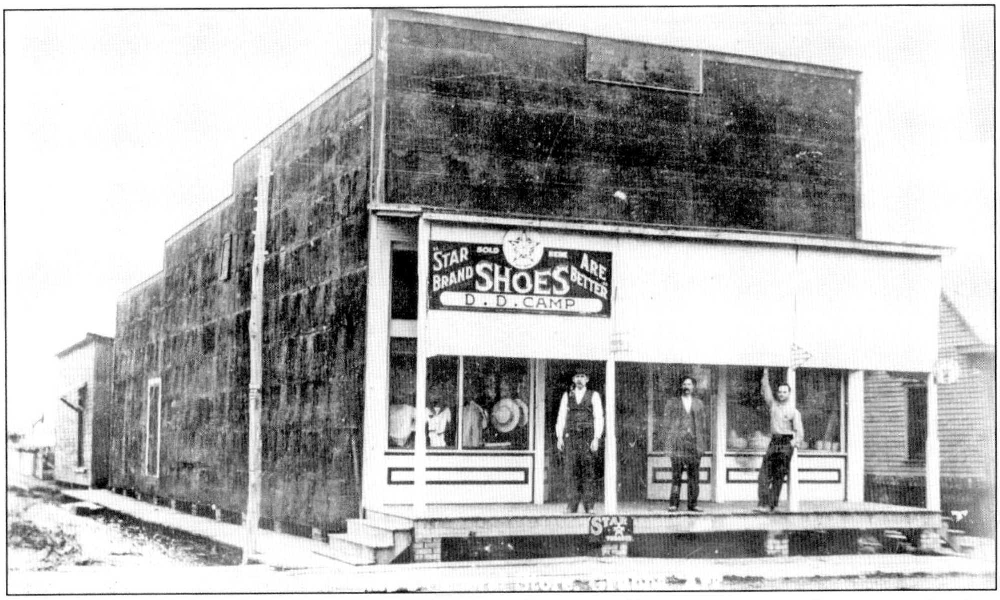

The D.D. Camp General Store in Grubbs, 18 miles east of Newport, was a favorite gathering place in this little farming community. D.D. Camp stands on the left and Hendrix Williams stands on the right in this image captured in 1916. The business is typical of general stores found all over the county.

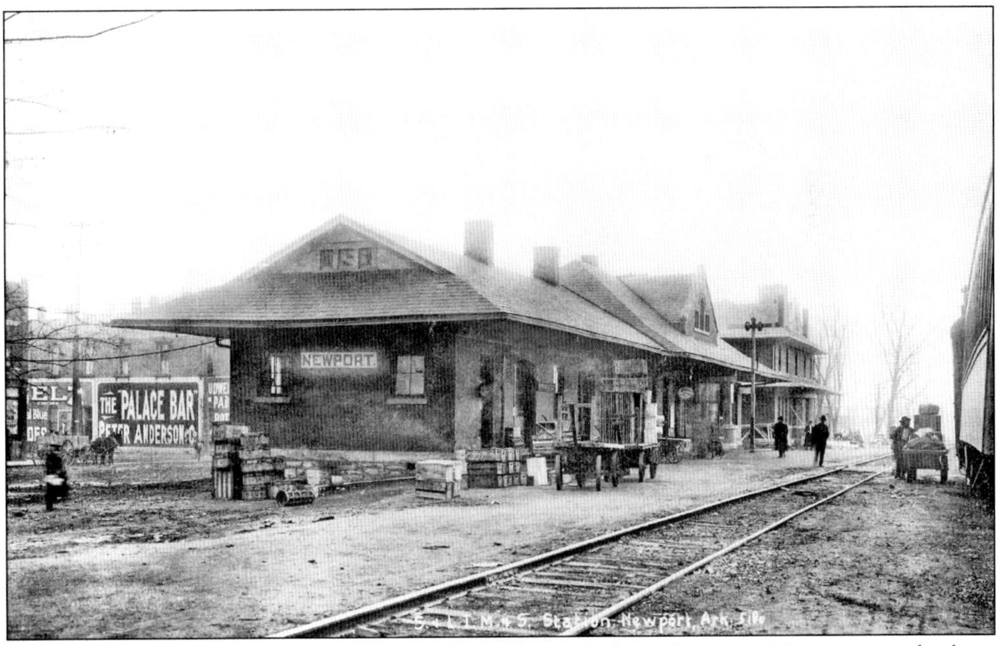

The second St. Louis, Iron Mountain, and Southern Railway Depot in Newport was built in 1916, and it was a busy place through the 1930s. As roads improved and automobiles became more accessible, passenger traffic declined, but the railroads still carried most of the cotton to market.

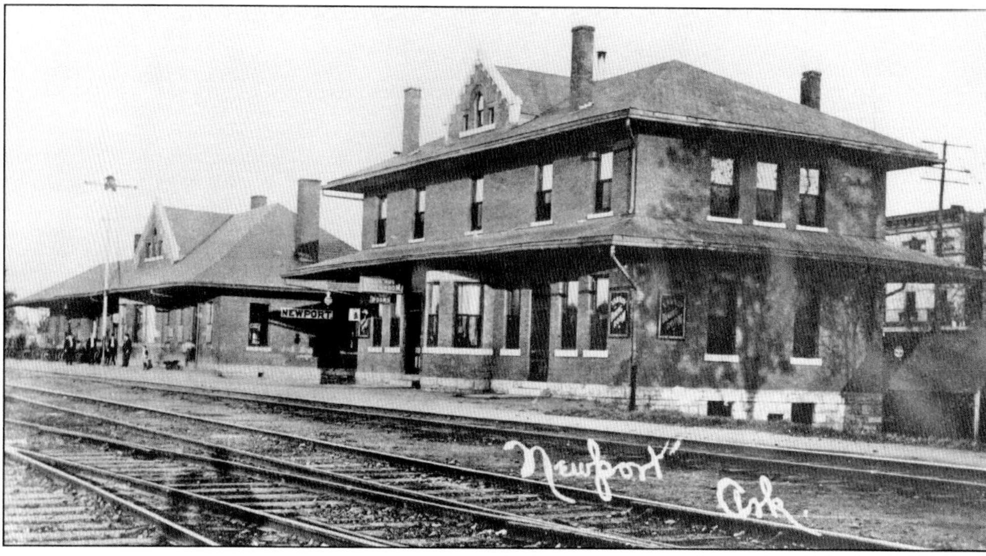

The Van Nuys Hotel and Restaurant next to the depot was built soon after the railroad station and was a popular restaurant in Newport. Men's clubs met here for weekly luncheons, people went for Sunday dinners, and it was the only restaurant in Newport that stayed open all night. It was torn down in the early 1970s. (Courtesy of Robert Craig.)

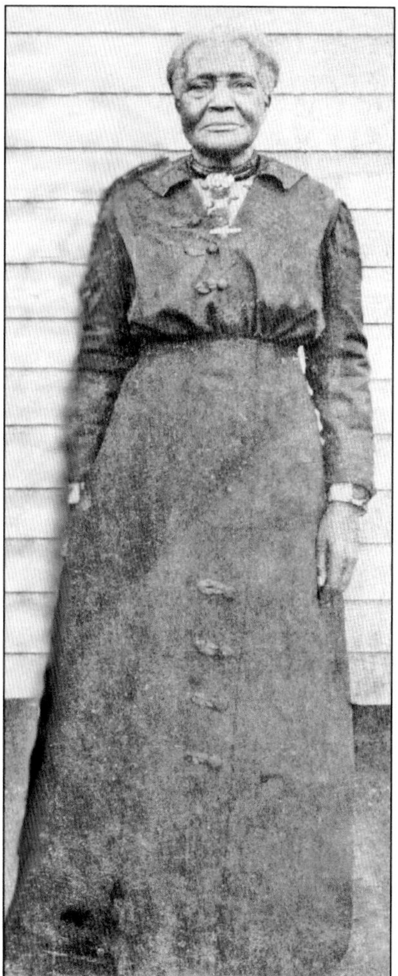

"Aunt" Caroline Dye was known throughout the region as a seer. At the time of her death in 1918, Dye's estate included numerous farms and exceeded $100,000. Memphis musician W.C. Handy sings about her in his 1923 "Sundown Blues": "I'm going to Newport, Arkansas, I'm going there to see Aunt Car'line Dye, Why she's a reader and I need her . . . She reads your fortune and the cards don't lie."

This World War I soldier is W.A. "Bill" Woods of Swifton. Many young men from Jackson County volunteered when the United States declared war on Germany and its allies in April 1917. And many more were drafted. (Courtesy of J.W. Hulen.)

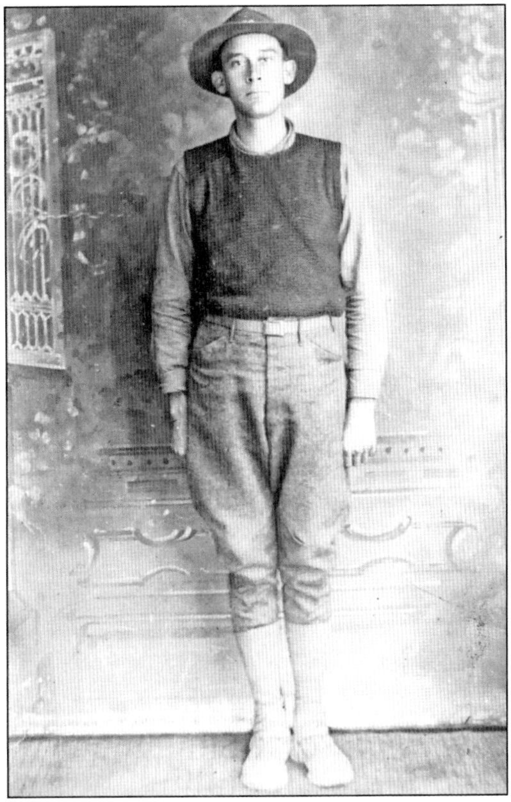

In World War I, Company E was a regiment that mustered out of Jackson County. Uniforms were not available; most of the men wore overalls and blue shirts, and Wolff-Goldman mercantile gave each man a cap. Among the soldiers pictured here are sons of the Shones, Coffin, Jones, Coleman, Knowles, Jones, Patton, Sprigg, Bevens, Foushee, Hurt, Hirsch, Sprigg, Littleton, Childers, Hubert, Shell, Long, Miller, Stallings, Brown, Mallory, Pettit, Fite, Yeay, and Parmley families.

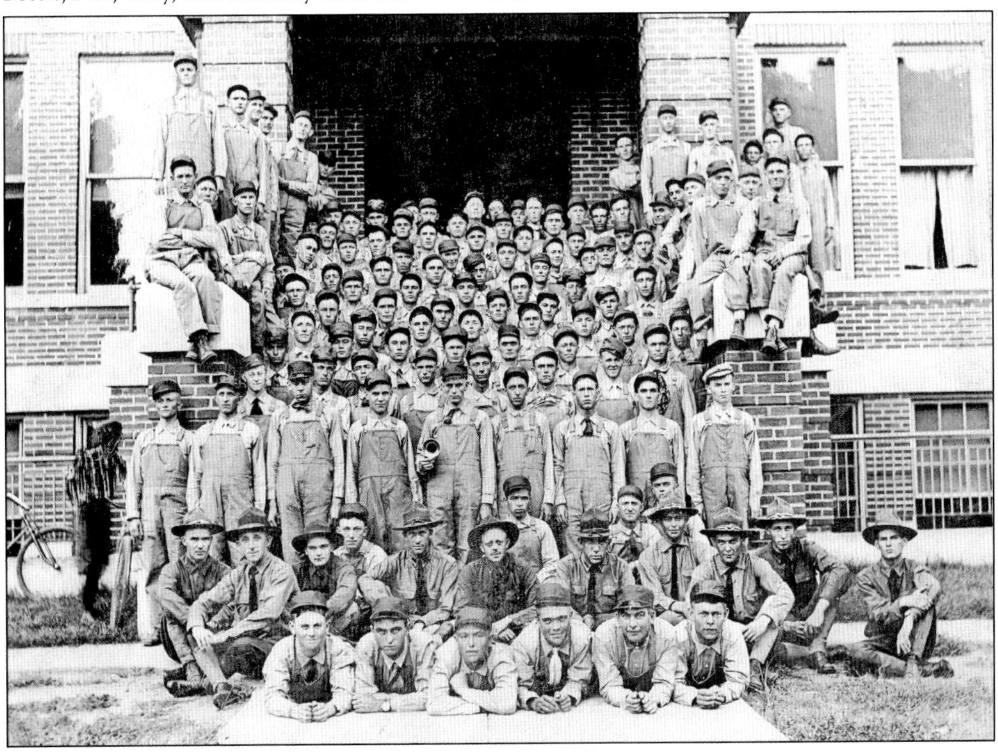

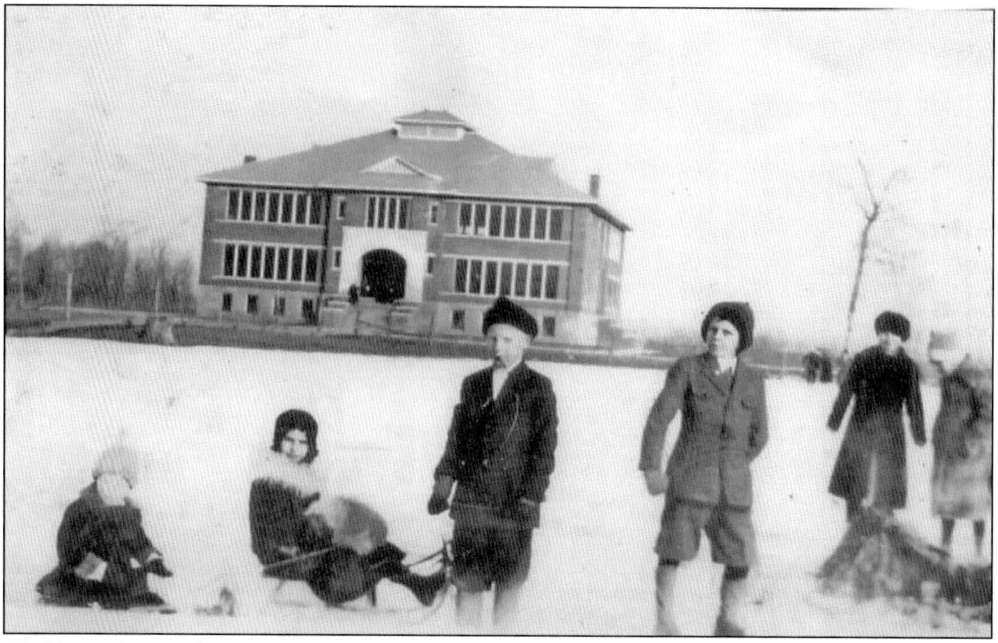

Children play in the unaccustomed snow on the grounds of the new Swifton High School in 1918. The substantial nature of the school building reflects the wealth that the ever-expanding cotton crop was bringing into Jackson County. (Courtesy of J.W. Hulen.)

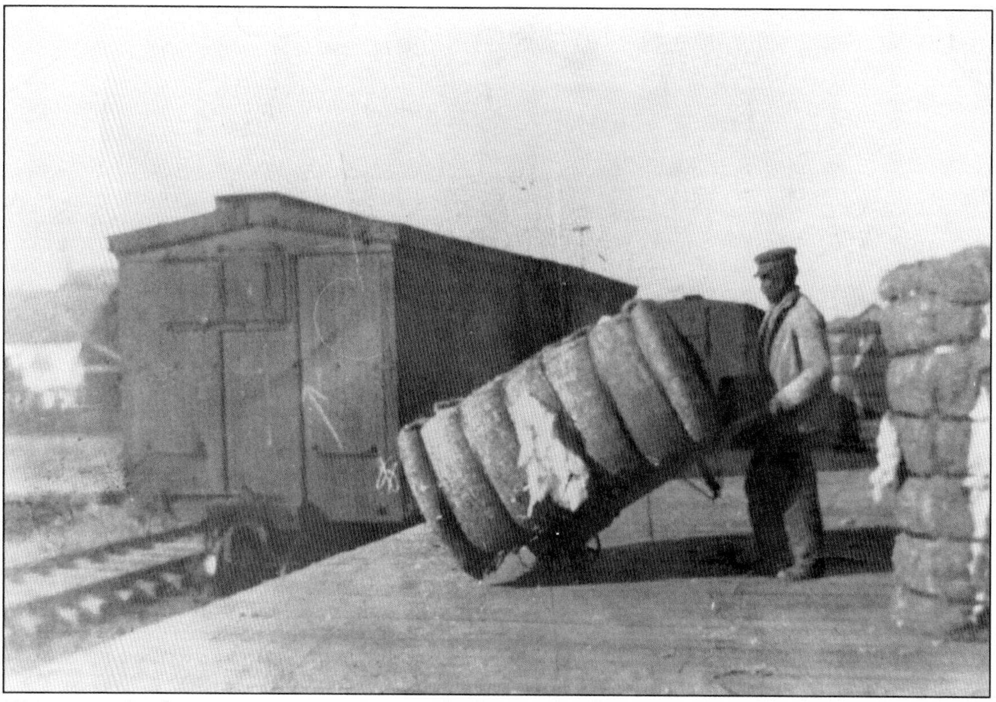

This man is loading cotton onto railcars at the Rock Island Depot in Tupelo. Running south from Newport, the Rock Island Line provided a connection between the tiny agricultural settlements in that part of the county and the Iron Mountain Railway in Newport, for transshipment to northern cotton mills and markets. (Courtesy of James Logan Morgan Jr. and the Butler Center.)

Five

New Challenges
The 1920s

The decade of the 1920s saw two devastating events in Jackson County. A destructive fire in Newport in 1926 followed by the great flood of the Mississippi River Valley in 1927 could have caused less-determined people to flee the area for better jobs and higher ground, but Jackson County actually continued its growth, if not its prosperity. Cotton was still king, though not as profitable, and life went on.

Entrepreneurs continued to clear more acres of virgin hardwood and drain the widespread swamps, thereby eliminating the illnesses and fevers that plague swampy land. Agricultural growth continued, despite the crash in the price of cotton that accompanied the South-wide agricultural depression of the 1920s. The old refrain "Cotton is down to a quarter a pound, and I'm busted" was almost literally true, as the aftermath of World War I played havoc with agricultural commodities.

The Great Fire of Newport, as old-timers once called it, happened on a windy March day, following a fire in a stave mill on the northwest side of town next to the river. High winds from the northwest lifted and scattered burning wood fragments over a large part of the residential area of Newport, causing many house fires when the roofs of those building were hit by the burning wood. The local fire department was quickly overwhelmed, and over 280 homes and other buildings burned to the ground. Newport quickly recovered, and most of the homes were replaced by new ones within six months of the fire. The next year, 1927, saw yet another flood in Newport and surrounding Jackson County, but this part of the state was not nearly as devastated by the great flood on the lower Mississippi as areas in southeast Arkansas were. Buildings were replaced and the floodwaters receded, and the life of the county moved forward.

The stock market crash in 1929 had no immediate impact on Jackson County, but the next decade, with its bank failures and high unemployment, were just around the corner.

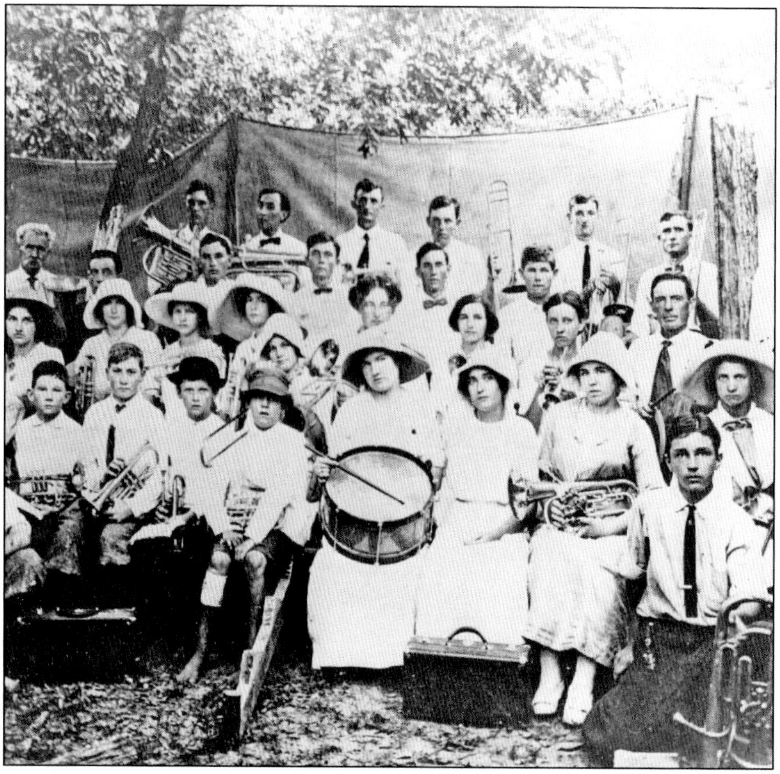

The Jacksonport Town Band seems to have been comprised mostly of youngsters, although some grown men seem to have entered into the fun. Probably a school group, this brass band surely made quite a spectacle when it marched in parades or played for celebratory occasions. A town band was a great source of pride in small-town America, and especially across the South.

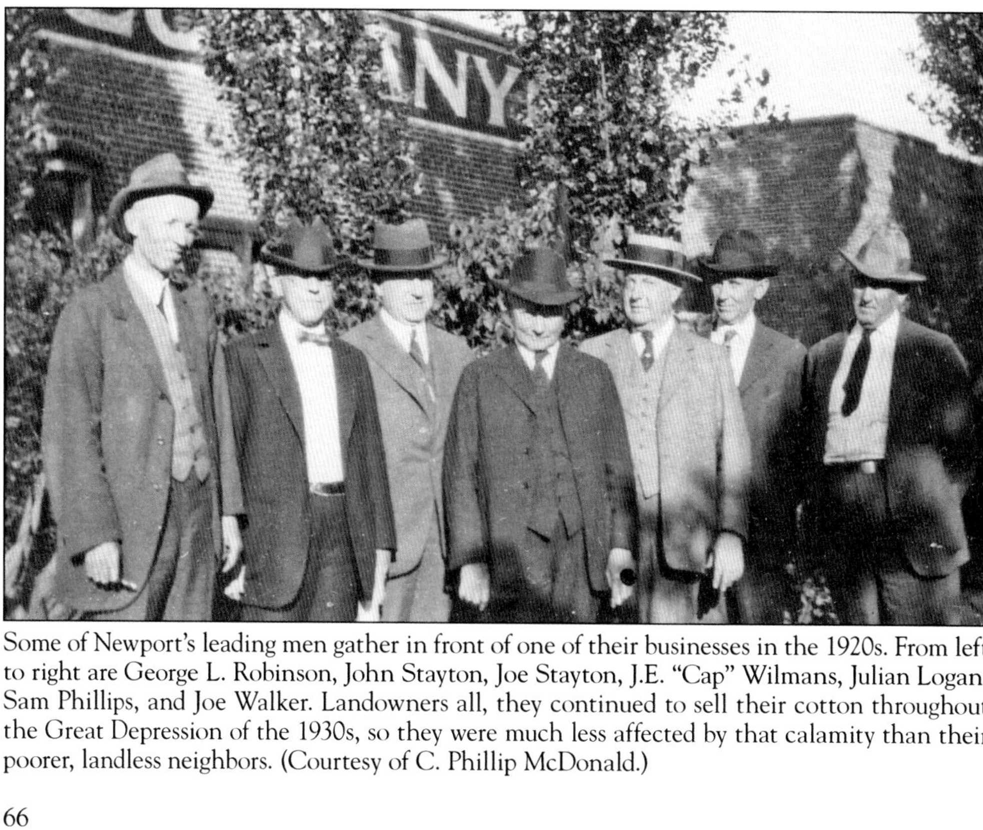

Some of Newport's leading men gather in front of one of their businesses in the 1920s. From left to right are George L. Robinson, John Stayton, Joe Stayton, J.E. "Cap" Wilmans, Julian Logan, Sam Phillips, and Joe Walker. Landowners all, they continued to sell their cotton throughout the Great Depression of the 1930s, so they were much less affected by that calamity than their poorer, landless neighbors. (Courtesy of C. Phillip McDonald.)

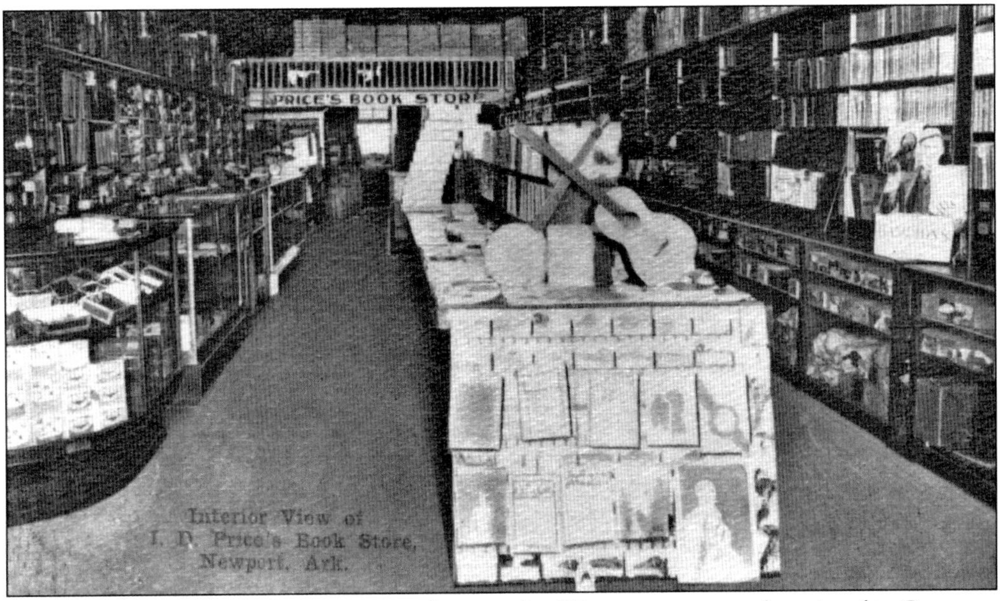

Bookstore owner I.D. Price commissioned postcards of Newport scenes to be printed in Germany and sold in his store, along with books, musical instruments, and other paper goods. Postcards from Price's store traveled all over the United States and are now valued collector's items.

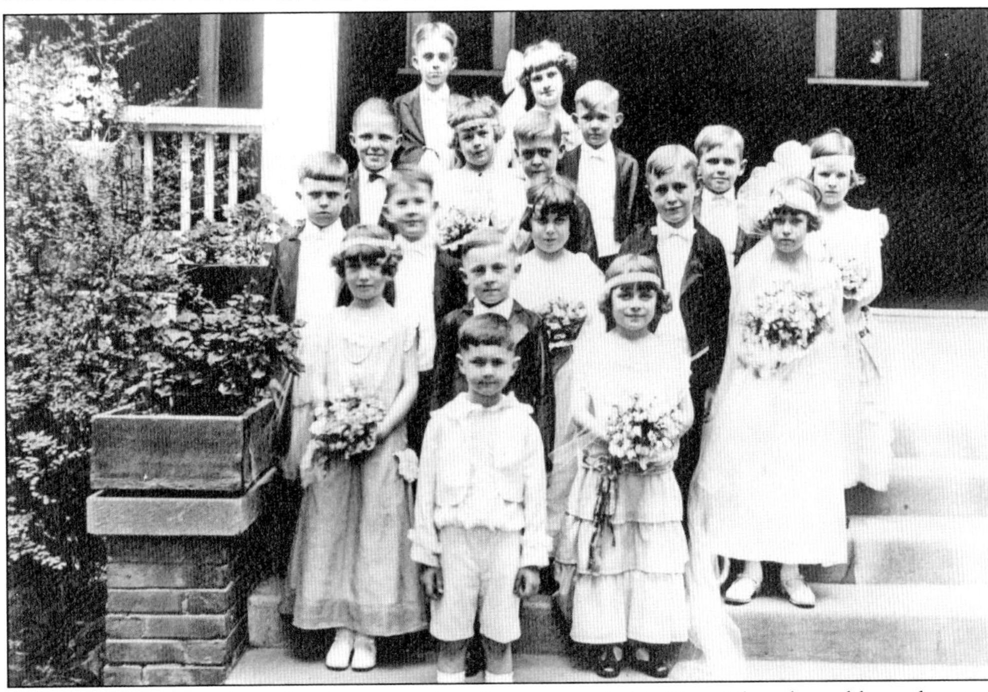

In 1923, the ladies of the Presbyterian church sponsored this Tom Thumb wedding, directed by Mrs. John Stayton. Pictured are, from left to right, (first row) Billy Stephens (ring bearer); (second row) Mary Wise, Fred M. Pickens, and Elizabeth Rossington; (third row) Luther Bob Harrell, Howard Ridley, Virginia Hinkle, Glenn Edgar (groom), Jane Bandy, (bride); (fourth row) Joe Findley, Maude Francis West, Walker Parish, Billy Bowie, Clay Gregory, and Emily Watson; (fifth row) Paul K. Holmes and Alma Davis.

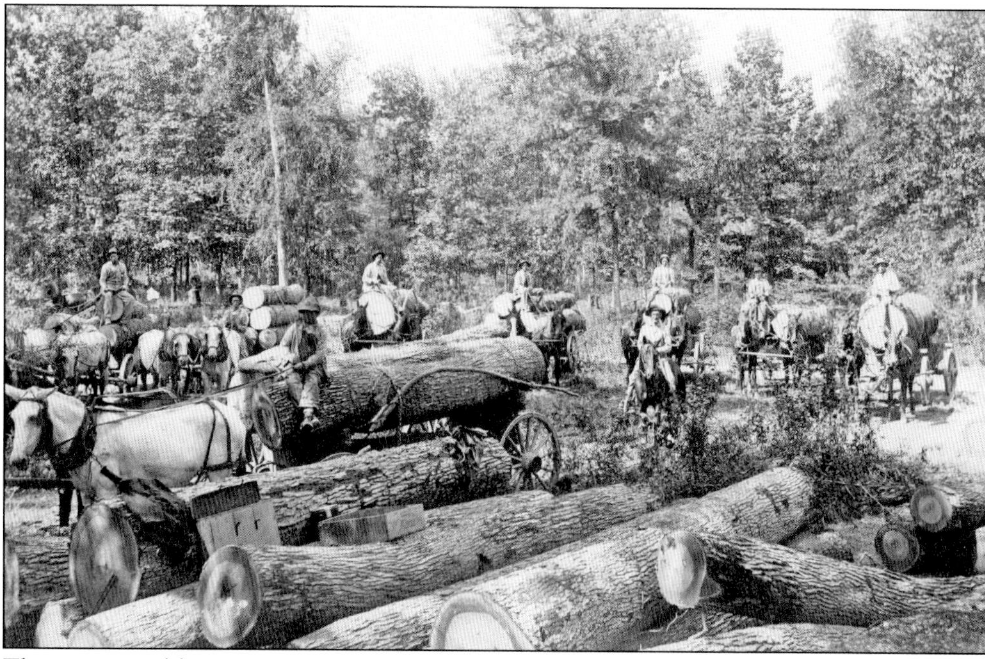

This is a typical logging camp in which men would set up for a few days or weeks to clear the trees from an area and then haul them to one of the numerous sawmills in the county. Mules were stronger than horses, though not as easily governed, and they were the livestock of choice used in clearing the land.

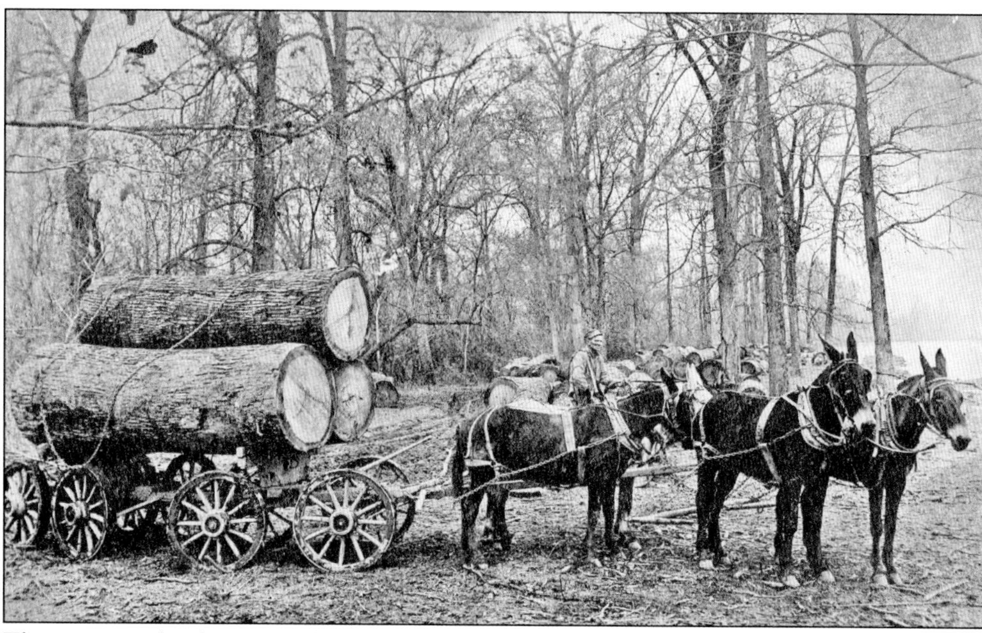

The virgin timber harvest yielded gigantic logs, which were very difficult to remove from the bottomlands where they were cut. Several small logging railroads solved the problem for many loggers of this era. One such line, the Bonnerville and Southern (later the Frisco), ran from the little community of Algoa in eastern Jackson County north through Amagon, Estico, and Grubbs and on to Jonesboro.

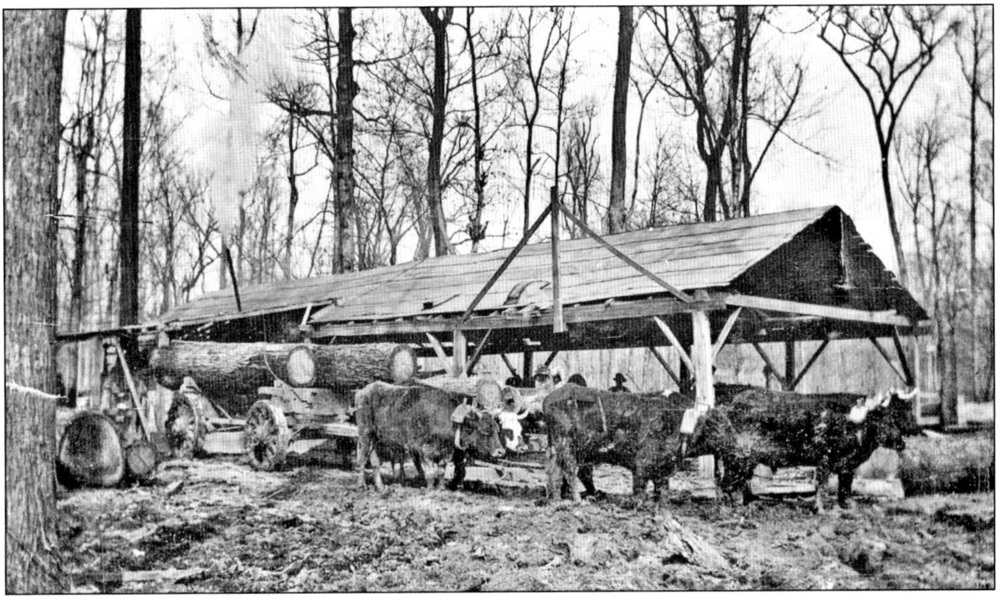

Oxen were often used to pull the heaviest loads, especially in muddy conditions, which were frequent since much of the land being cleared was along the river, and the river usually overflowed its banks twice a year, contributing to the outstanding fertility of the land. This 1924 scene shows large logs being hauled into Bob Logan's mill in Newport.

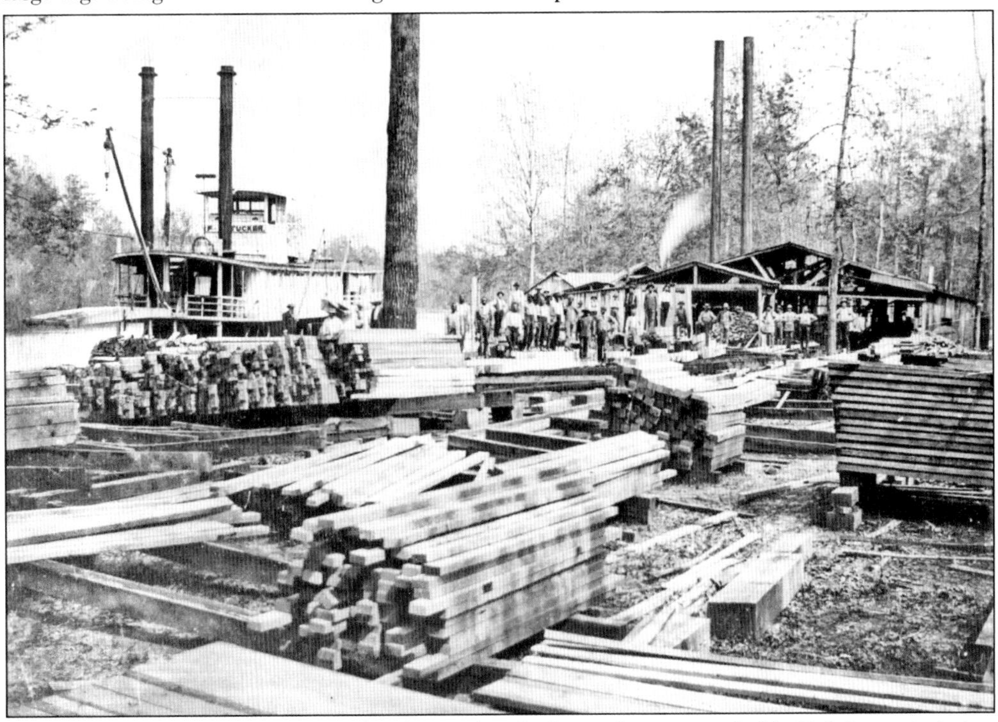

The steamer *F.W. Tucker* sits at a lumberyard in Jackson County, probably Bob Logan's, being loaded in the 1920s. African American laborers are standing by waiting to load the cut lumber onto barges that the steamboat will push down the White River to Memphis, New Orleans, and beyond.

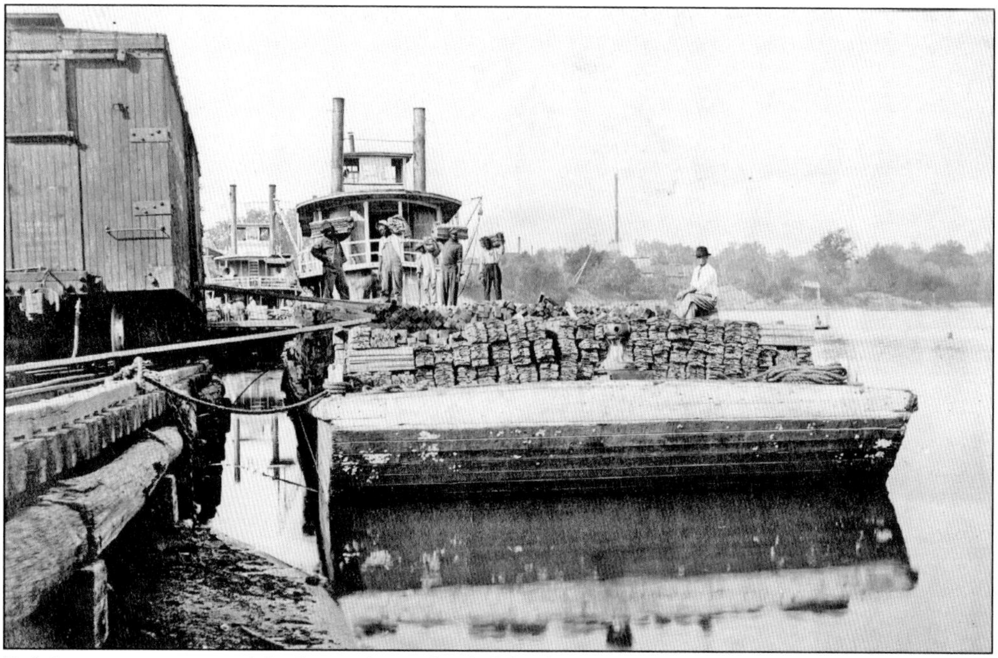

Bob Logan sits on one of the barges being loaded for shipment from his mill in 1924. Railcars also stand by waiting to be loaded, as does another steamboat docked at the river's edge in Newport. Strong arms and broad shoulders were needed to do this backbreaking work, as were balance and endurance.

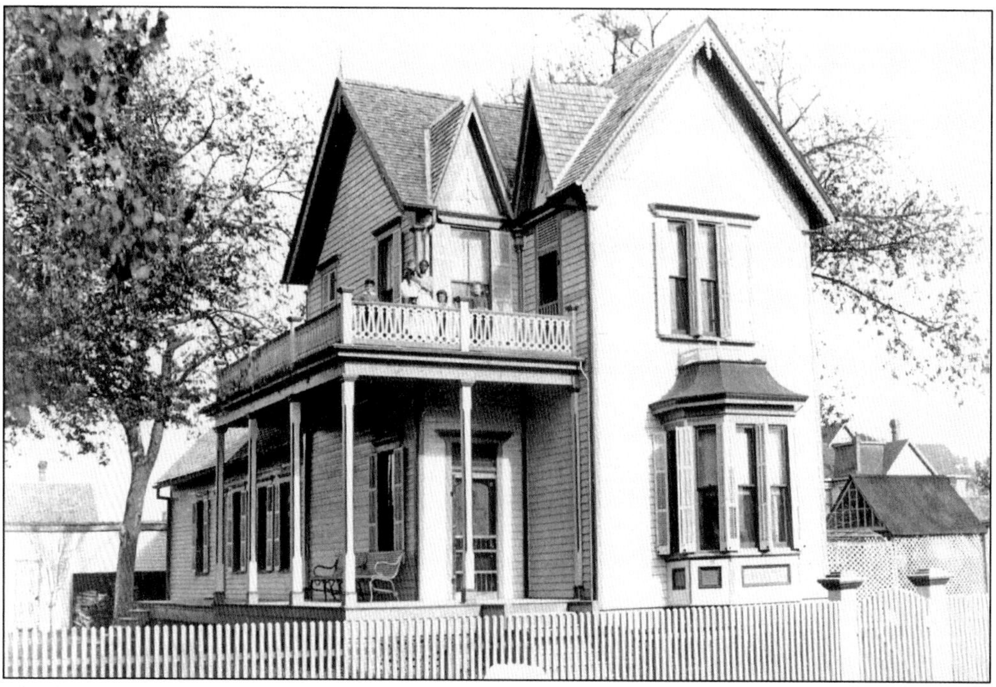

The home of Sigmund and Elise Wolff was one of the fine homes in downtown Newport that soon would fall prey to the fire of 1926. Note the unidentified black nursemaid, a fixture in every prosperous white home at the time.

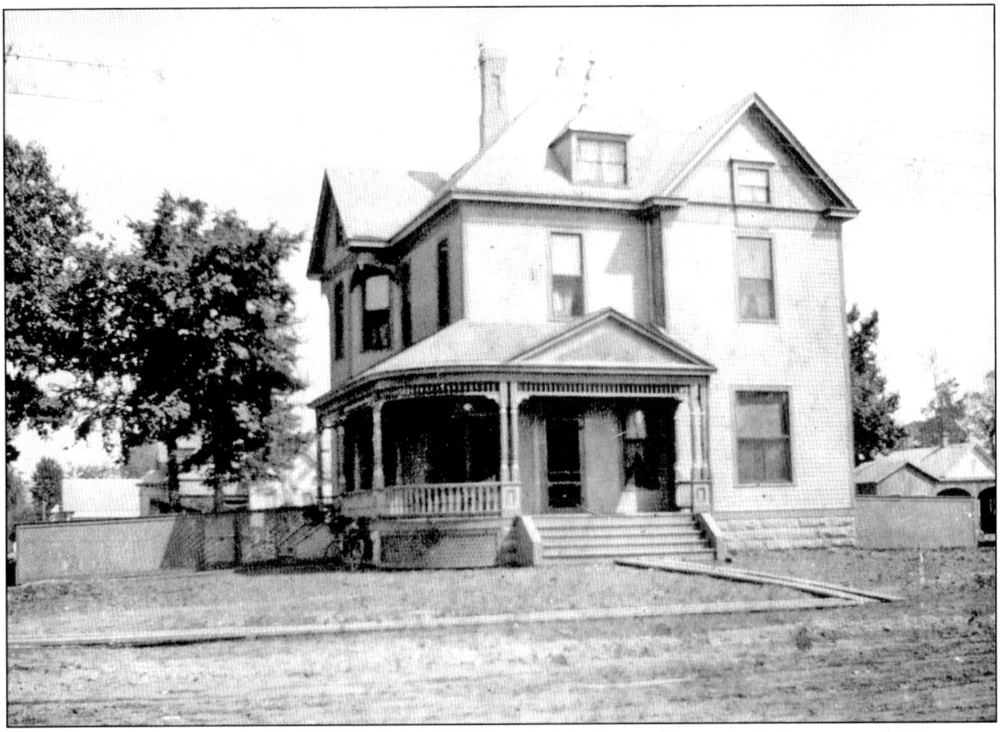

The John Stayton home was another lovely structure—and one that mercifully survived. Historian Marvin Schwartz writes, "Wealthy families celebrated their good fortune, building large, expansive homes with elaborate parquet flooring, railings, and wall panels." Those families also filled their homes with Oriental carpets, fine linens, china, and silver.

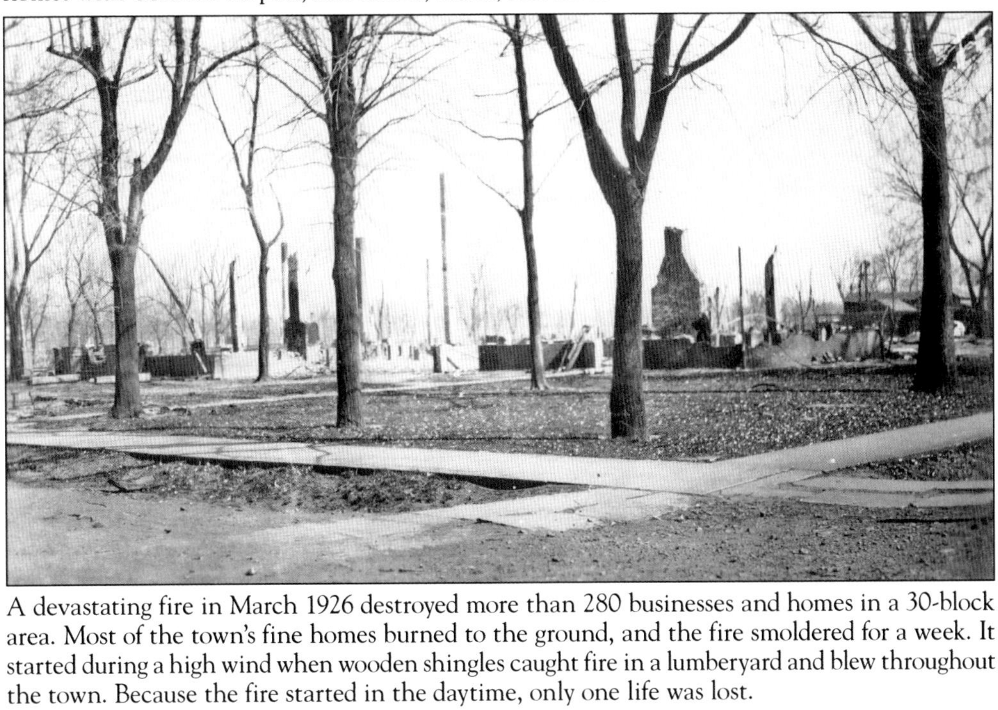

A devastating fire in March 1926 destroyed more than 280 businesses and homes in a 30-block area. Most of the town's fine homes burned to the ground, and the fire smoldered for a week. It started during a high wind when wooden shingles caught fire in a lumberyard and blew throughout the town. Because the fire started in the daytime, only one life was lost.

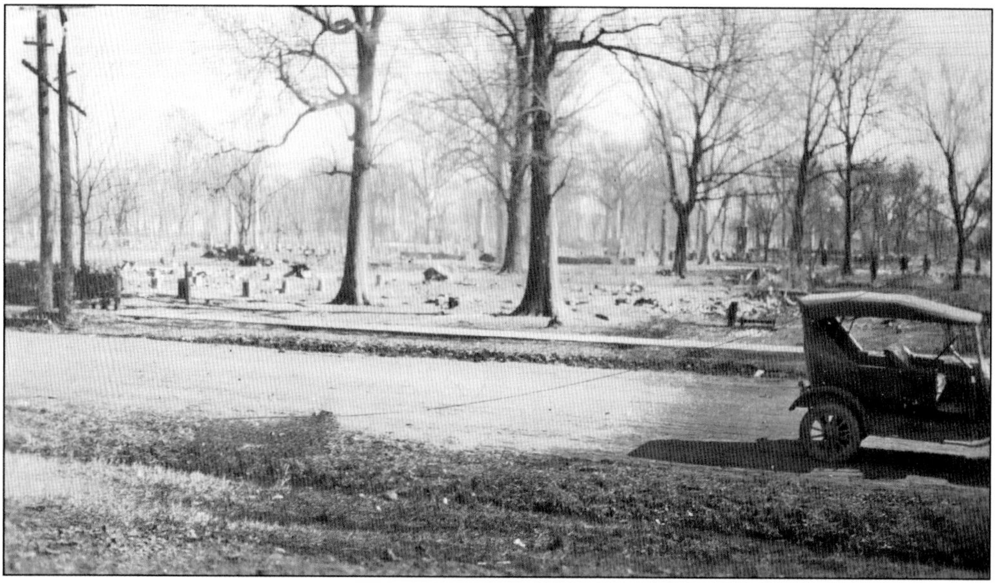

Newport's old-timers remembered for years how eerie the town seemed after the fire—looking to the veterans like scenes they had witnessed during World War I. Whole blocks were swept clean of homes, and then suddenly it would be evident that the wind had shifted and a home here and there had been spared. "The Fire" came to mean the fire of 1926, just as "the War" had always meant the War between the States.

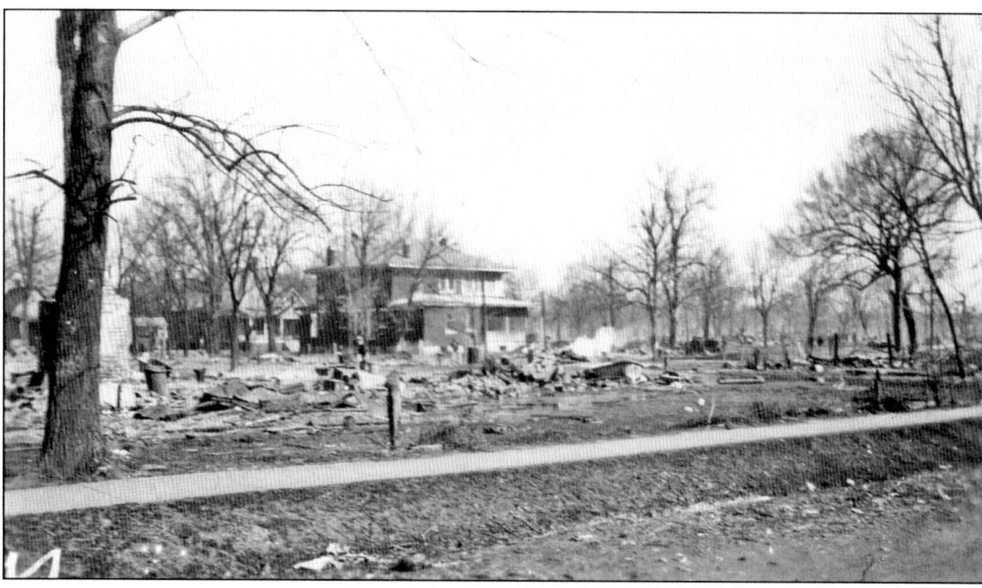

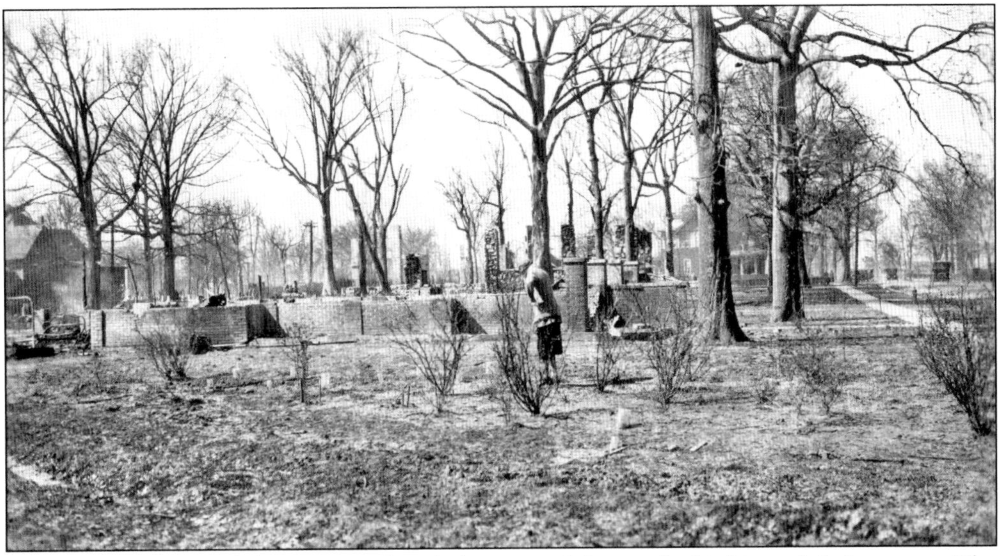

A few homes survived the carnage, largely because of the quick thinking of their owners. The Wilmans house (not pictured) was spared only because R.D. Wilmans brought his farmhands in from the fields and stood them on top of his house with wet towels and blankets to brush away the blazing shingles that landed on his roof. Located at Third and Pine Streets, it was directly in the path of the blaze.

This map shows the area that succumbed to the fire, as it was obviously being driven by the wind. Newport bounced back with strong-willed determination. The town astounded the entire state with its optimism and energy, winning the nickname "Plucky Newport" in news accounts over a wide area.

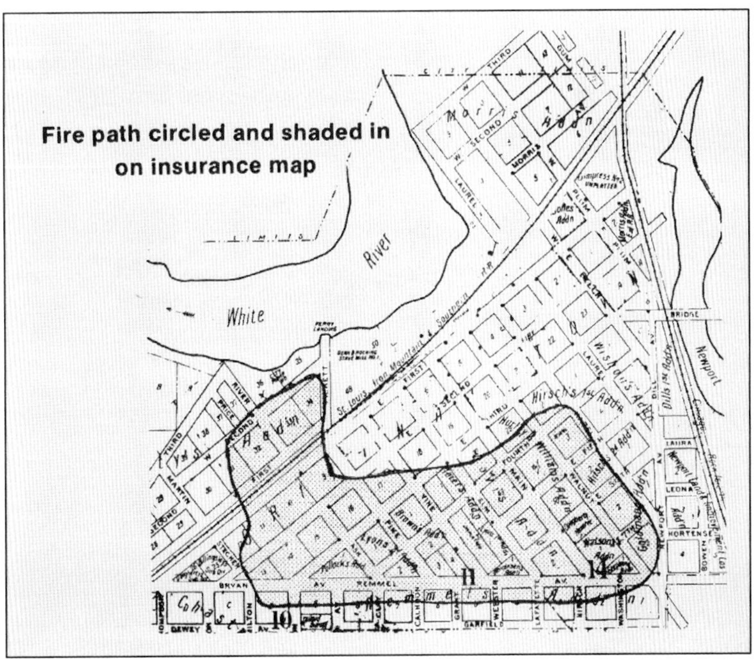

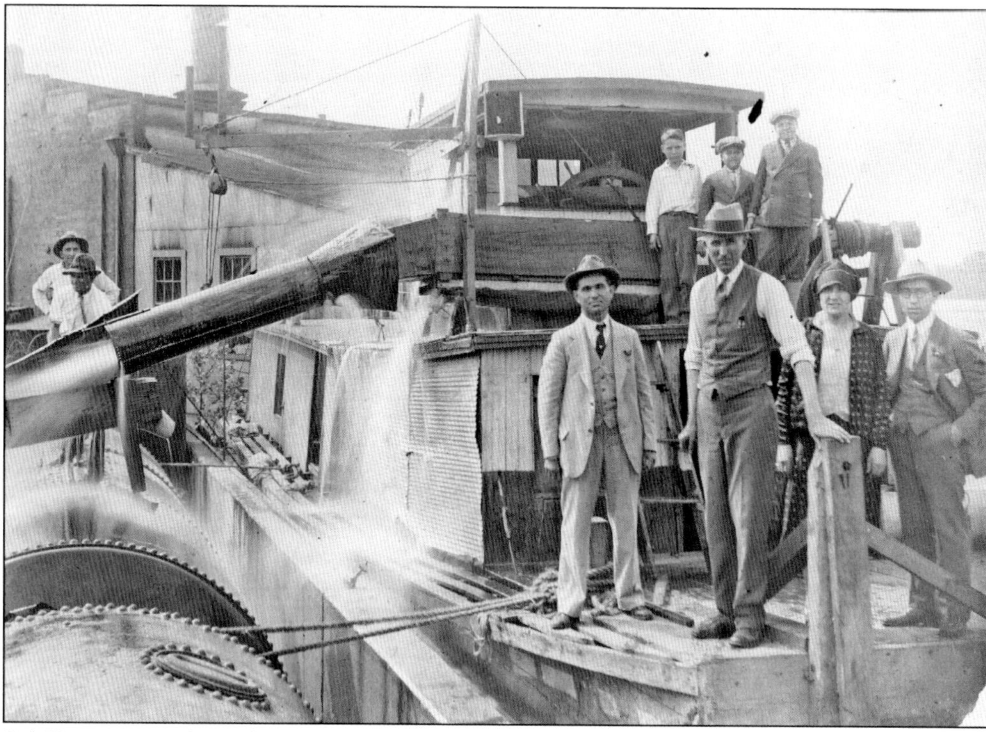

Sol Heinemann's barge brought fresh water into Newport during the flood of 1927. Shown in this picture are, from left to right, two unidentified, J.E. Wilmans (mayor), Heinemann, Hattie Heinemann, and a Mr. House. The boys are identified only as Sol and Sylvan Heinemann and a friend. (Courtesy of Jackson County Historical Society, Mildred Minor Gregory Collection.)

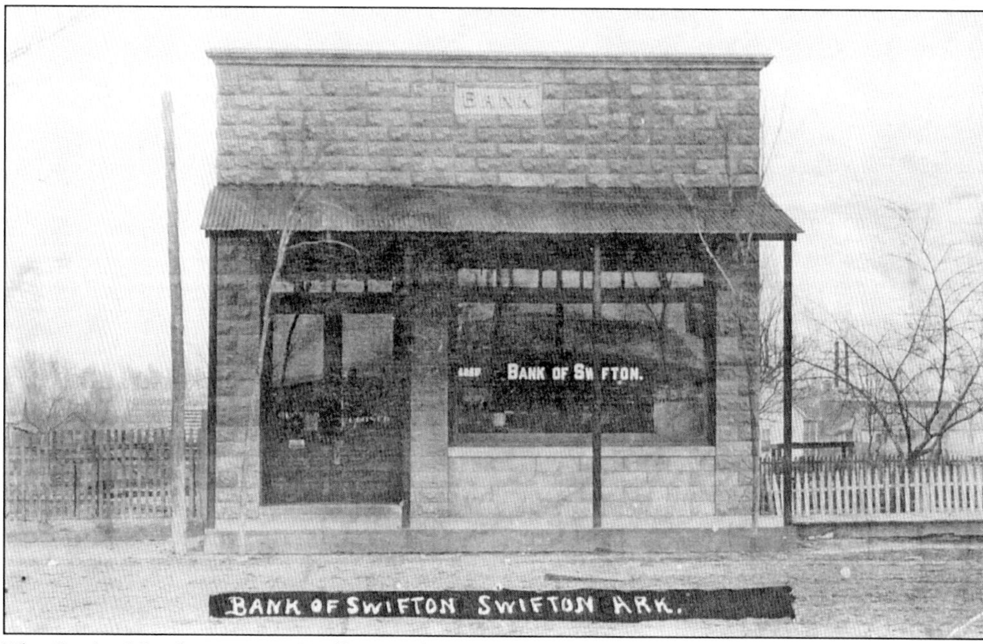

The Bank of Swifton was no Wall Street bank, but it did a brisk business in this prosperous little north Jackson County farming community. (Courtesy of Ray Hanley.)

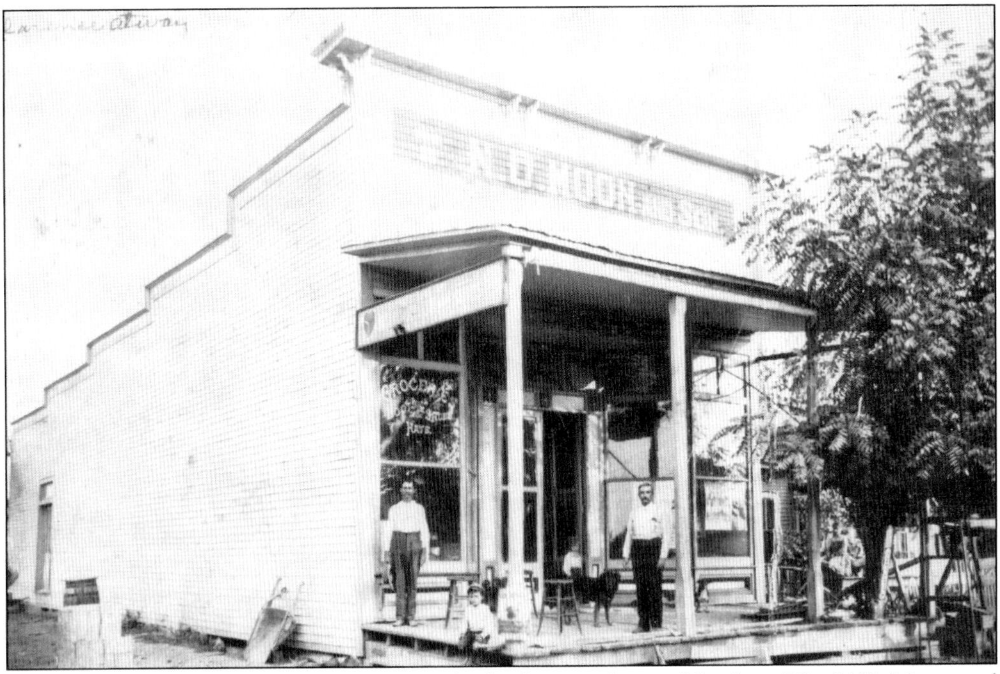

Members of the Moon family were among the leading residents of Swifton. The N.D. Moon and Sons Store offered groceries and dry goods. Almost every small community in the county had its own general merchandise store that sold everything from buttonhooks to bacon and made the lives of the townspeople and those from the surrounding countryside much easier. (Courtesy of J.W. Hulen.)

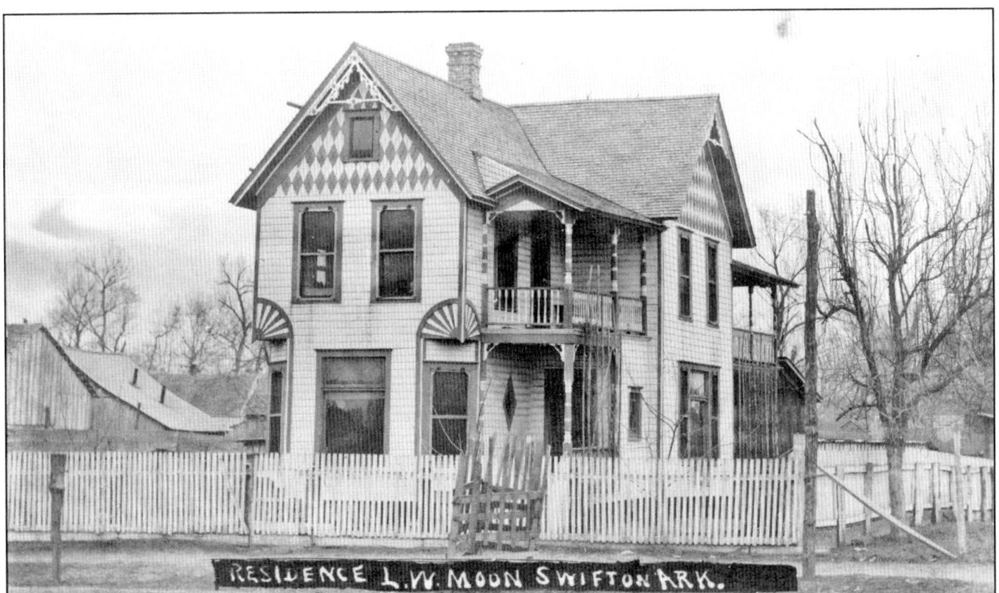

The L.W. Moon home was perhaps the most intriguing of the many fine homes that Swifton's farmers and merchants built for their families. (Courtesy of Ray Hanley.)

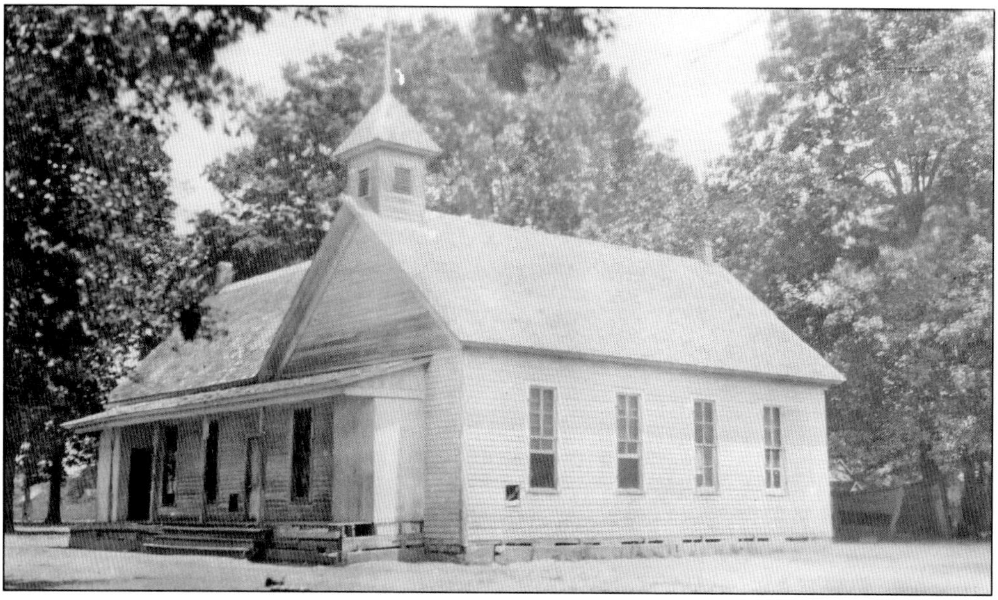

In the southern part of Jackson County, the white children of Weldon attended school in this wood-frame schoolhouse through the first half of the 20th century. Small rural schools like this one dotted the countryside all over the county. School consolidation later caused the closure of all such centers of learning, so that now there are only two school districts remaining. (Courtesy of Jackson County Historical Society, Mildred Minor Gregory Collection.)

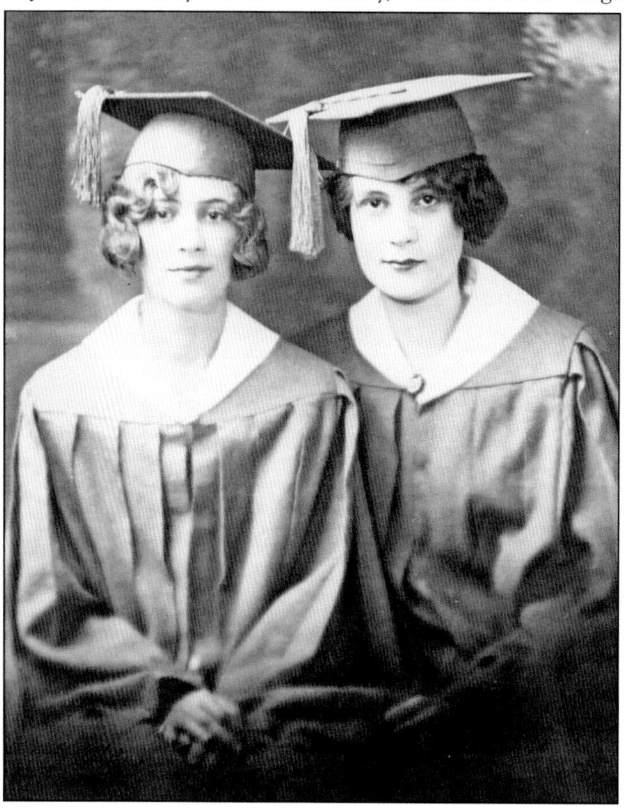

Best friends Lady Elizabeth Watson (later Luker), left, and Clare Phillips (later Dowell) graduated from Newport High School in 1928. Lady then spent a year at Miss Madeira's School in Washington, DC, in preparation for college at Wellesley. Clare attended Goucher College in Baltimore, Maryland, at the urging of her brother Neill Phillips, who had graduated from Annapolis and later became an admiral in the US Navy. (Courtesy of Tim Watson Sr.)

Six

New Demands
The 1930s

Jackson County suffered through the Great Depression of the 1930s along with the rest of the nation. Agriculture continued to be the lifeblood of the county, despite the near-ruinous low commodity prices, and the landowners continued to prosper. Newport finally built an extensive levee system completely encircling the town following the 1927 flood that devastated so much of the Mississippi basin, and the new levee has kept the waters at bay ever since (along with the help of four dams on the upper White River).

The year 1930 saw the completion of the first highway bridge across the White River at Newport, greatly diminishing the time needed to cross at the old ferry site. The US Army had originally created the Highway 67 roadbed as a military road and called it the Southwest Trail. The new bridge opened to much fanfare, as businessmen and farmers saw great possibilities stemming from the improved transportation into and out of their county. In the 1960s, the bridge acquired a coat of blue paint.

In the 1930s, Newport became a production center for pearl buttons. The mussels from the White River that occasionally yielded valued pearls now came to be valued for their shells as well, and plugs from these shells were used to make buttons for clothing. Reportedly, Newport's button factories could handle 76,000 pounds of mussel shells per day, which required 1,000 shell fishers to keep them active. Another industry that developed in the 1930s was rice production, which in the years since has become one of the major sources of income in the county. Rice growing is much less labor-intensive than tending to King Cotton.

Pickens Black, a freed slave who came to Jackson County in the 1870s, continued to buy land that the timber companies had cleared in the eastern part of the county, and his unincorporated town of Blackville now sported schools, churches, cotton gins, retail businesses, and many homes—all for his extended family and fellow African Americans. Most Jackson County blacks were not as fortunate as Pickens Black, and as they had only their labor to sustain them, their lives during the Depression years were especially hard.

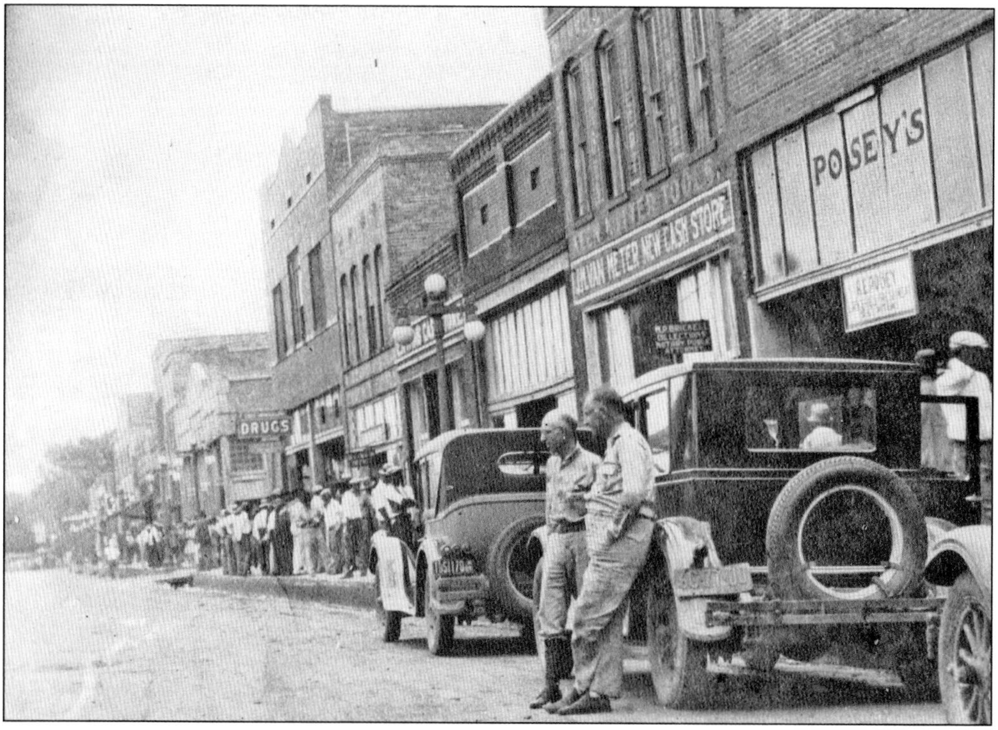

Obviously captured on a Saturday, this image shows the throngs of people who collected on Front Street in downtown Newport every weekend as the folks from the country came into town to do their shopping. One old-timer remembers rushing downtown as a teenager to get a good parking spot in front of the drugstore, because they would deliver a Coke on ice to the car window. (Courtesy of C. Phillip McDonald.)

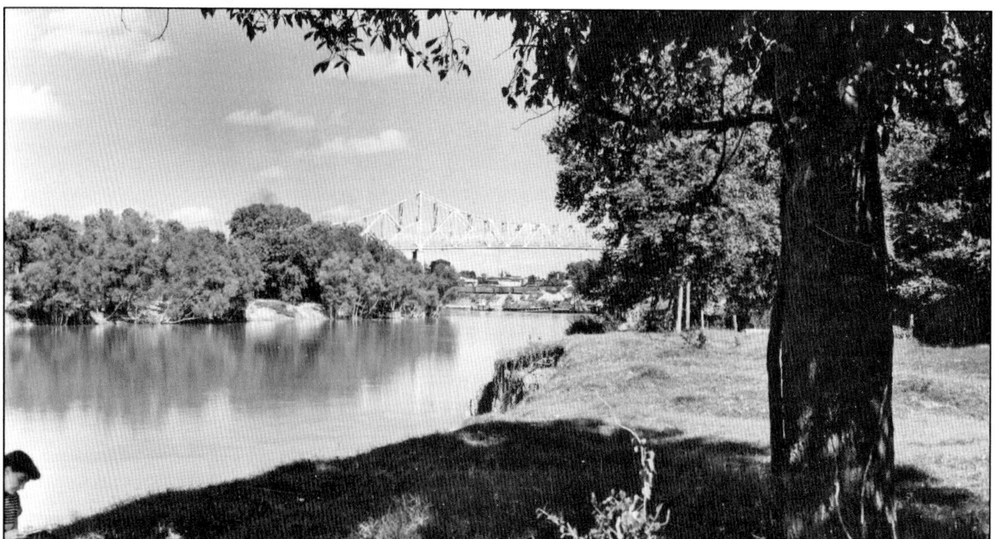

Opened in 1930 to much fanfare, the bridge over the White River in Newport was constructed at the location of the old Newport, or upper ferry. Ferry service had existed at this point on the White River since approximately 1835. The new bridge helped speed traffic on Highway 67 south toward Little Rock and beyond.

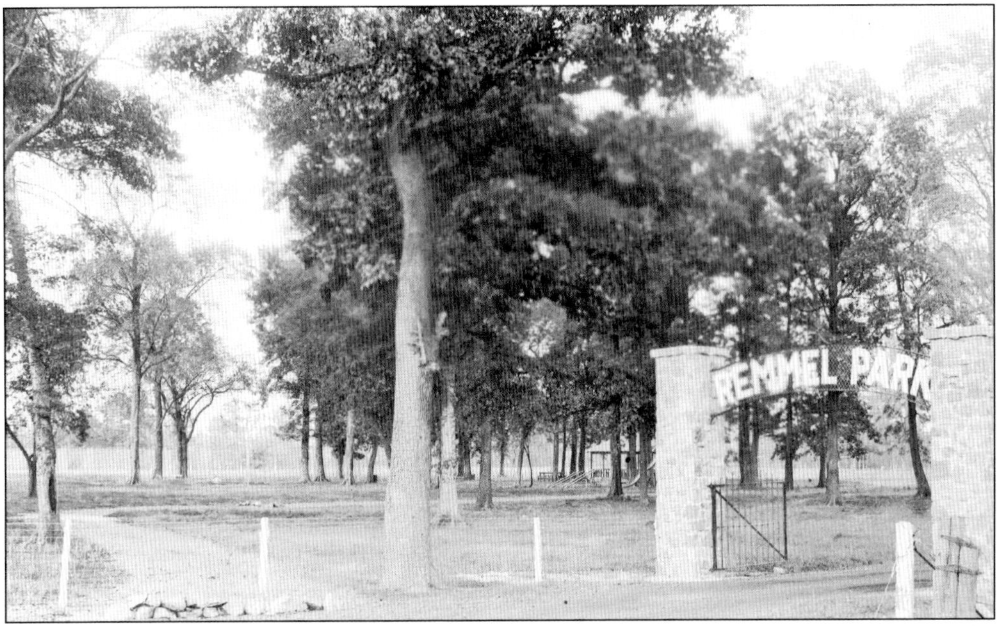

Situated on beautiful tree-shaded land bordering Newport Lake, Remmel Park, given by the Remmel family around 1930, was the first city park for Newport's citizens. The park provided picnicking, tennis, and fishing for locals, and is still much in use. In 1932, Huey Long made an appearance there for Arkansas senator Hattie Carraway, haranguing the large crowd gathered there to return the "little woman" to the US Senate. (Courtesy of Jackson County Historical Society, Mildred Minor Gregory Collection.)

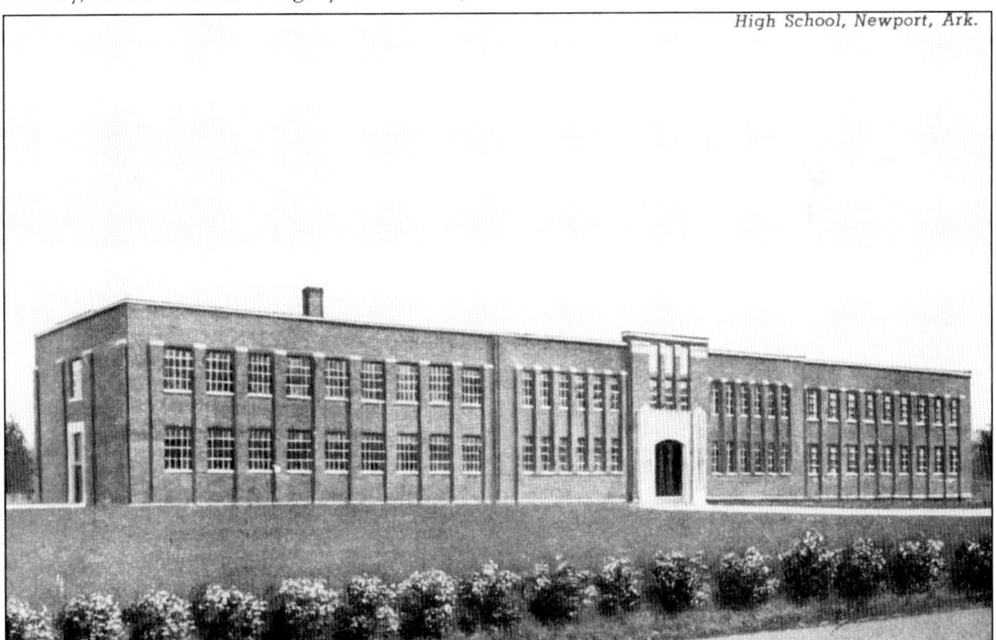

Built in 1930, Newport High School replaced the Walnut Street School, which continued to be used for grades one through six until 1951. This school building is still in use as Newport High School. (Courtesy of Robert Craig.)

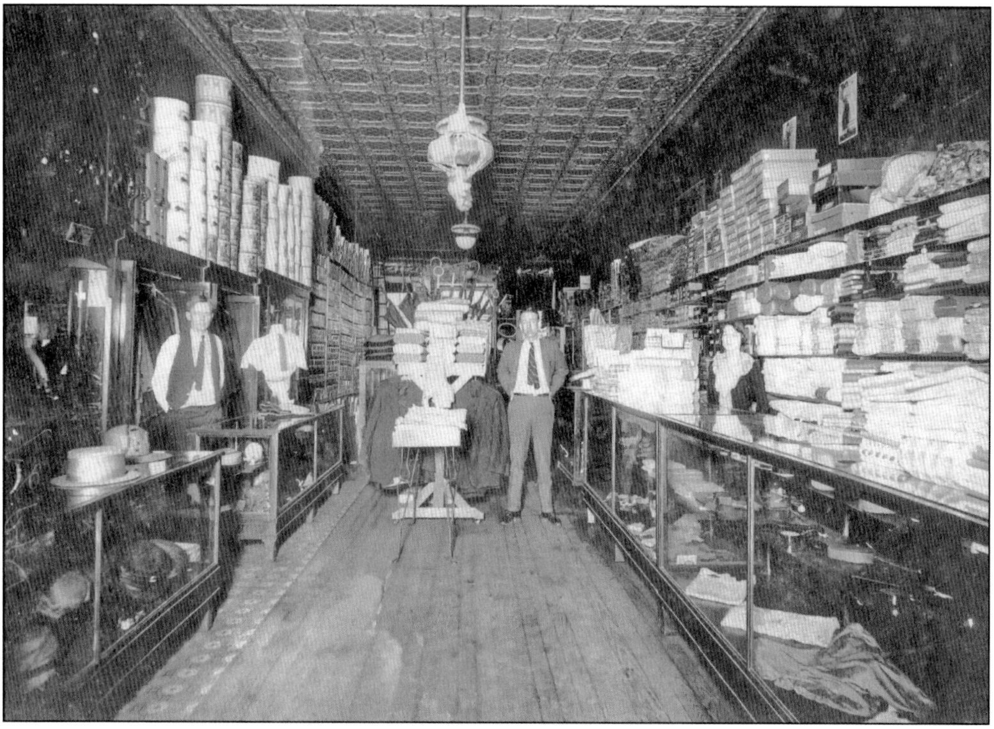

Sol Heinemann Sr. operated the Heinemann Department Store in the 400 block of Front Street from 1903 to 1929, then sold it to P.K. Holmes Sr., who changed the name but operated in that location for over 40 years. In 1972, Holmes's son moved his P.K. Holmes Men's Store two doors from the original location and operated a fine gentlemen's clothing store for many years.

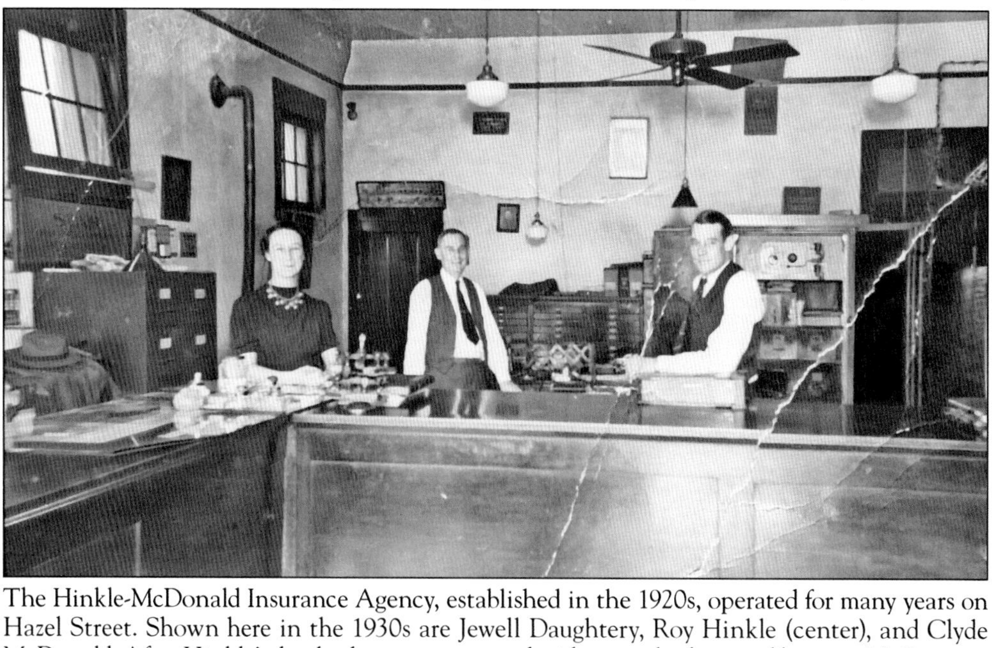

The Hinkle-McDonald Insurance Agency, established in the 1920s, operated for many years on Hazel Street. Shown here in the 1930s are Jewell Daughtery, Roy Hinkle (center), and Clyde McDonald. After Hinkle's death, the agency merged with several others and became McCartney, Manning, McDonald, and Guinn. (Courtesy of C. Phillip McDonald.)

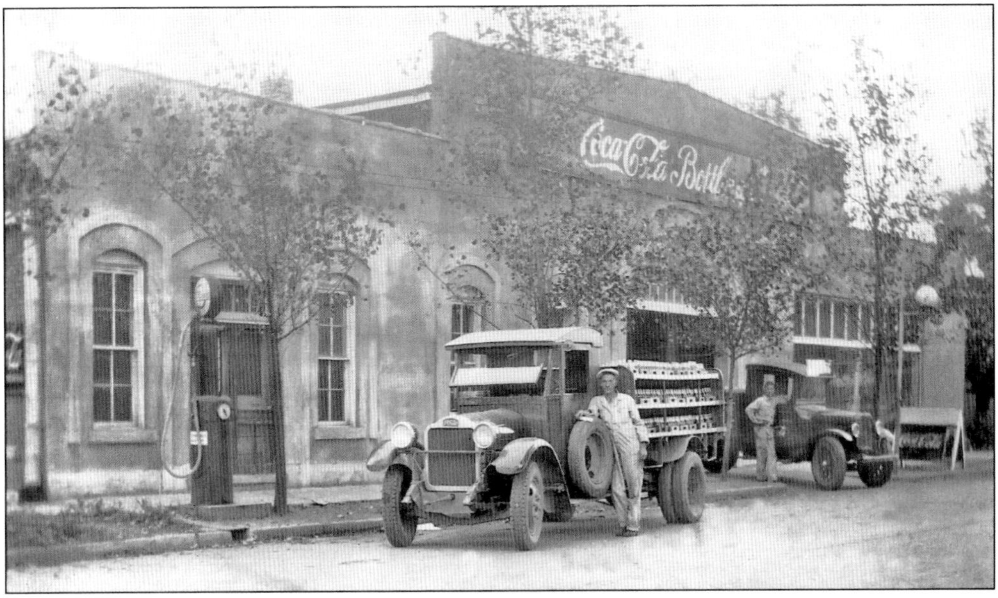

Newport's Coca-Cola Bottling Co. plant delivered cases of Cokes to stores all over the county. In April 1931, Dewitt Scraggs and John Robinette pose for an informal portrait. Scraggs, in the driveway, had the in-city route; Robinette, by the truck in the street, had the county route. This building was located in the 200 block of Beech Street in downtown Newport.

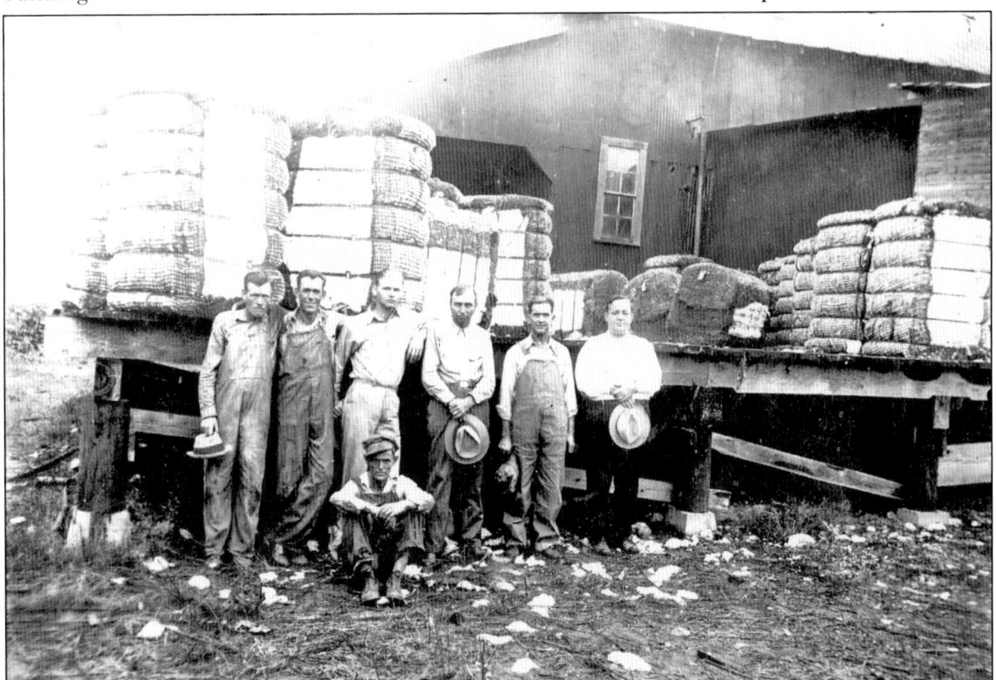

Taken in 1934 at the Swifton cotton gin, this photograph shows cotton bales that are ready for shipment. The proud workers and serious businessmen are, from left to right, John Jordan, Herbert Duncan, Troy Montgomery, Loyd Mosley, Harry Wyatt, Jim Haney, and Bill Atway, seated in front.

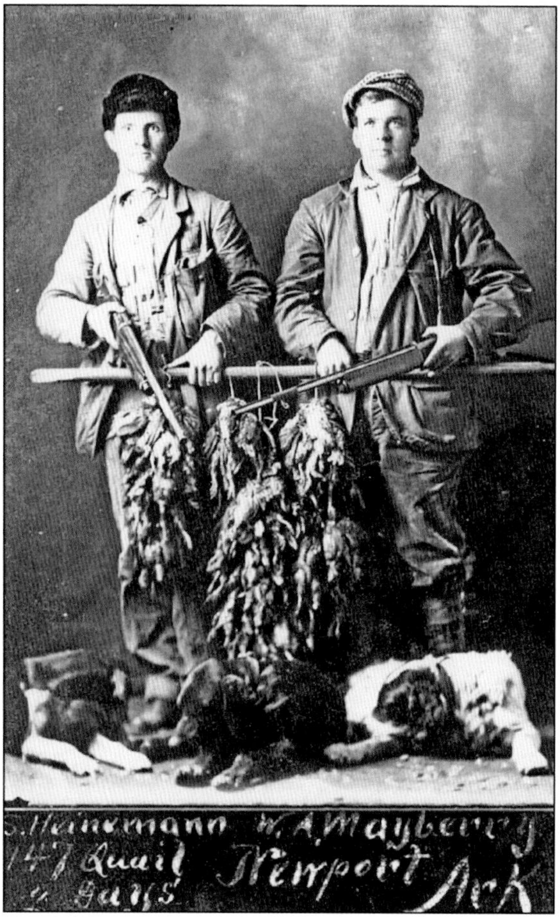

These young men chose to memorialize their prodigious hunting by having a postcard printed carrying their images. Clearly, there were no state-imposed limits in those days. Signed by Sol Heinemann Jr. and W.A. Mayberry, the note reads, "147 quail, 2 dogs." Hunting of every variety was always a major masculine endeavor in Jackson County. (Courtesy of Ray Hanley.)

Newport had discovered a new source of wealth in the early 1900s. Beautiful irregular freshwater pearls from the White River became a national and international sensation, bringing new riches to those who had the technology and the tenacity to harvest them. After being steamed open, the mussel shells were either sold to the button factories or crushed to be used in paving Newport's streets. (Courtesy of Robert Craig.)

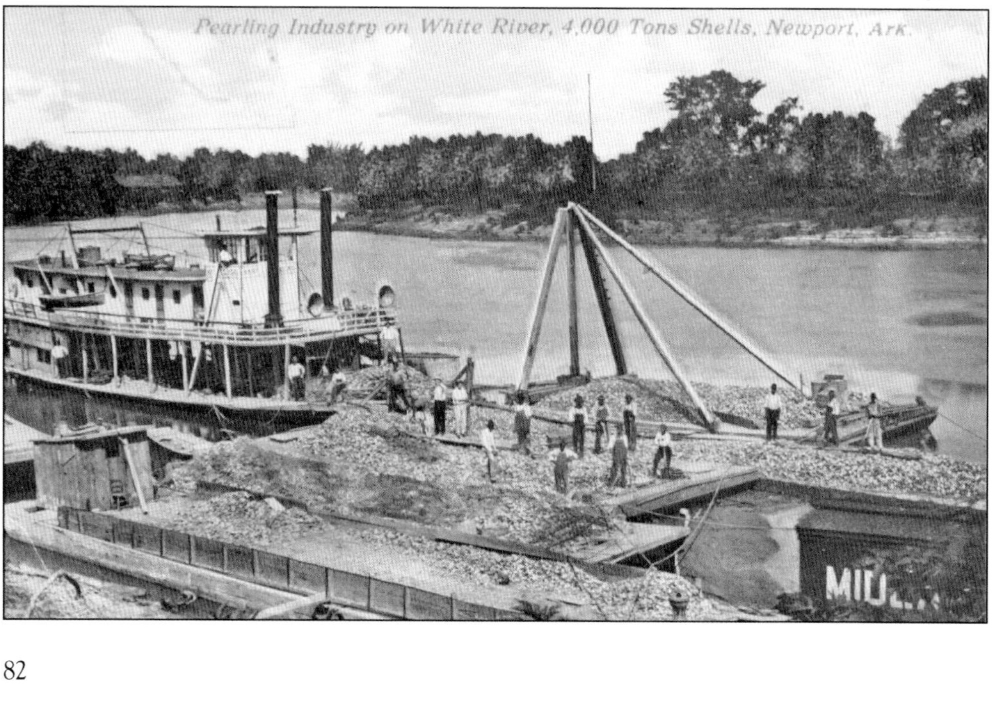

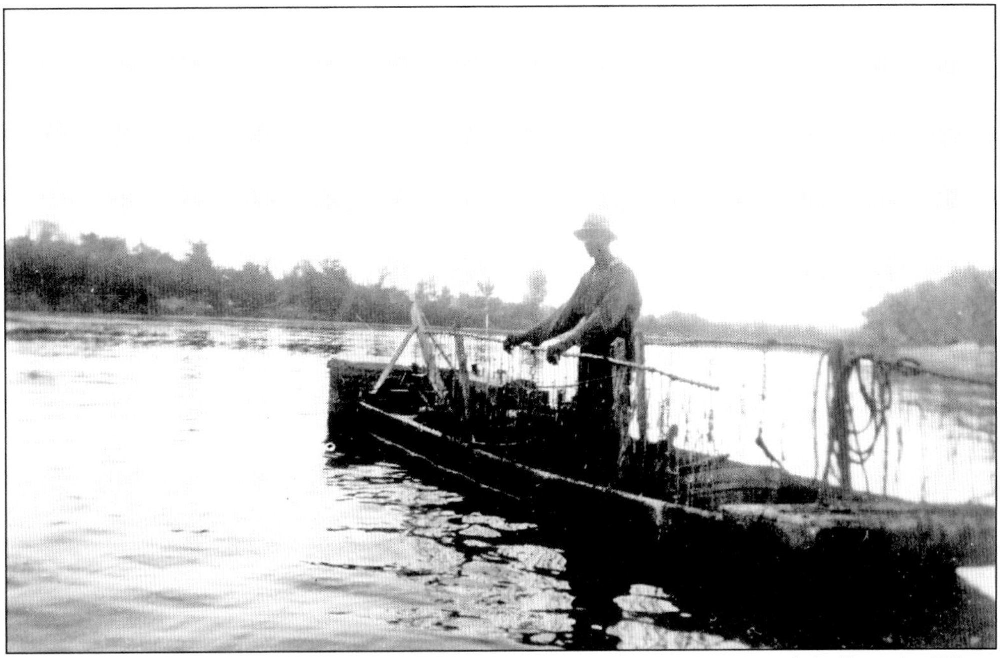

Robert Monroe rigged his flatboat with suspended hooks for harvesting mussel shells in the White River about 1936. Hooks were suspended from a pole and dragged along the bottom of the river. The work was tedious and usually beset by mosquitoes and the vagaries of the weather, but the rare bonanza of a beautiful and valuable pearl made it all worthwhile.

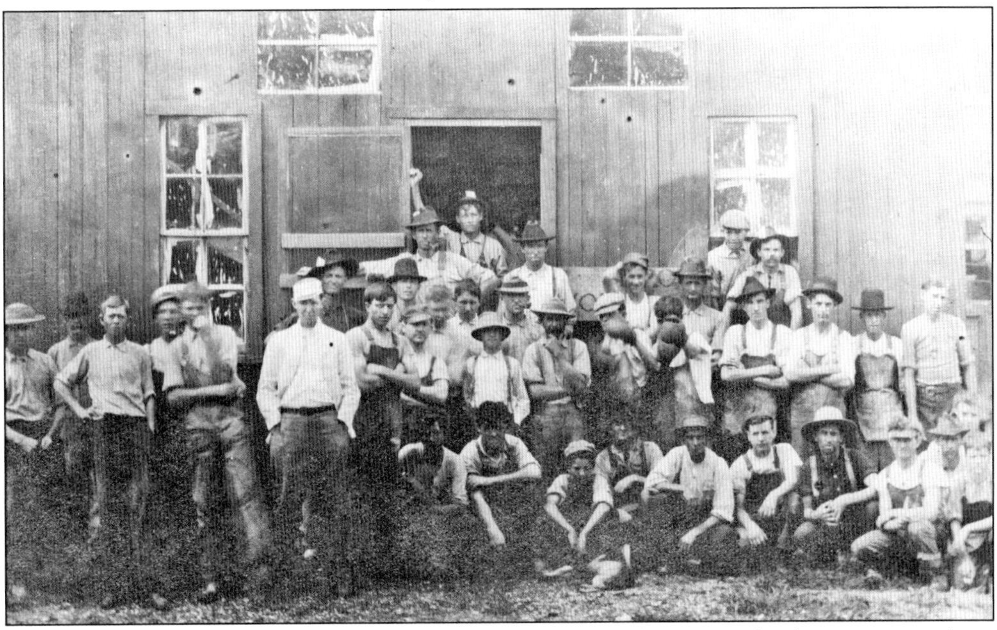

The workers outside one of the button factories in Newport ham it up for the camera, perhaps aware that they will soon appear on postcards that will travel all over the country. They seem blissfully unaware that their industry is overharvesting the White River's mussel shells and button production in Jackson County will soon come to an abrupt halt. (Courtesy of James Logan Morgan Jr. Papers and the Butler Center.)

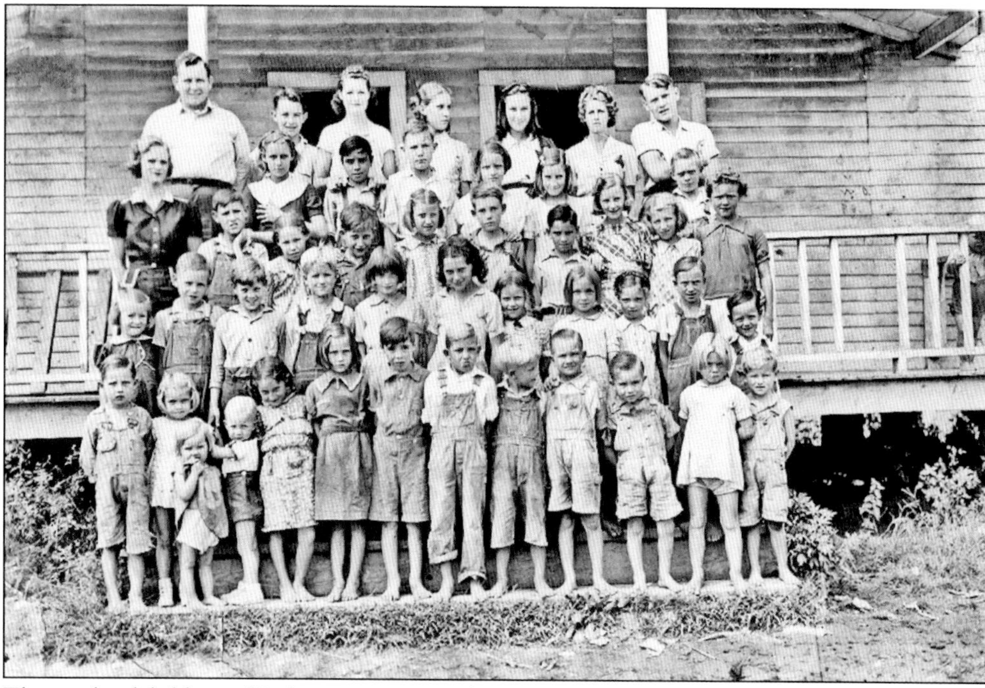

These schoolchildren of Jacksonport pictured in 1939 with their teachers, Charles and Thelma Warlow, are identified by last names only. They are, from left to right, (first row) Seymore, Gullett, unidentified, Wilson, unidentified, Eliott, Seymore, Adams, Fortune, Dunham, Jones, Jones, unidentified, and Davis; (second row) Dyke, Turner, Wilson, Dunham, Caldwell, Eliott, Odom, Dunham, Jordan, Street, and Odom; (third row) Turner, McBee, Eliott, Wilson, Street, Jeffery, Caldwell, and Davis; (fourth row) Smart, Jeffery, Jones, Ferguson, Rutherford, and Jordan; (fifth row) Jones, McLendon, Freeman, Jeffery, Smart, and Stuart.

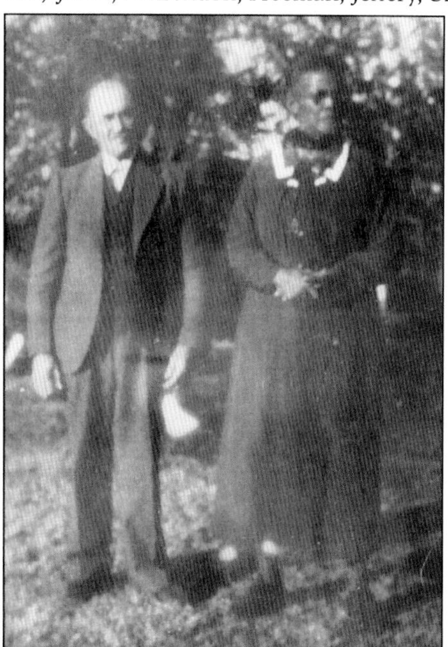

Born a slave in Alabama about 1861, Pickens Black Sr. moved to Arkansas as a teenager, worked on the railroad, and started buying land, eventually amassing more than 8,000 acres. Black and his sons ran a plantation that included a cotton gin, sawmill, and grain elevator. He employed 360 families as sharecroppers, whites as well as blacks, to work the land around his unincorporated town of Blackville. Black died in 1955. The woman in the photograph is unidentified.

Seven

NEW POSSIBILITIES
THE 1940S

As the nation emerged from the Great Depression with the coming of World War II, Jackson County returned to growth and prosperity. The war touched Jackson County more directly than its neighbors because the Army established a flight-training facility east of Newport in 1942, bringing in so many young soldiers that the population of the town doubled. The influx of youthful energy and dollars made Newport an exciting and prosperous town during the war years. With the end of the war and the removal of the flight school, the Army gave the airfield to the City of Newport to use as its first industrial park.

The decade of the 1940s was a transitional period in the economic life of the county, from one almost wholly dominated by agriculture to the beginnings of the era of new plants and factories, providing more jobs to the people of the county than ever before. This phenomenon would come to full fruition in the next decade, but its roots were in the 1940s, with the donation of the Army airfield and the beginnings of farm mechanization—especially the introduction of larger and more powerful tractors that would usurp the jobs of so many of the county's farm laborers.

By the 1940s, Jacksonport had become a ghost town, but the villages of Tuckerman, Grubbs, and Swifton grew along with the county, as did Newport. The old farming communities of Weldon, Shoffner, and Tupelo also returned to prosperity, but the days of all these farming communities were numbered, as ensuing decades would see their labor forces begin to drift away into the cities and to the North.

For now, the county's citizens went back to work, building more schools and churches to accommodate the growing population. The levee around Newport, which had been raised to its current height in the 1930s, the concrete embankment along the river, and the coming of the first large dams on the upper White River kept Newport dry, and have ever since.

In politics, Jackson County was as "Yellow-Dog" Democrat as any other county in the South. The Republican Party simply did not exist in Jackson County, and it would not for many more decades. As a result, party politics as such was nonexistent. Factions within the Democratic Party vied in the primaries, and as the old saying went, success in the primaries was "tantamount to election."

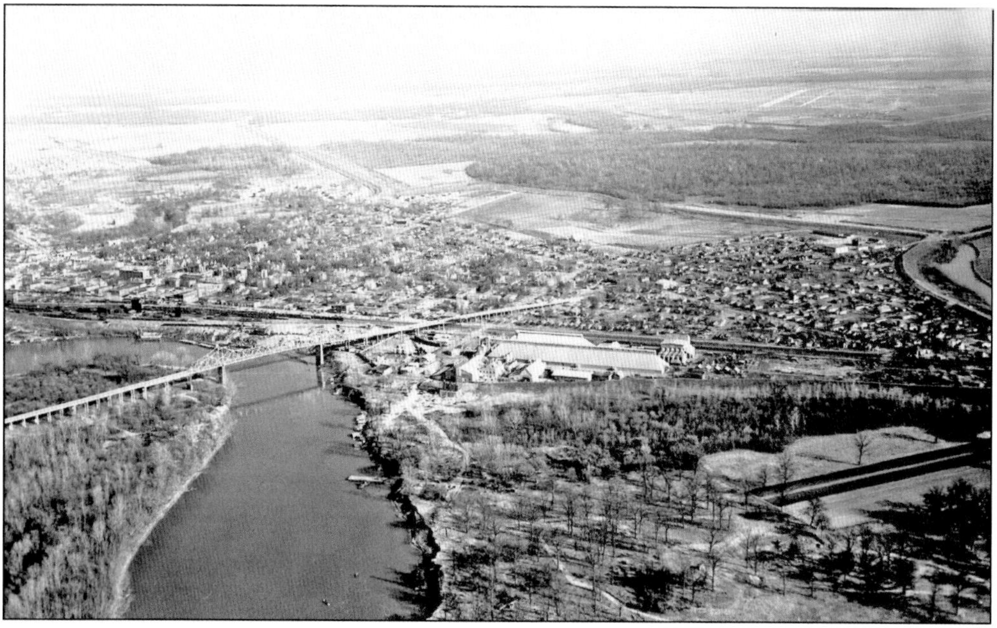

An aerial view of Newport shot in 1940 shows the bend in the White River on the north side of town, with the blue bridge spanning the river and leading into the business district. Clearly, the devastation of the 1926 fire has been overcome, and a prosperous little town and fertile fields spread out where virgin hardwood forests used to stand. The Southern Cotton Oil Company is seen is the right center. Cottonseeds were cooked and crushed for their oil.

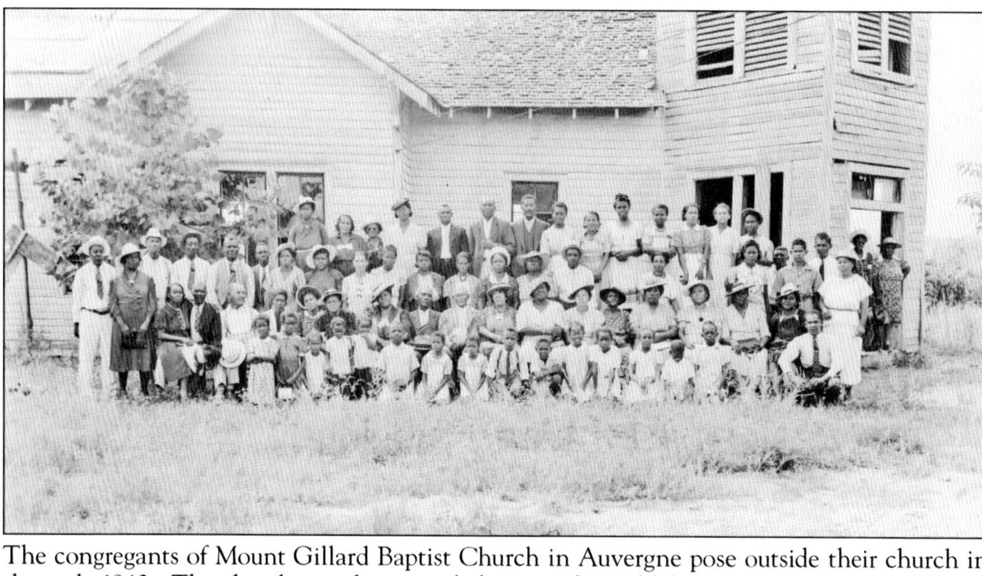

The congregants of Mount Gillard Baptist Church in Auvergne pose outside their church in the early 1940s. The church was the central element of social life in most parts of Arkansas at this time, in white communities as well as black. (Courtesy of James Logan Morgan Jr. and the Butler Center.)

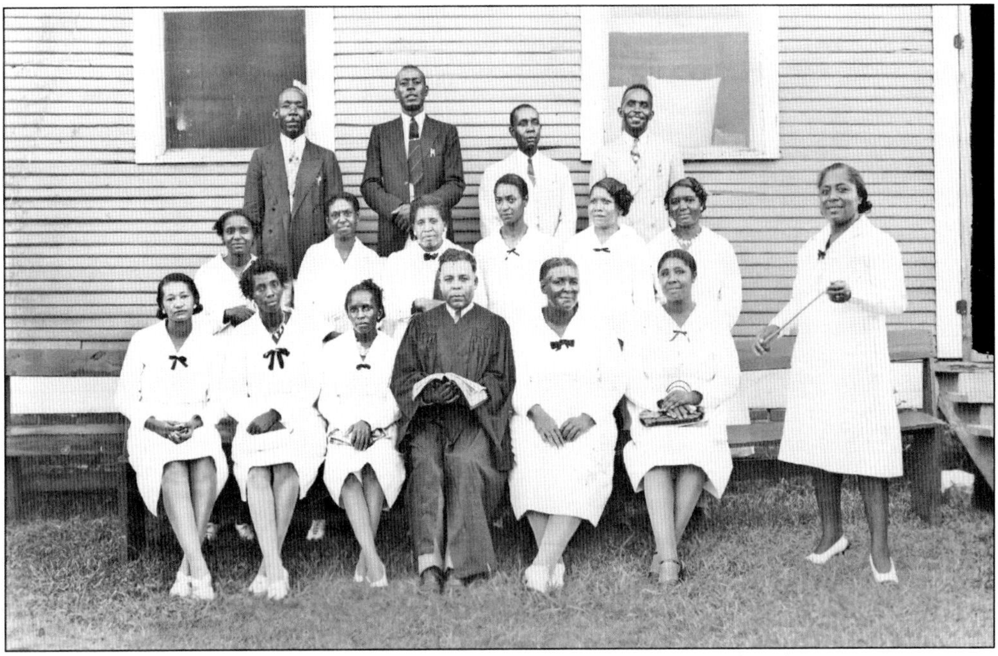

Above, members of the senior choir of the Morning Star Baptist Church in Newport poses proudly with their pastor, Rev. R.S. Jones. Pictured are, from left to right, Ruth Cagle, Edith Seales, Thaddeus Walker, Reverend Jones, Hattie Whittenhill, Sally Boyd, and director Deborah Daniels (standing); (second row) Lillie Battie, Sophia Ware, Erma Alexander, Lottie Mae Smith, Lizzie Hose, and Vasa Holmes; (third row) Aaron Daniel, David Reed, William McBride, and Jessie Hill. Below, the elders of the Morning Star Baptist Church in Newport include, in no particular order, Frank Burton, Witt Warren, Reverend Jones, Henry Holmes, Felix Whittenhill, G.W. Oates, Aaron Daniel, William McBride, Robert Patrick, and Jessie Hill. (Both, courtesy of James Logan Morgan Jr. and the Butler Center.)

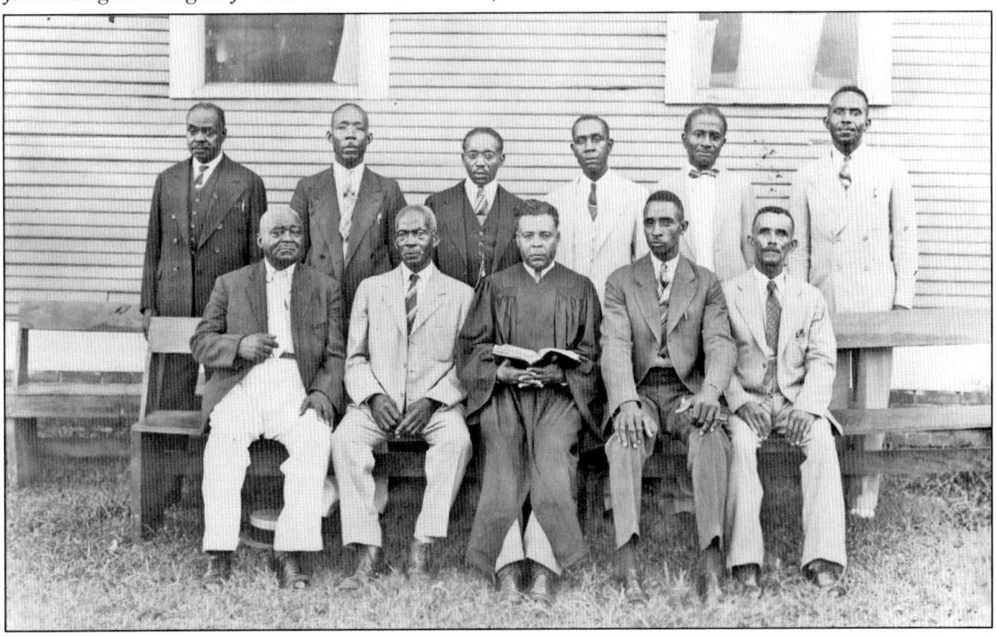

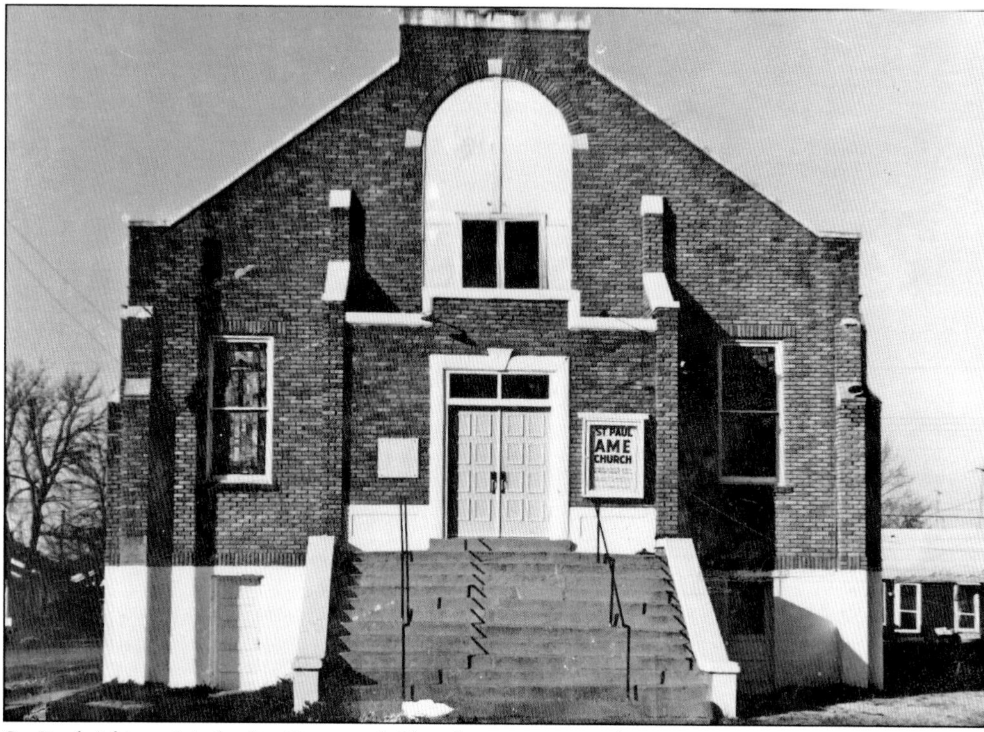

St. Paul African Methodist Episcopal Church was organized in 1880, and the congregation built this fine structure in 1914 at the corner of Sixth and Main Streets. Long the home of a vibrant congregation, the church moved "out on the highway" (away from downtown), and this building was torn down in 2012. (Courtesy of James Logan Morgan Jr. and the Butler Center.)

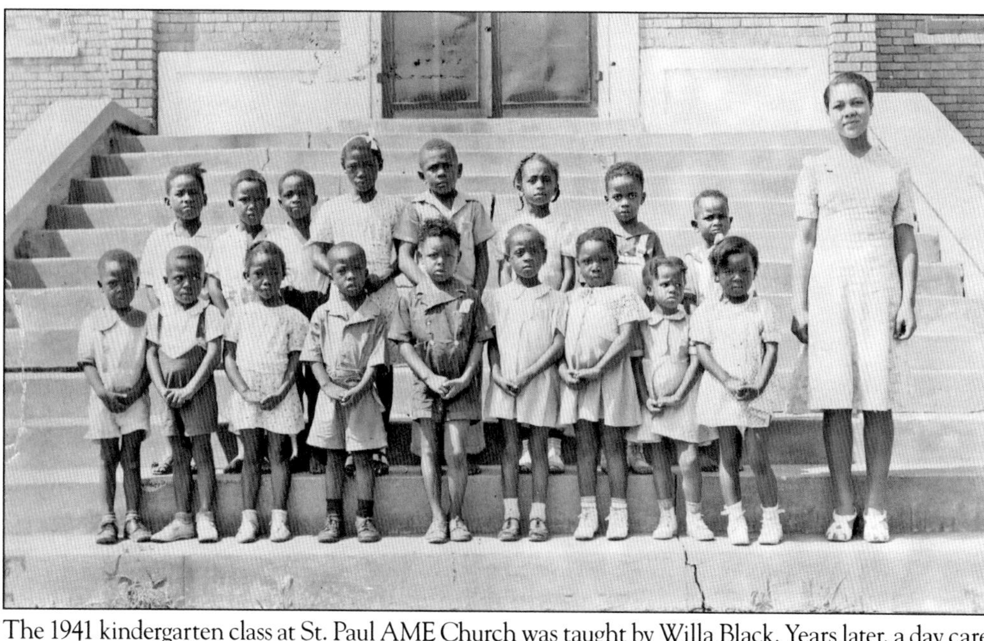

The 1941 kindergarten class at St. Paul AME Church was taught by Willa Black. Years later, a day care center was named in her honor. (Courtesy of James Logan Morgan Jr. and the Butler Center.)

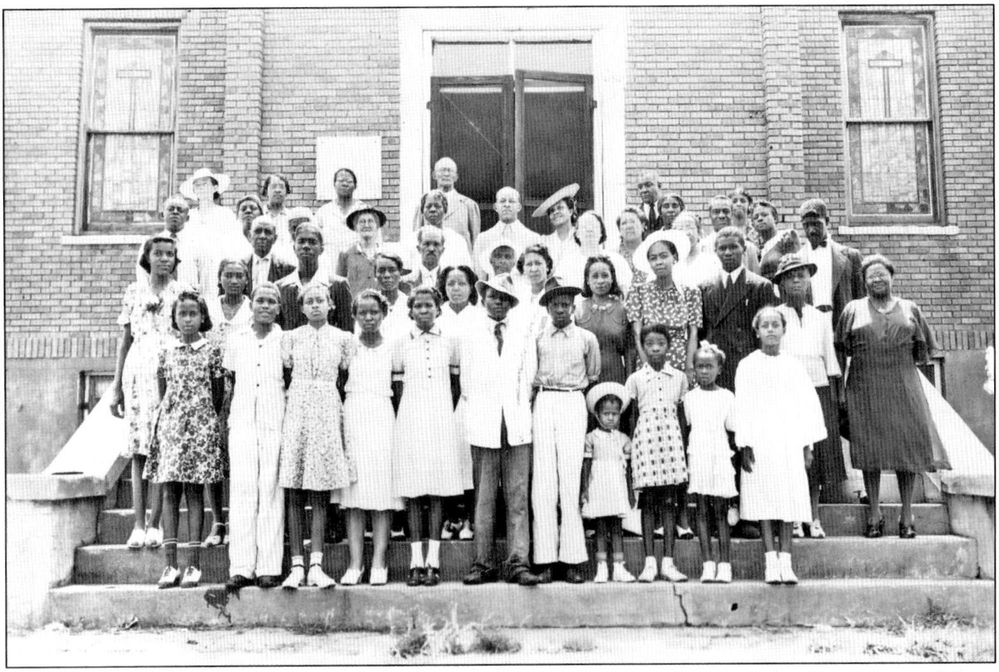

Unidentified members of St. Paul AME Church's congregation stand on the front steps of their church sometime in the 1940s, among them many of the leaders of Newport's black community. (Courtesy of James Logan Morgan Jr. and the Butler Center.)

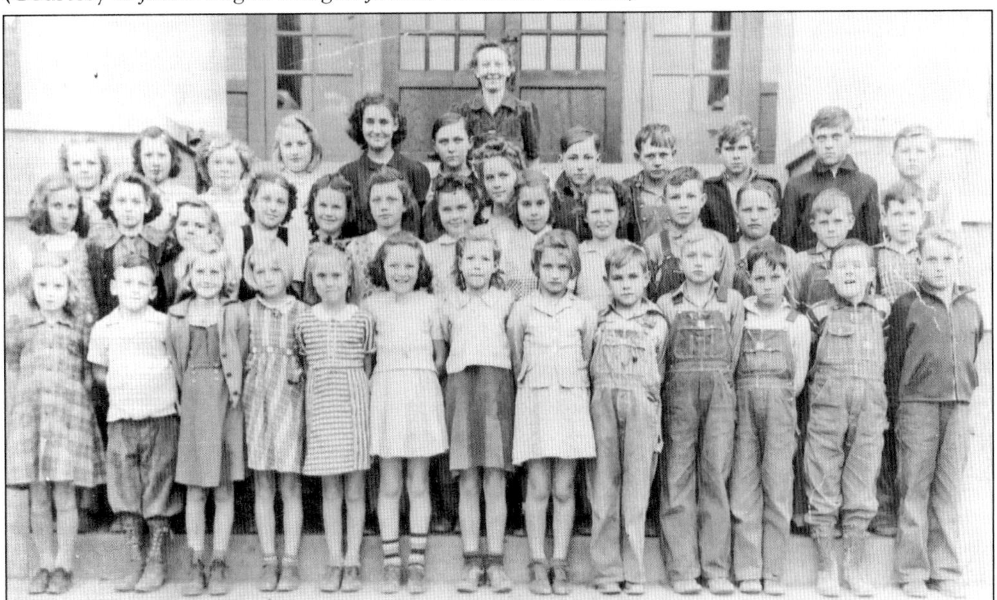

Swifton's fourth-grade class in 1941–1942 seems to be a happy lot, and they all have shoes. Standing with their teacher, Jewell Eldridge, are, identified by last names and from left to right, (first row) Cason, Moon, two unidentified, Harvey, Barker, Cross, Duncan, McGee, Harvey, King, and House; (second row) unidentified, Lovelace, Bailey, Wilson, Wyatt, unidentified, Haygood, two unidentified, Norton, Paton, Jordan, and Taylor; (third row) Fowler, Smith, two unidentified, Callahan, Norris, Gale, Sudduth, Vaughn, Templeton, Morton, and Smith. (Courtesy of J.W. Hulen.)

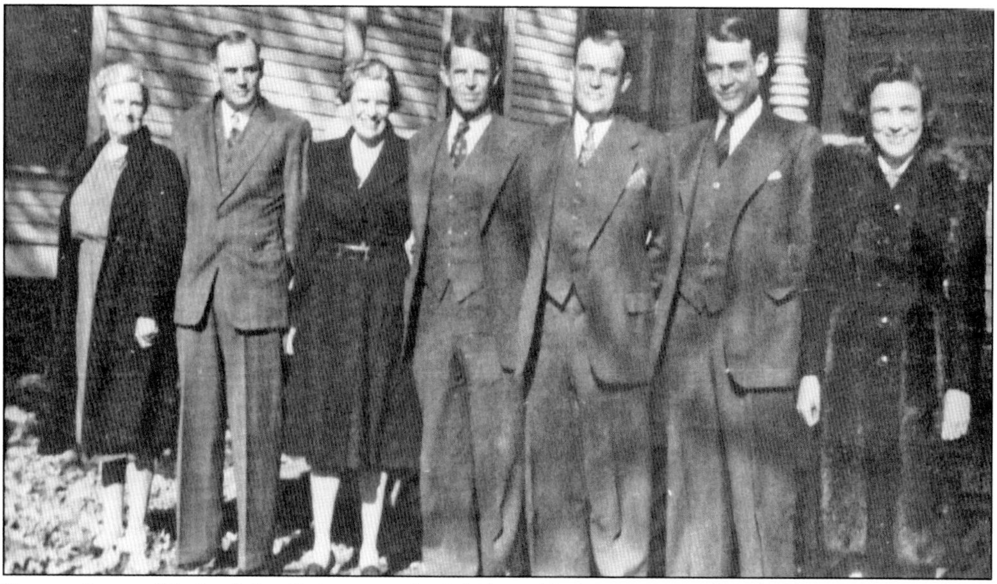

Descendants of Judge John Robinson, the McDonald siblings were the children of Alvin Tobe McDonald and Mary Susan Johnson McDonald. They are, from left to right, Sue McDonald Robinson, Robert Haas McDonald, Lottie McDonald McCartney, Joseph Johnson McDonald, Ralph McDonald Sr., Clyde Phillip McDonald, and Helen McDonald Chaney. (Courtesy of C. Phillip McDonald.)

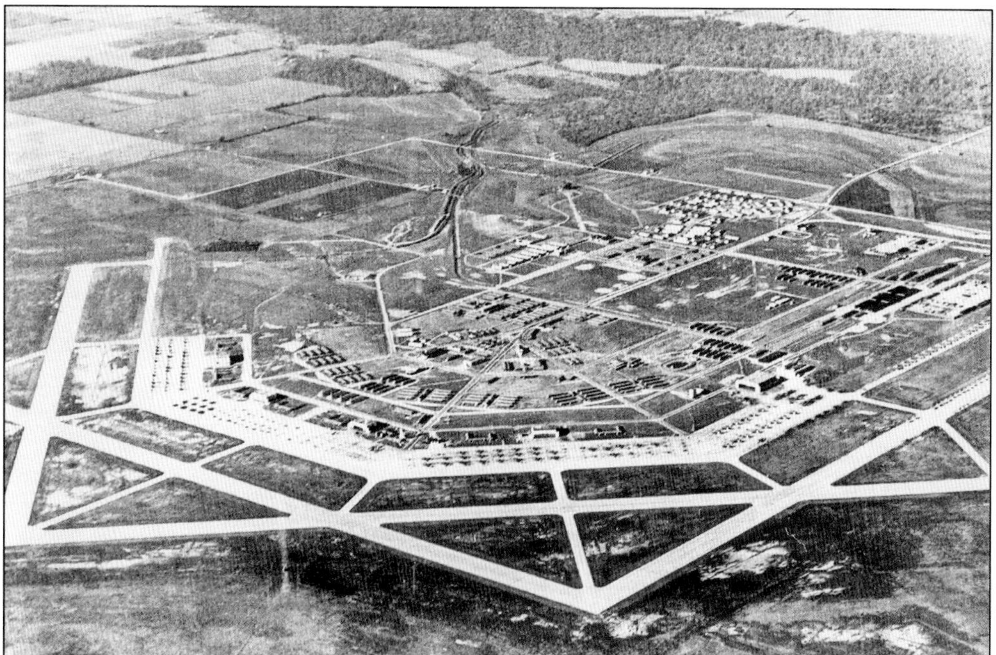

In November 1942, the Newport Army Airfield sprang into existence after only one year of intensive effort to clear rice fields and marshes, build barracks and training centers, and recruit potential pilots from all branches of the military services to participate in air combat during World War II. The airfield became another bonanza for Newport's thriving economy. (Courtesy of Robert Craig.)

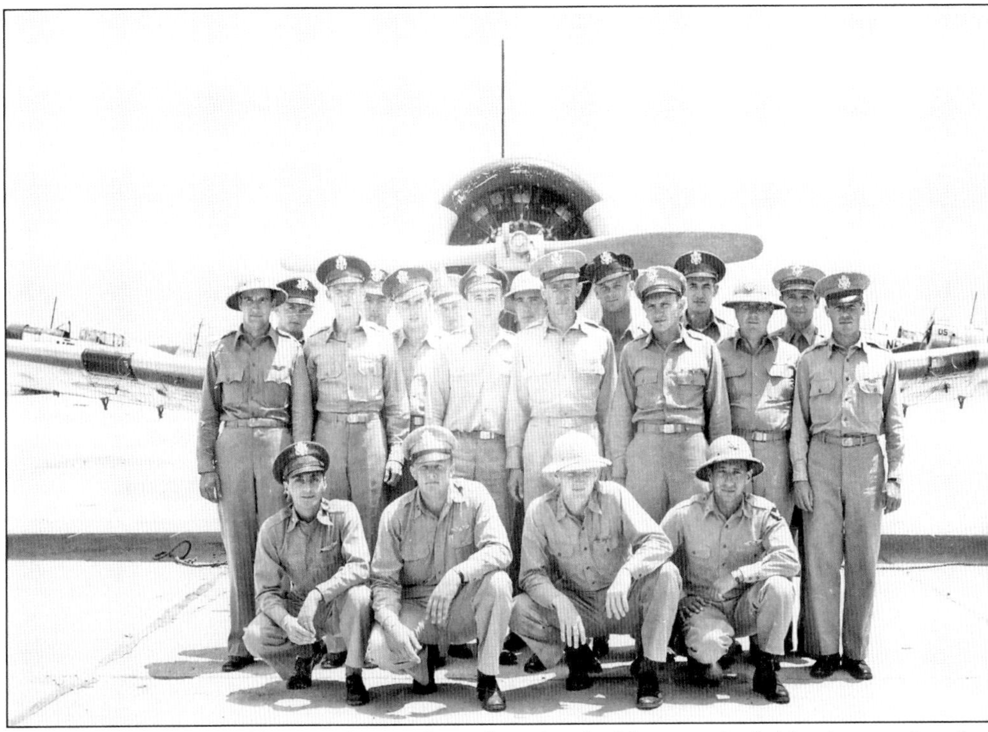

These are a few of the officers and men who gathered at the Newport Airfield to learn to be pilots and to maintain airplanes. The sudden arrival of thousands of young men in Jackson County contributed mightily to the nightlife in a county with legalized alcohol sales and a tolerant attitude toward gambling. The town's many roadhouses provided dancing and socializing for the soldiers. (Both, courtesy of Robert Craig.)

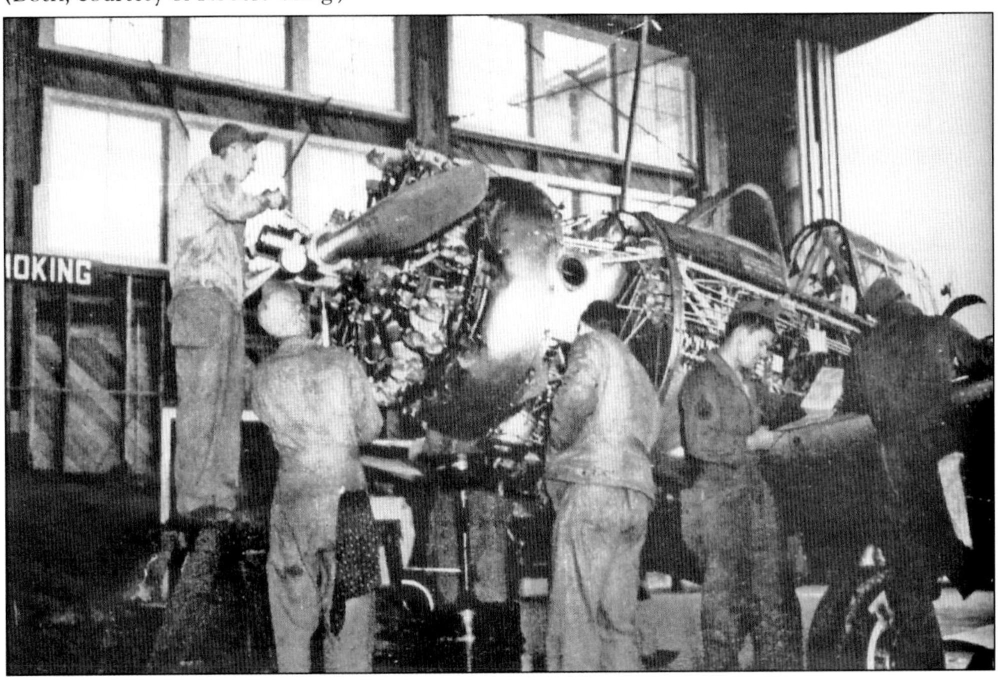

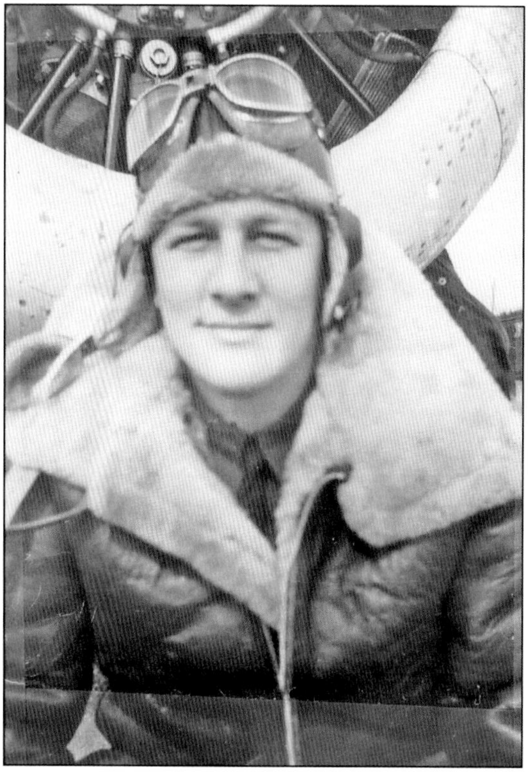

Cullus Walker was one of the pilots who won the heart of a Newport girl and returned after the war to spend his life in Jackson County. Movie-star handsome, he could have been a poster boy for the whole war effort. (Courtesy of Jackson County Historical Society, Mildred Minor Gregory Collection.)

Wiley Albright was one of several Jackson County boys who earned their wings at the Newport Airfield. From 1942 to 1946, Wiley was a fighter pilot in the Pacific, flying off the carrier *Antietam*. His father owned a construction business in Newport, and after the war Wiley spent the rest of his life in Newport, serving proudly for many years as the chairman of the airport commission. (Courtesy of Jackson County Historical Society, Mildred Minor Gregory Collection.)

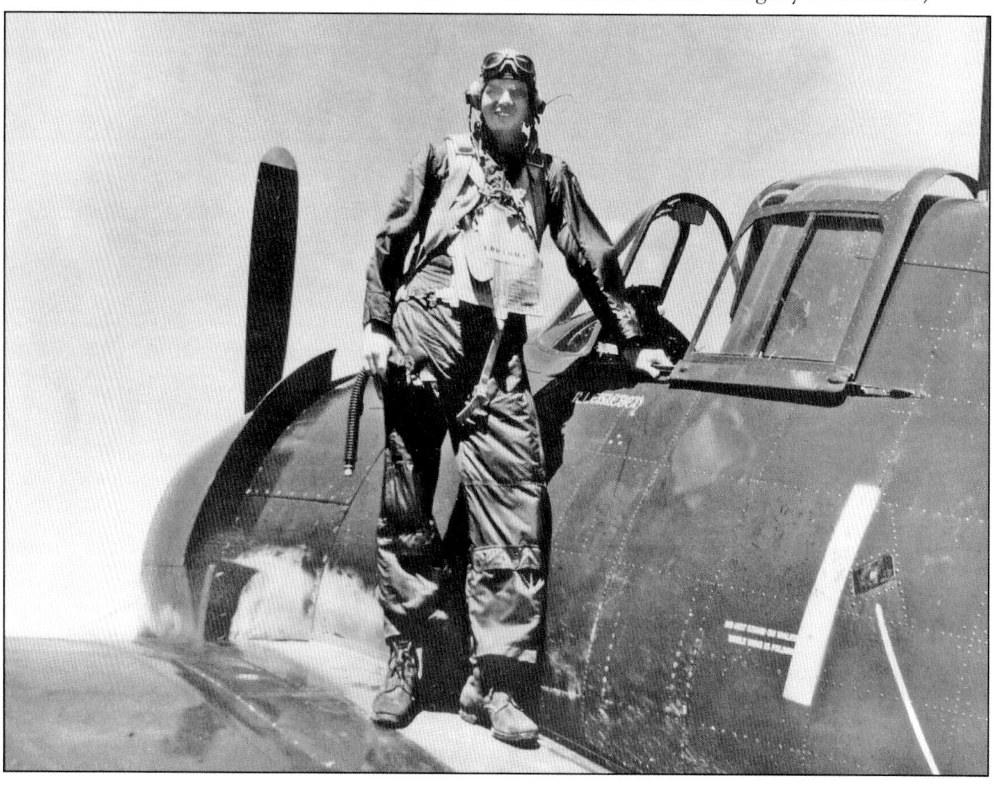

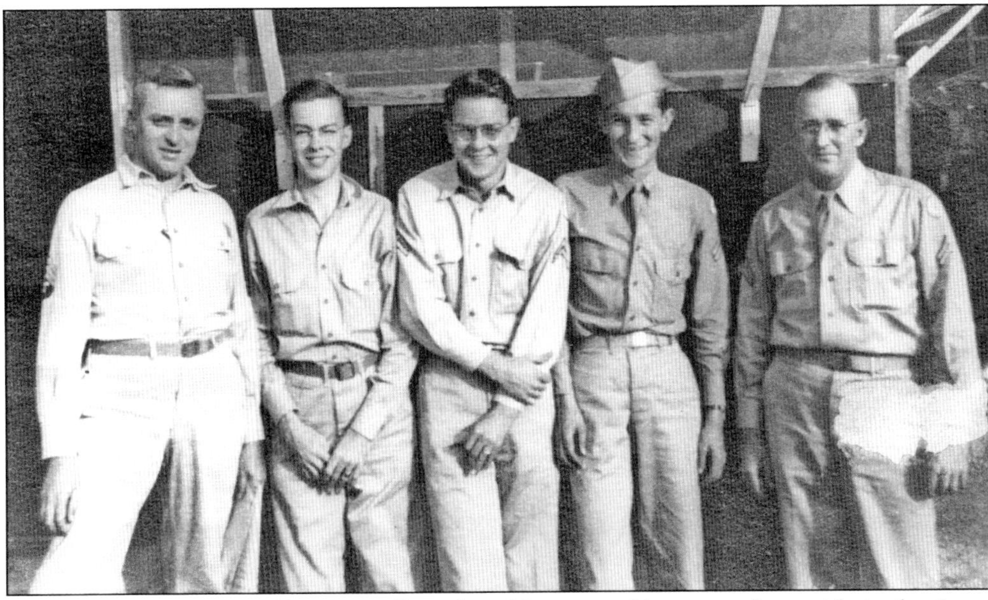

In other areas of the World War II effort, these Newport soldiers served stateside in the Army. From left to right are Roy Evans, ? Landrum, ? Anders, John Burke, and Ralph Monroe. Evans published the *Probe*, an Army newspaper, at Wakeman Hospital in Indianapolis. (Courtesy of Jane Parnell.)

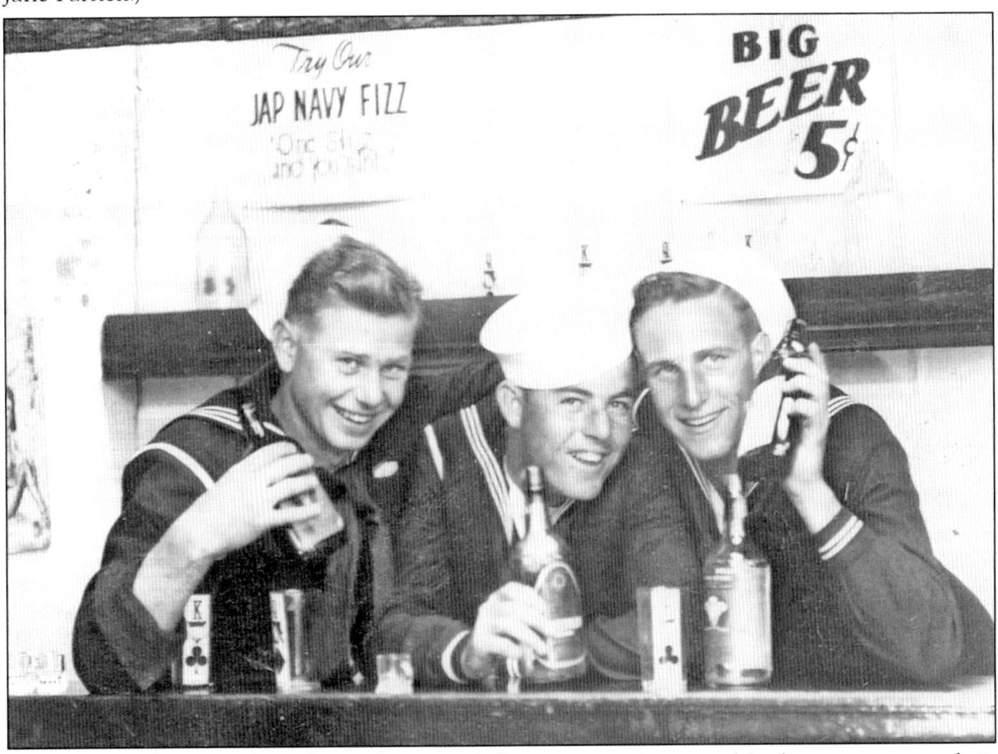

These sailors from Swifton obviously enjoyed their time on leave and had someone snap their photograph for Mom. From left to right are Johnny Tharp, Billy Gale, and J.W. Willmuth. (Courtesy of J.W. Hulen.)

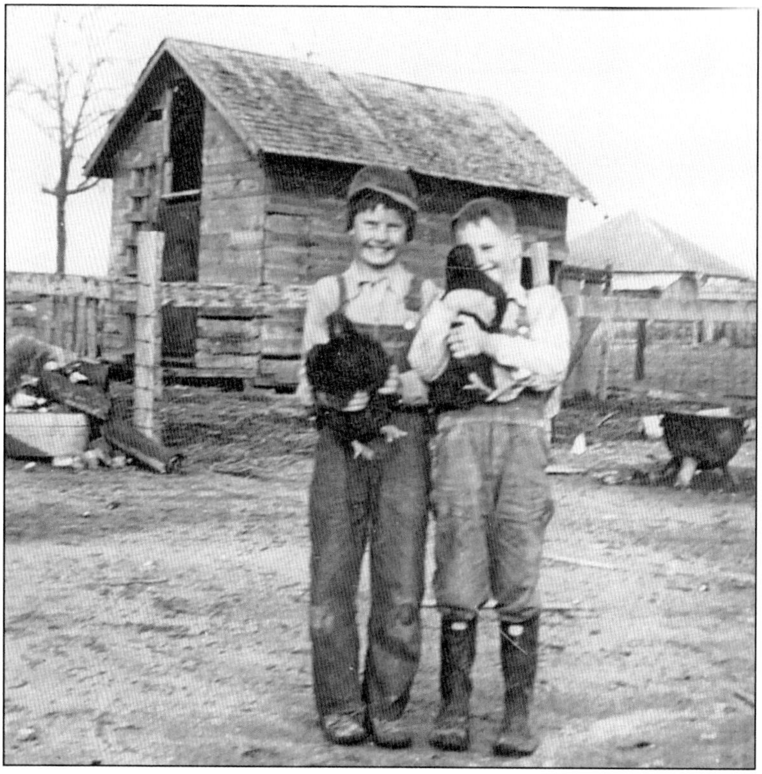

On the home front, life went on as usual for most Jackson County residents. These two little Swifton boys, James Tinsley (left) and J.W. Hulen, enjoy playing with the chickens in the backyard of the Hulen home. Raising chickens for their eggs, and for Sunday dinner when the preacher came, was a South-wide practice at this time. (Courtesy of J.W. Hulen.)

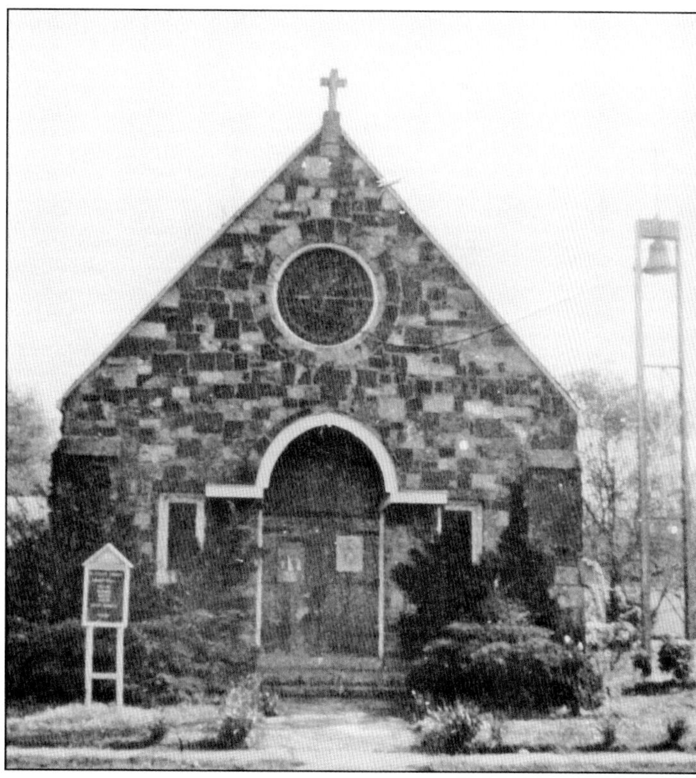

St. Cecelia's Catholic Church in Newport started out in the 1890s as the Church of St. John the Evangelist. Parishioner Christian J. Saenger was instrumental in raising construction funds, and the church building was completed in 1896. The first church burned in the 1926 fire, and the new church, St. Cecelia's Roman Catholic Church, was completed in 1934. St. Cecelia's continues to this day, although in a new location. (Courtesy of Jane Parnell.)

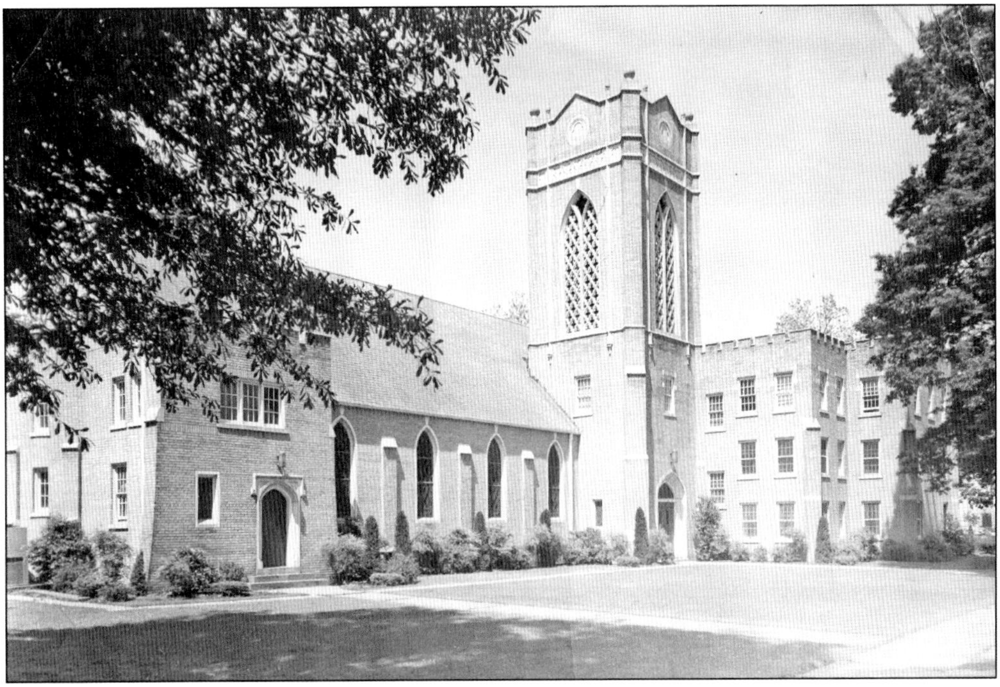

The First Baptist Church in Newport was organized in 1892 and the sanctuary pictured here, which is still in use, was built in 1946. (Courtesy of Jane Parnell.)

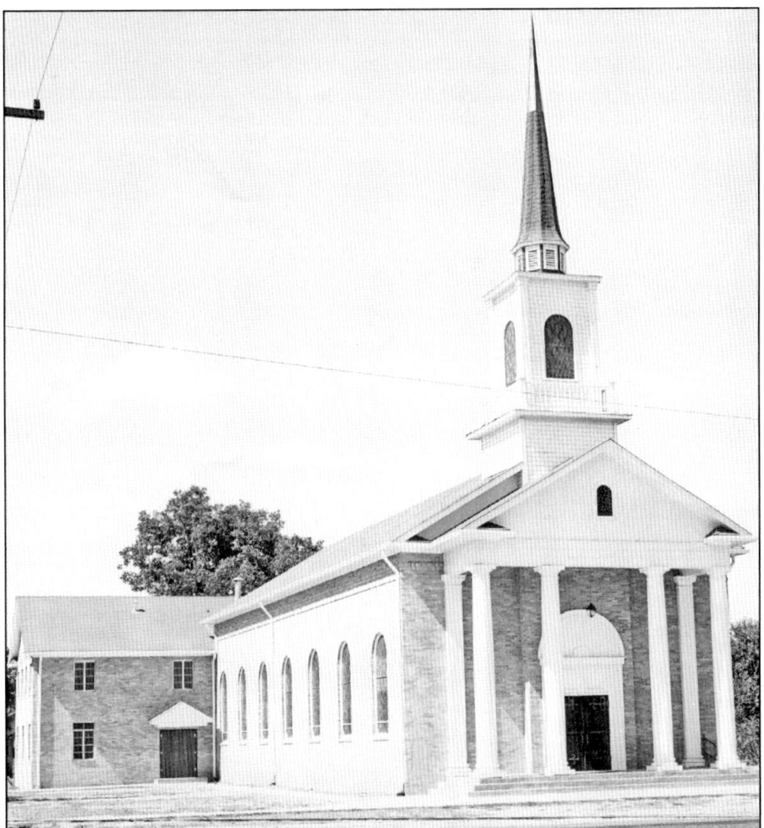

One of the largest congregations in Newport was the Holden Avenue Church of Christ. The Church of Christ had come to Jackson County in the mid-1800s and had flourished to the point that by the 1940s there were more than 25 congregations in the county. (Courtesy of Ron Michaels.)

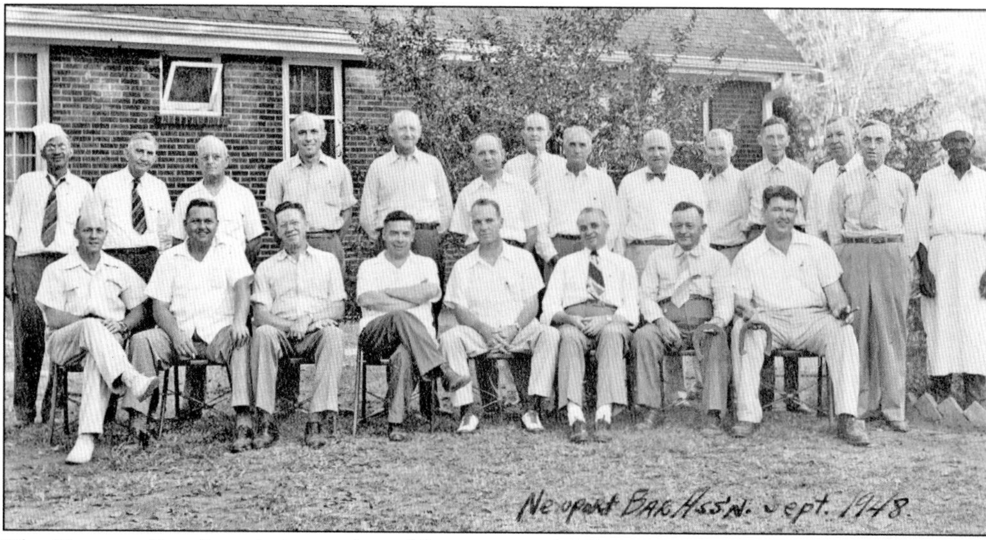

The Newport Bar Association gathered for its annual fall party in 1948. Pictured are, from left to right, (first row) Fred Pickens Jr., Jud Hout, J. Fred Parish, Harold Erwin, Kaneaster Hodges Sr., Roy Evans, W.H. Reid, and Millard Hardin; (second row) Jessie Berry (cook), Joe Armstrong, Ben White, Bernard Rosen, Wesley Bengel, Vernon Ridley, Fred Ball, Andrew Jackson, Fred Pickens Sr., Ras Priest, Paul Ward, Jim Johnson, ? Hurley, and Bud Parrott (cook). (Courtesy of Harold Erwin.)

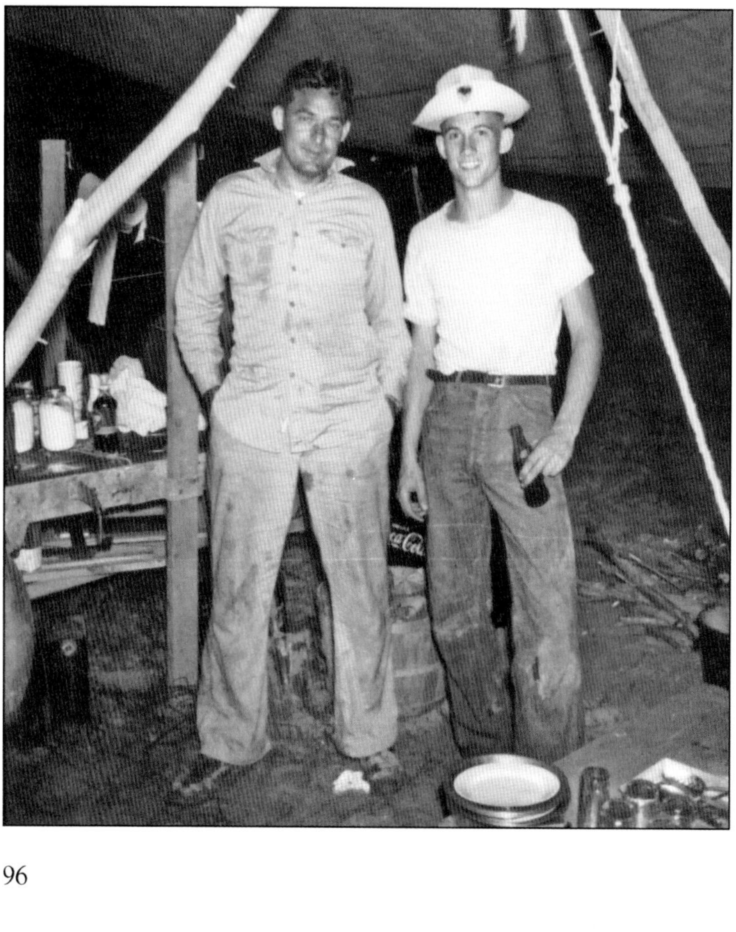

A 15-year-old John Minor (right) stands with his pal Sam Walton at a nearby fishing camp. Walton was manager of Newport's Ben Franklin Store, and he soon became president of the chamber of commerce and a community leader. Unfortunately, Walton was not able to renew his lease when it expired, and as a consequence, he left Newport and moved to Bentonville, Arkansas, where he later founded Wal-Mart Stores, Inc. Newport lost the opportunity to become the world headquarters. (Courtesy of John Minor.)

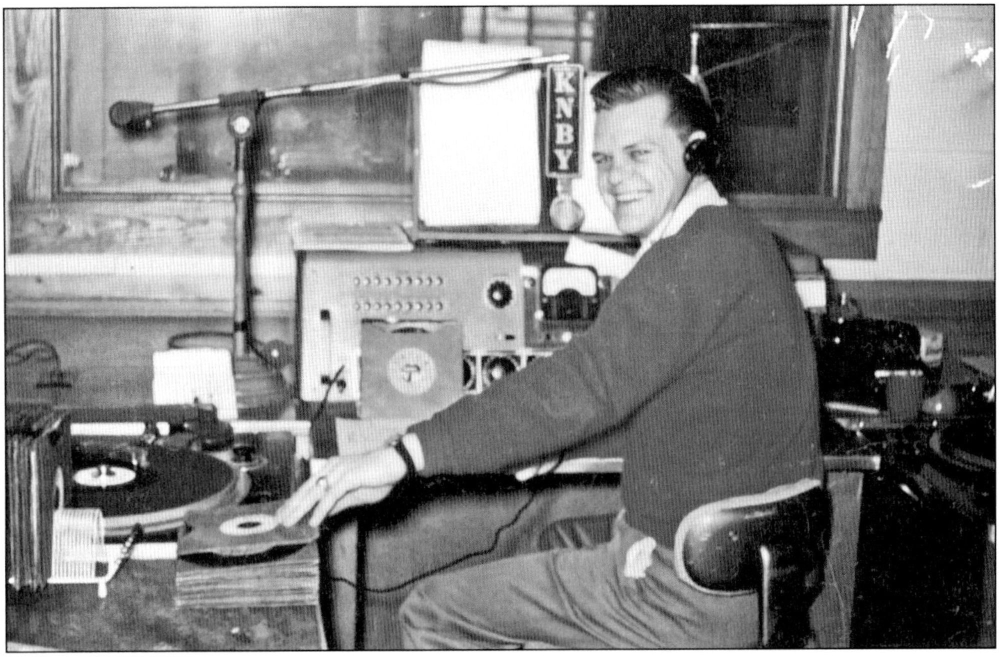

Newport High School senior Steve Stephens showed an early talent for the entertainment industry when he worked as a disc jockey at Newport's radio station, KNBY. Stephens later went on to statewide fame as the host of the weekday afternoon television dance party in Little Rock, *Steve's Show*. (Courtesy of the Stephens Papers and the Butler Center.)

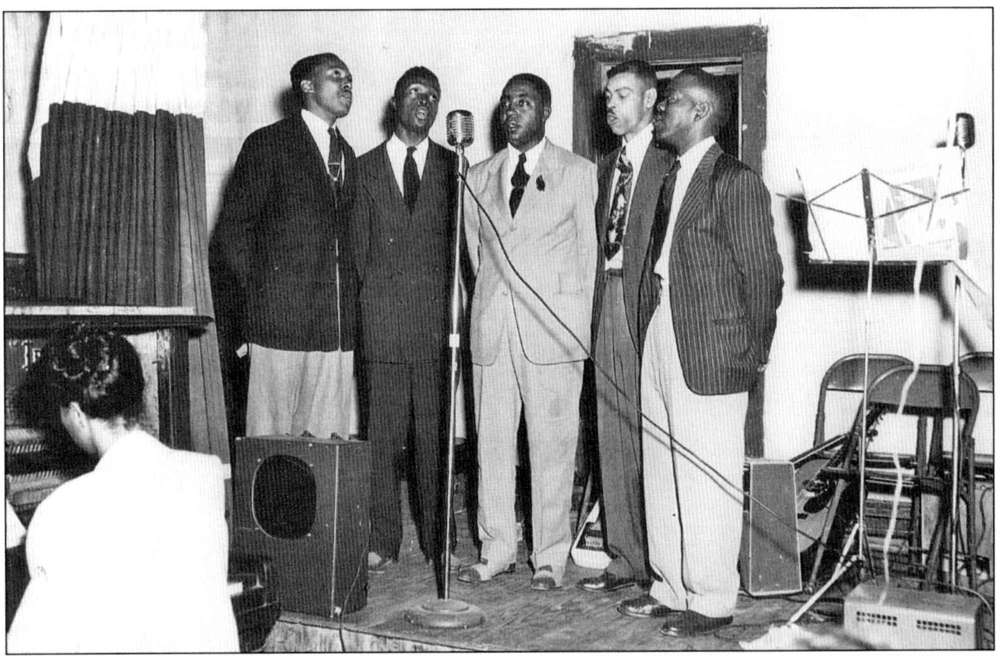

The first black group to have a program on radio station KNBY was the United Harmonizers, organized in 1948. Pictured are, from left to right, Ted Hatchett, Norris Stephenson, Theophilus Henderson, Gus Hatchett, and T.A. Watson. Minnie Bell Stephenson sits at the piano. (Courtesy of James Logan Morgan Jr. and the Butler Center.)

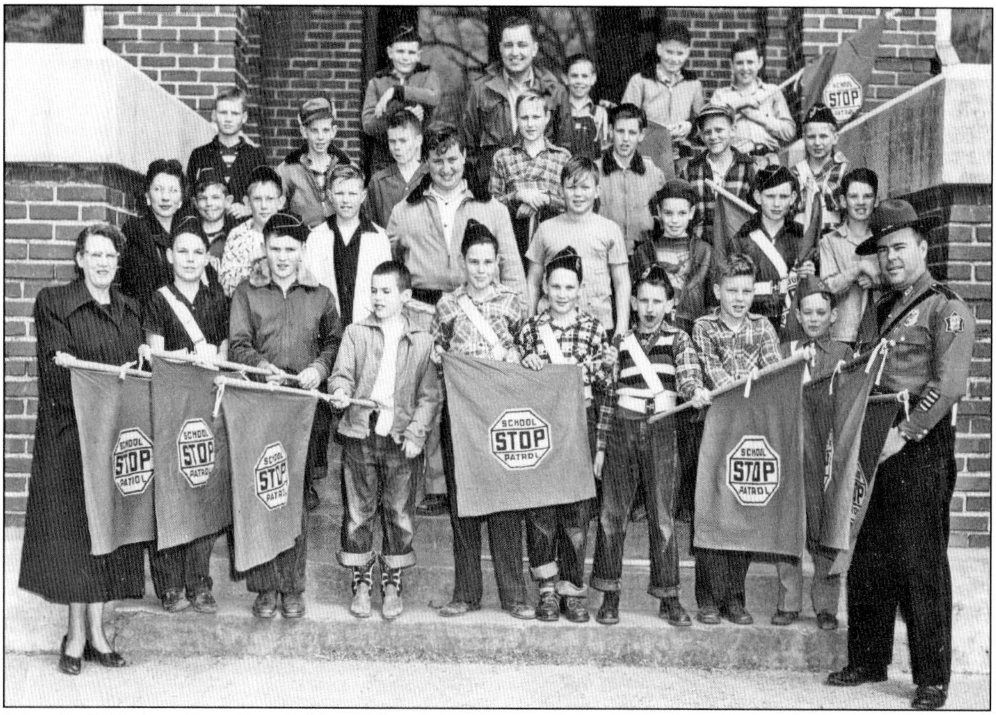

The 1949 Safety Patrol at Gibbs Albright Elementary School in Newport was composed of a group of proud young boys who had been selected for their good grades and good deportment. As in other towns, girls were not eligible to serve on the Safety Patrol—often to their chagrin. (Courtesy of Jane Parnell.)

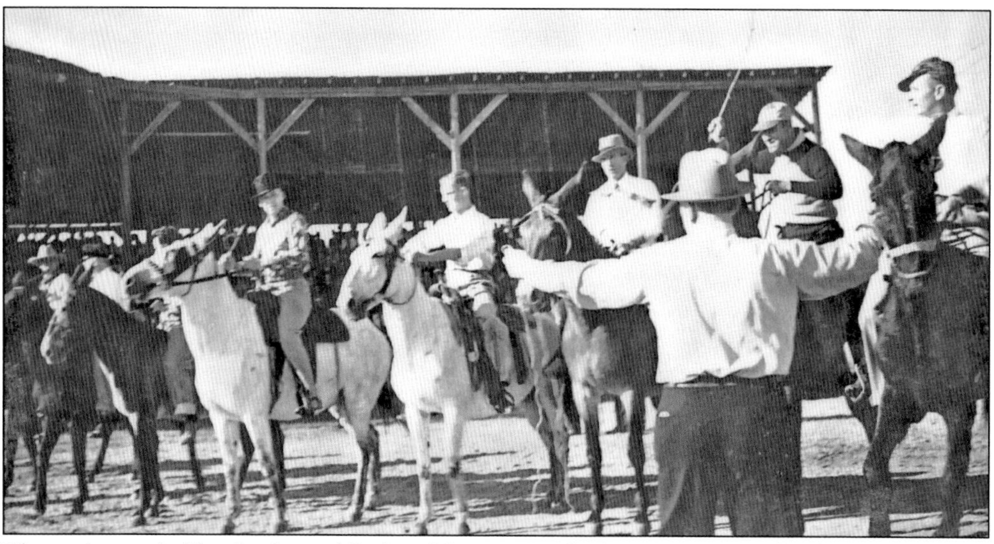

The mule race held at Lockwood Park in Newport in the late 1940s was a fundraiser for a local business. Mules were famously ungovernable and obstinate, so the prospect of watching local leaders try to make them race was one that promised hilarity and an uncertain outcome. Pictured here on their balky steeds, are, from left to right, Ed Baum, Skippy McDonald, Alcorn Minor Sr., unidentified, and Lockwood Burkett, with Boss Birmingham in charge of the start whistle. (Courtesy of John Minor.)

Eight

New Hopes
The 1950s

The 1950s saw Jackson County, with its strong agricultural base, emerge as one of the wealthiest counties in the state and region. As historian Marvin Schwartz writes, "Newport had reason to believe in its prosperous future. In May 1951, the newspaper cited an industrial survey that showed Jackson County as one of the wealthiest counties in the nation, the bulk of its income from agriculture. Jackson County was listed as eighth in the nation in rice production, tenth in cotton, and eleventh in soybeans. Each of the crops was valued at several million dollars."

In the 1950s, the county's agricultural wealth was augmented by the coming of factories producing aluminum foil, trailers, toothpaste tubes, and more. These factories employed thousands of Jackson County residents, increasing the per capita income dramatically. One of Newport's energetic young business leaders, Sam Walton, became president of the chamber of commerce, and he worked tirelessly to attract industries to plant their factories at the airbase. Unfortunately, Walton was not able to secure the lease on his building, and so what could have been another major windfall for the Jackson County economy, the future Wal-Mart Stores, Inc., was established in northwest Arkansas.

In the 1950s, the local Rural Electrical Cooperative, Farmers Electric, began to sponsor an annual Farmers Day at Remmel Park in Newport that for many years remained wildly popular throughout the county. At its peak, the day attracted 10,000 visitors, who came to hear live music of every variety, watch demonstrations of the wonderful new household and farming machinery that electricity made possible, listen to politicians, enter raffles for intriguing prizes, and meet and greet friends.

The birth of rock and roll touched Jackson County directly, with the establishment of more roadhouses out on Highway 67 (later dubbed the Rock 'n' Roll Highway), from Porky's Rooftop and Bob King's in the north end of the county to the many honky-tonks in Newport. The legendary Silver Moon north of Newport attracted patrons from as far away as Memphis. All the early rockers played these roadhouses—from Elvis to Fats Domino and many in between.

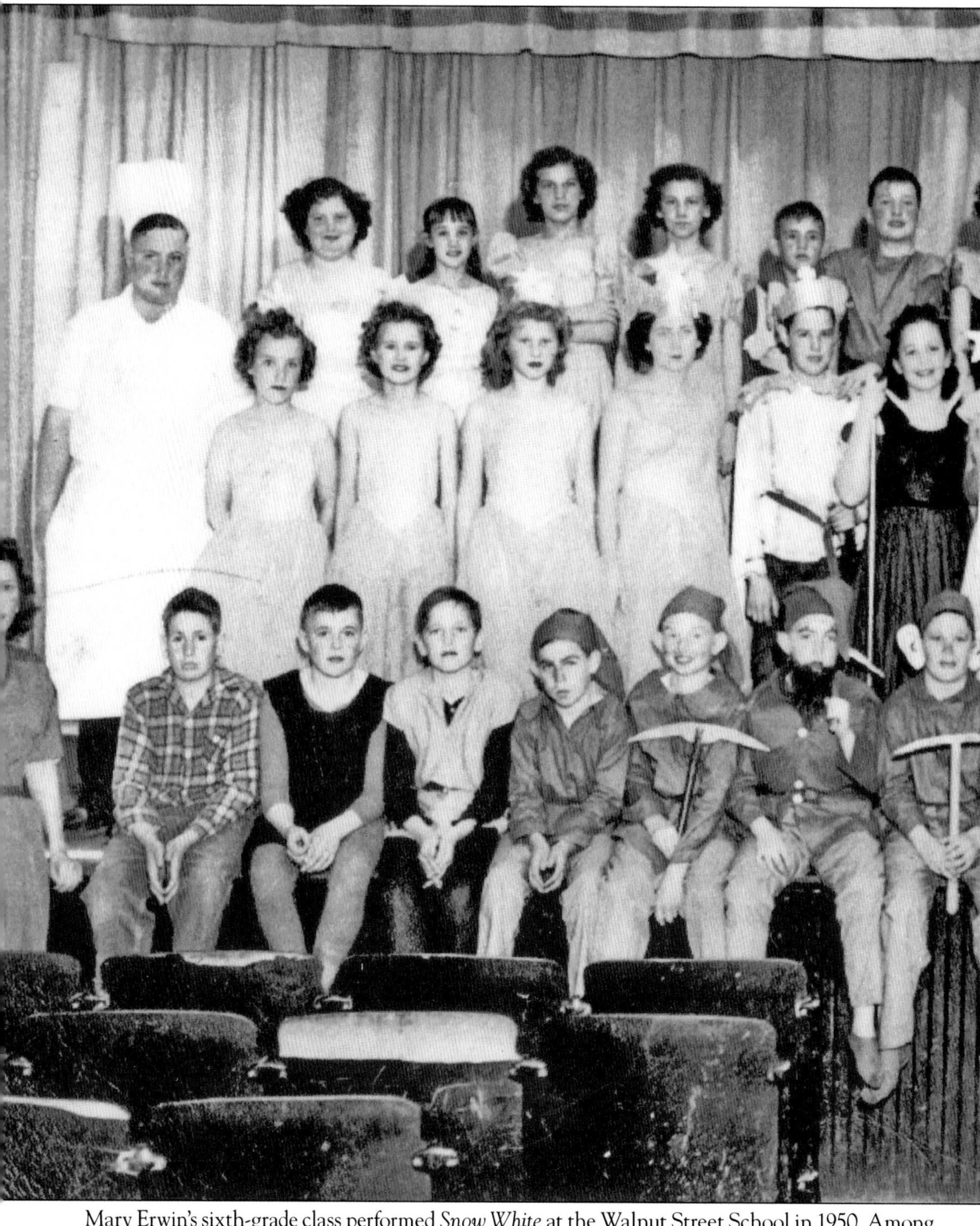

Mary Erwin's sixth-grade class performed *Snow White* at the Walnut Street School in 1950. Among the cast members are, from left to right, (first row) Aubrey Burgess, Duane Egnis, Leo Davis, James Edward Morris, Dallas Burrow, David Adcox, Earl Jones, Wayne Orsborn, Kaneaster Hodges as Dopey, Billy Byrd, Conway Landrum, Melvin McDonald, James McEwing, Harold Jones, and Billy Ray Gray; (second row) Alphie ?, Ann Miller, Patricia Ball, Melissa Magness, Bobby Ray Gay,

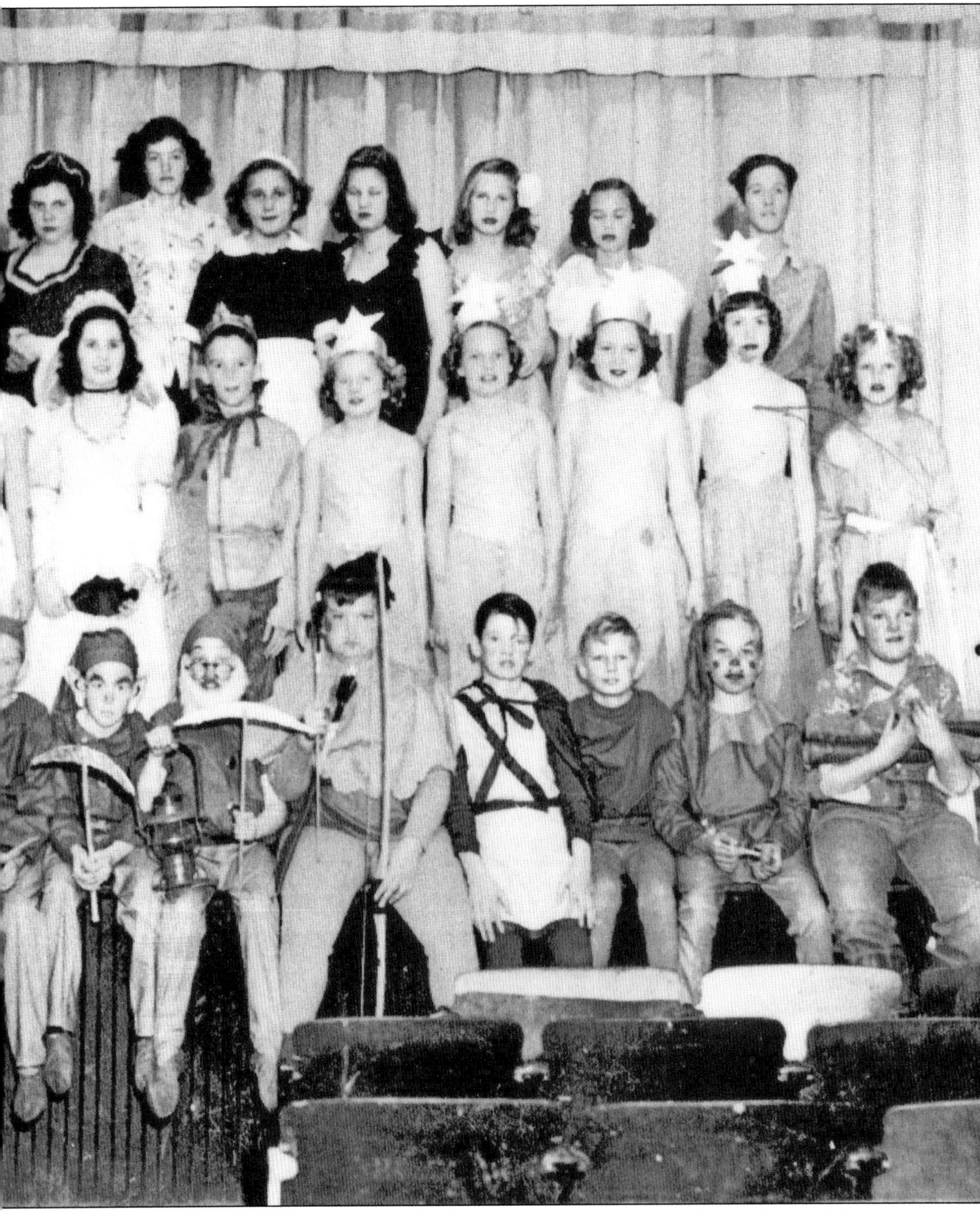

Lindley Williams as Snow White, Camille Watson, Jo Alice Stephens, Toby McDonald, Peggy Jones, Sharon Campbell, Phyllis Mantooth, Mary Ann Carruth, and Jonathan Ward; (third row) Richard Lovell, Lois Orsborn, Betty Lou Stoner, Fay White, Maxine White, Charles Doyle, Bobby Jackson, Elois Rupe, Barbara Welch, Geraldine ?, Ella Sue East, Virginia Selvidge, Mary Alice ?, Jerry Lee Binnington, and LeRoy ? (Courtesy of TheoBeth Jones Beckett.)

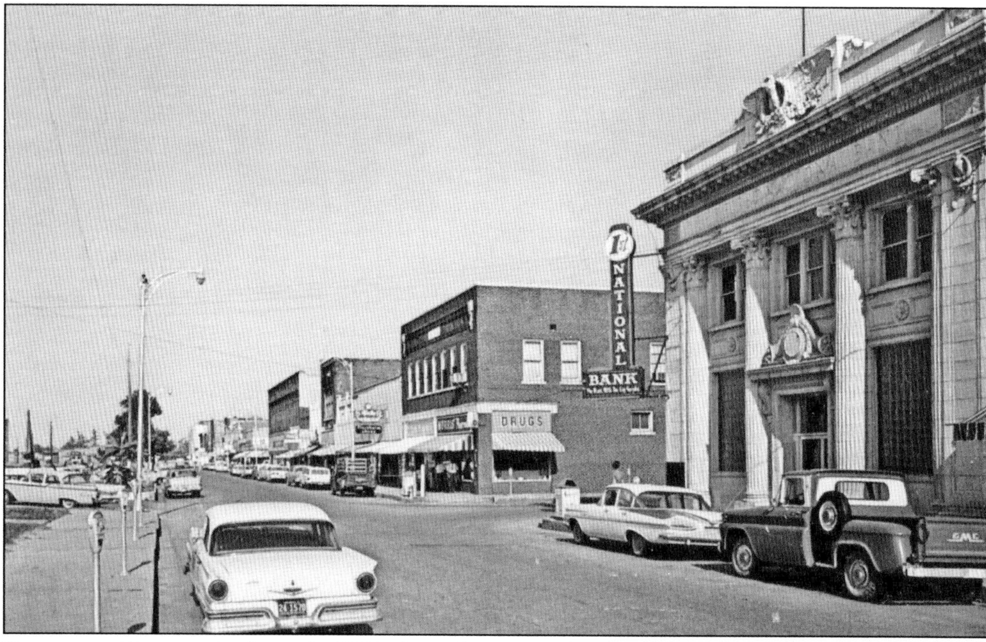

Downtown Newport in the early 1950s showed many improvements over earlier years, as evidenced by this postcard. On Saturdays, this stretch of Front Street was crowded with shoppers and moviegoers, as everyone came to town for a day of socializing. "Out on the highway" had not yet developed, and almost all commerce took place downtown. (Courtesy of Jane Parnell.)

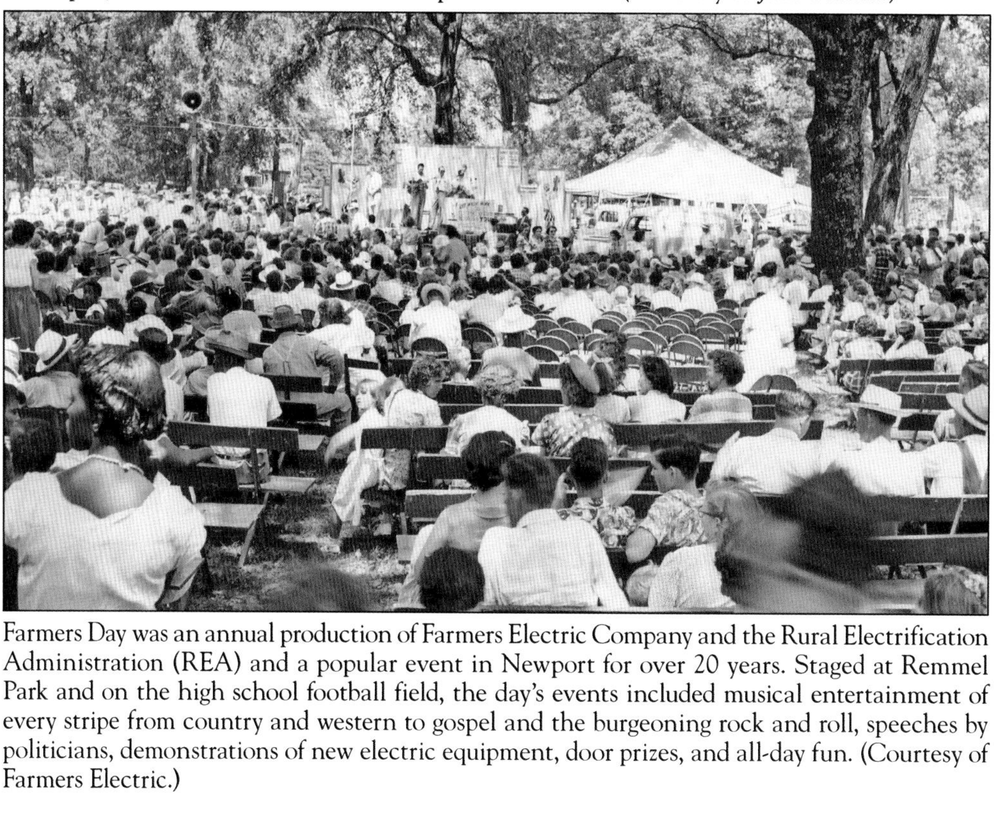

Farmers Day was an annual production of Farmers Electric Company and the Rural Electrification Administration (REA) and a popular event in Newport for over 20 years. Staged at Remmel Park and on the high school football field, the day's events included musical entertainment of every stripe from country and western to gospel and the burgeoning rock and roll, speeches by politicians, demonstrations of new electric equipment, door prizes, and all-day fun. (Courtesy of Farmers Electric.)

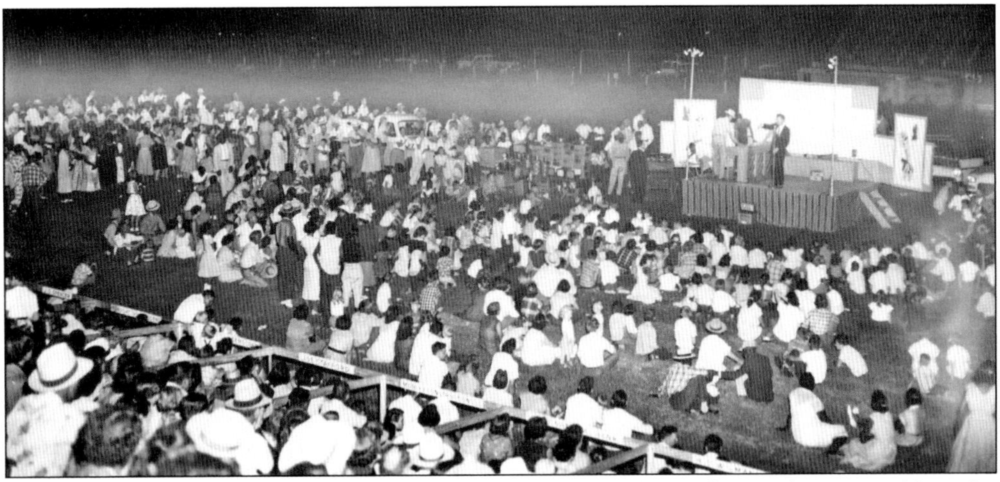

Farmers Day extended into the night and drew huge crowds from all over the county. Note the level of racial integration in a town that had experienced very little racial tension to this point. (Courtesy of Farmers Electric.)

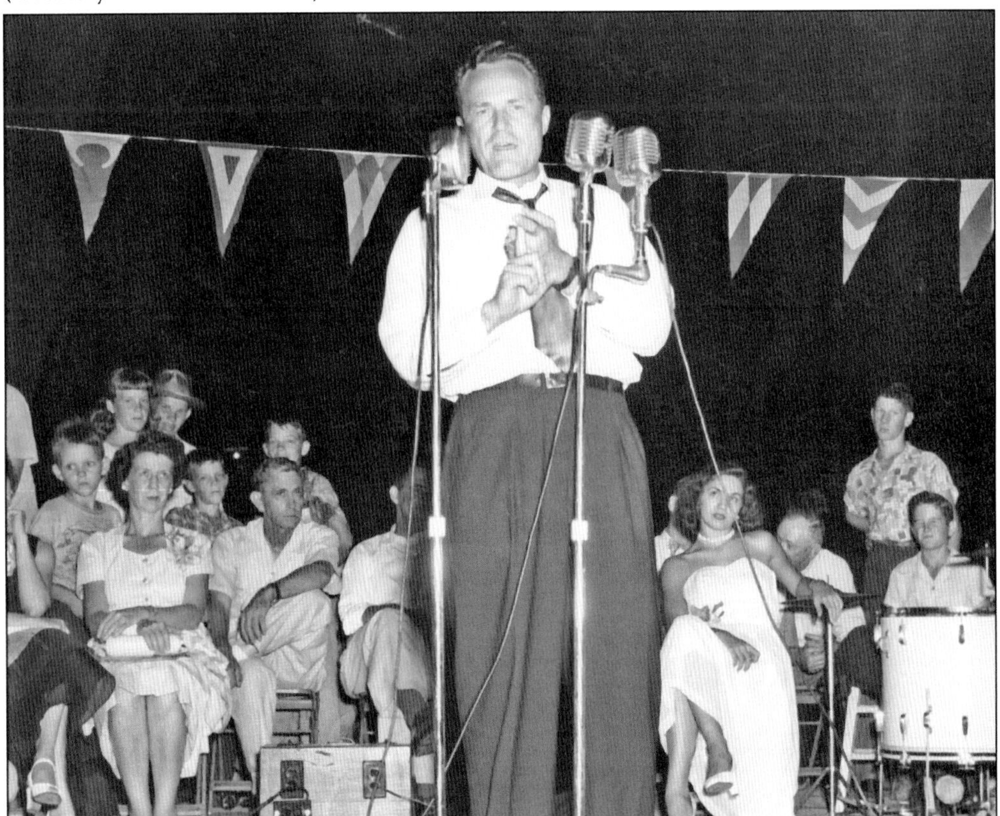

Gov. Sid McMath came to speak at the fifth Farmers Day in 1951, when he was running for reelection. A record crowd of 10,000 people was reported that year. Eleanor Jowers, on the left, seems to be less than impressed. Miss Newport Betty Castleberry, on the right, sang as a part of the night's entertainment. McMath lost the election to Francis Cherry, from Jonesboro. (Courtesy of Henry Boyce.)

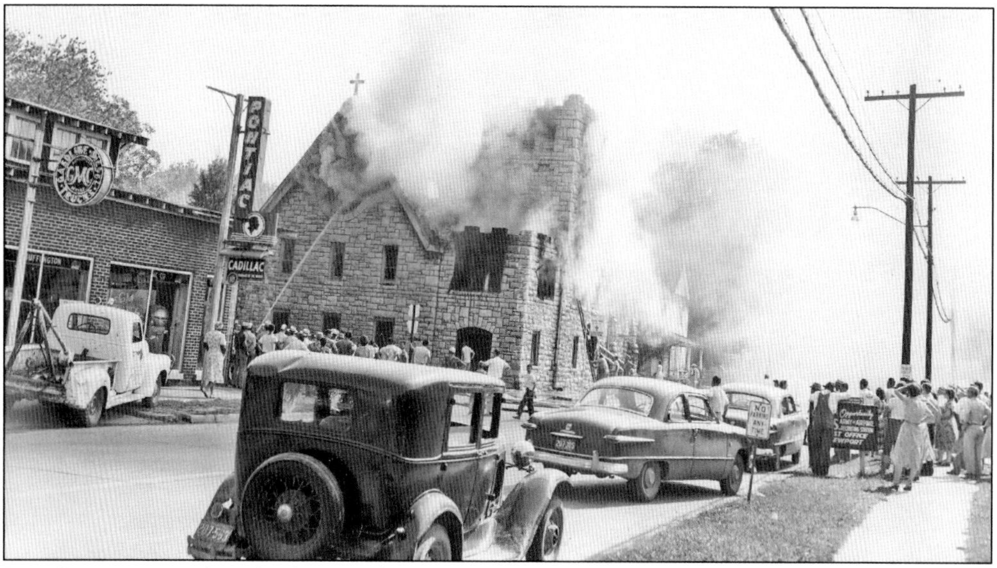

In 1951, two young boys broke into the sacristy of St. Paul's Episcopal Church and started a fire in the sanctuary, perhaps accidentally. The ensuing blaze gave the townspeople quite a scare, but the Newport Fire Department was able to extinguish the fire without tremendous loss. To this day, visitors to the church can discern charred stains along the top of the high altar. (Courtesy of Ron Michaels.)

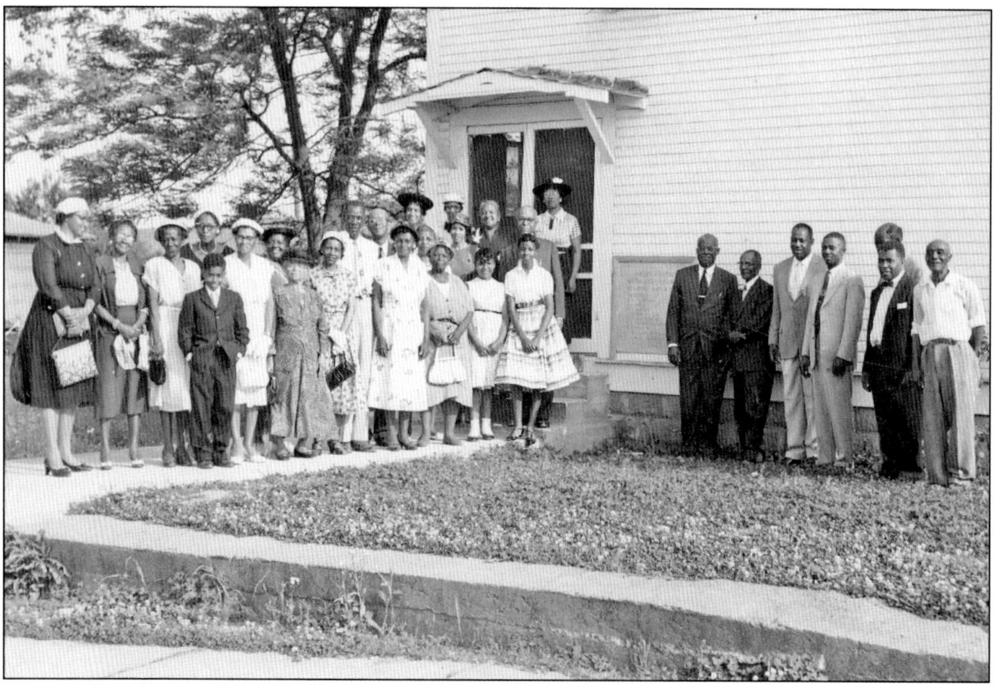

Emory Chapel United Methodist Church in Newport was originally a congregation of the northern Methodist Episcopal Church. Established in 1881, the first church on Front Street was traded in 1897 for a lot on Remmel Avenue, where it is still in operation. The church building was almost destroyed in the 1926 fire, but it was rebuilt. Here, members of the congregation pose outside their building in 1952. (Courtesy of James Logan Morgan Jr. and the Butler Center.)

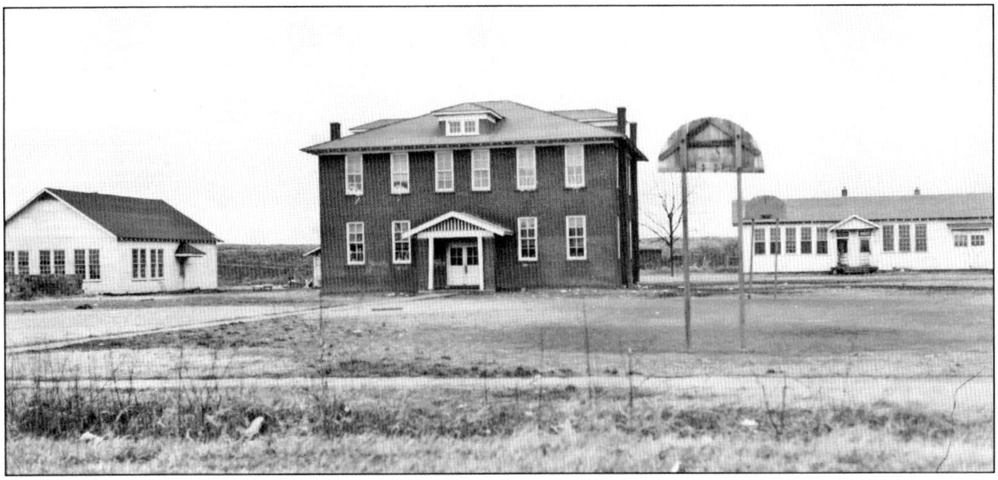

W.F. Branch High School, the Newport school for African American children, was imposing. In the wake of the 1954 *Brown* decision by the US Supreme Court, the Newport School Board constructed additional modern school buildings in an attempt to stave off school desegregation, but the city's schools were formally integrated in 1968, and Branch High School closed shortly thereafter. (Courtesy of James Logan Morgan Jr. and the Butler Center.)

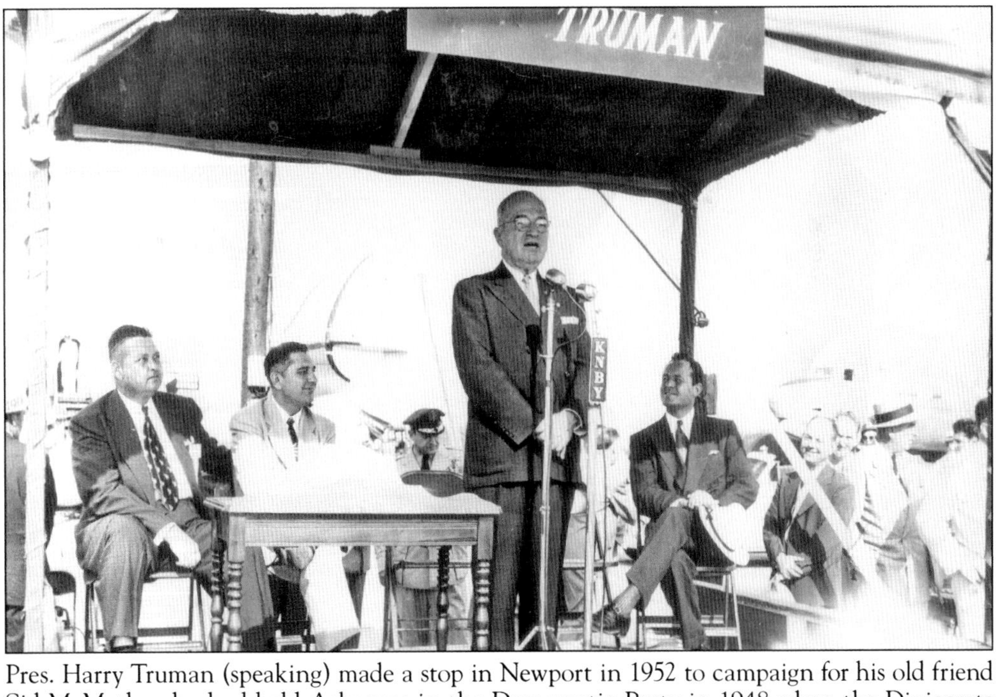

Pres. Harry Truman (speaking) made a stop in Newport in 1952 to campaign for his old friend Sid McMath, who had held Arkansas in the Democratic Party in 1948 when the Dixiecrats bolted and almost cost Truman his election. Sitting on the platform with Truman are, from left to right, Newport mayor Jud Hout, congressman Wilbur Mills from nearby Kensett, and Governor McMath. (Courtesy of Ann Hout.)

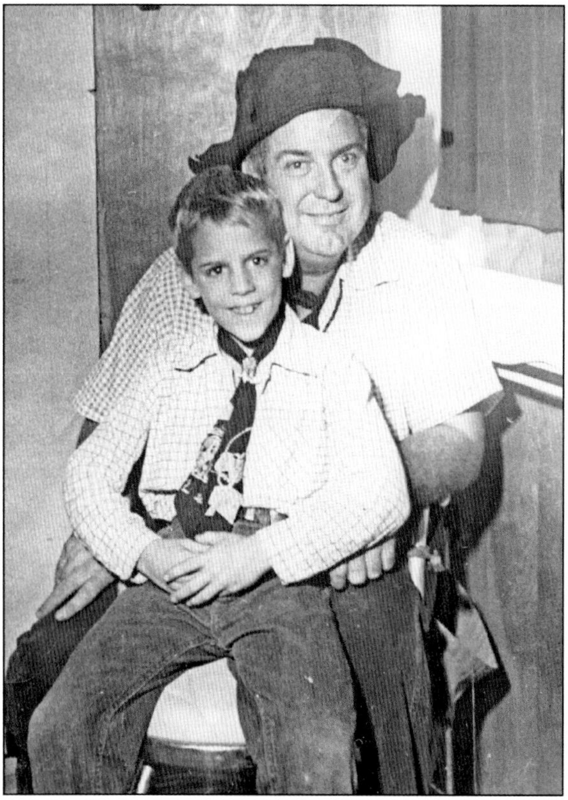

Nine-year-old Tim Watson won the Smiley Burnett Look-Alike Contest in 1953. Burnett was a film star who played in the cowboy movies many children loved to watch on Saturday afternoons. Young Tim came home from the movie with his prize, a mean little Shetland pony, which his mother immediately locked in the coal bin for the night. (Courtesy of Tim Watson Sr.)

Gov. Francis Cherry (front row, fourth from right) visited Newport in 1953 to meet with the town's business leaders. Chamber of commerce executive director Maude Hinkle escorted him around and undoubtedly apprised him of the many industrial development opportunities available at the abandoned Newport Airfield. (Courtesy of Judge Harold Erwin.)

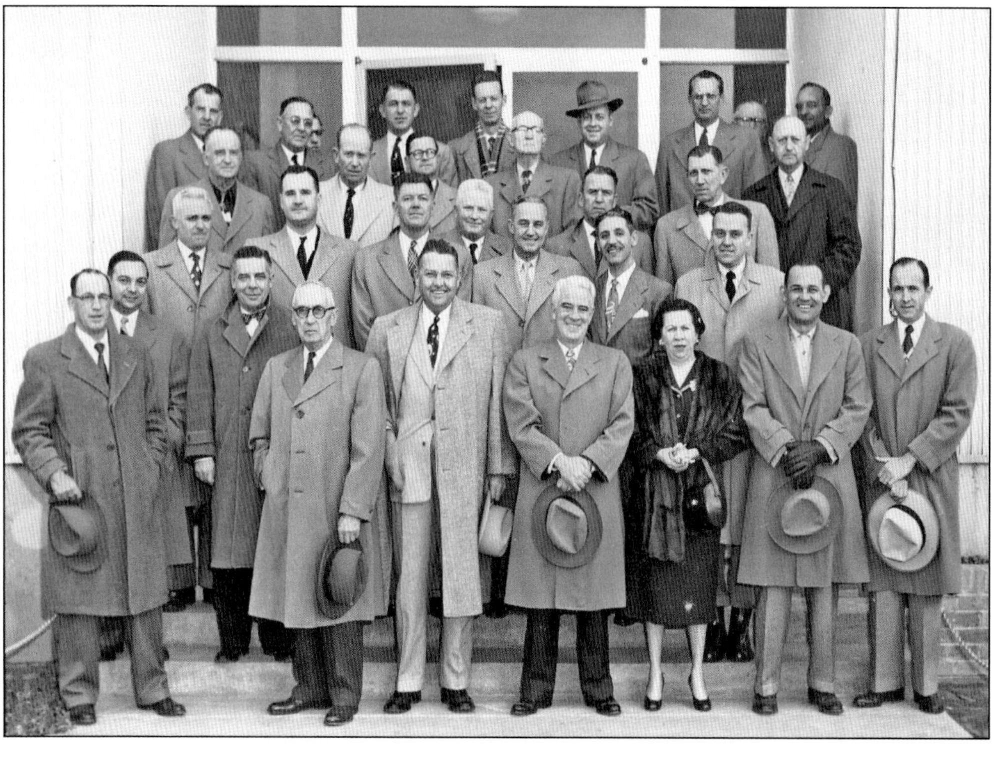

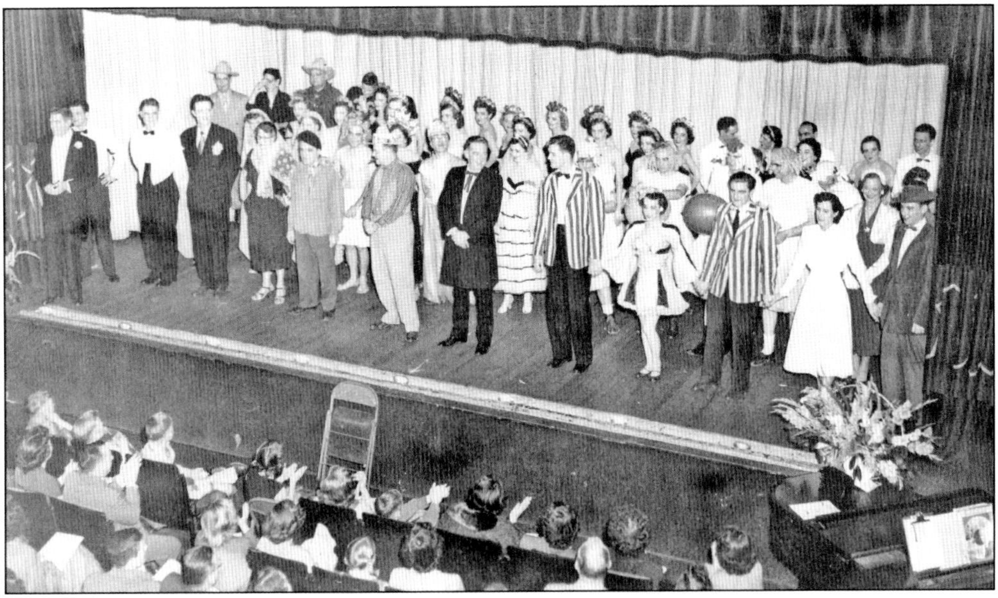

For many years, the Newport Service League put on an annual follies to raise money for its many charitable projects. This was always a popular enterprise, both for the many citizens who loved the opportunity to strut their stuff onstage under the direction of a professional theater manager and for the enthusiastic audiences. This image is from 1953. (Courtesy of Tim Watson Sr.)

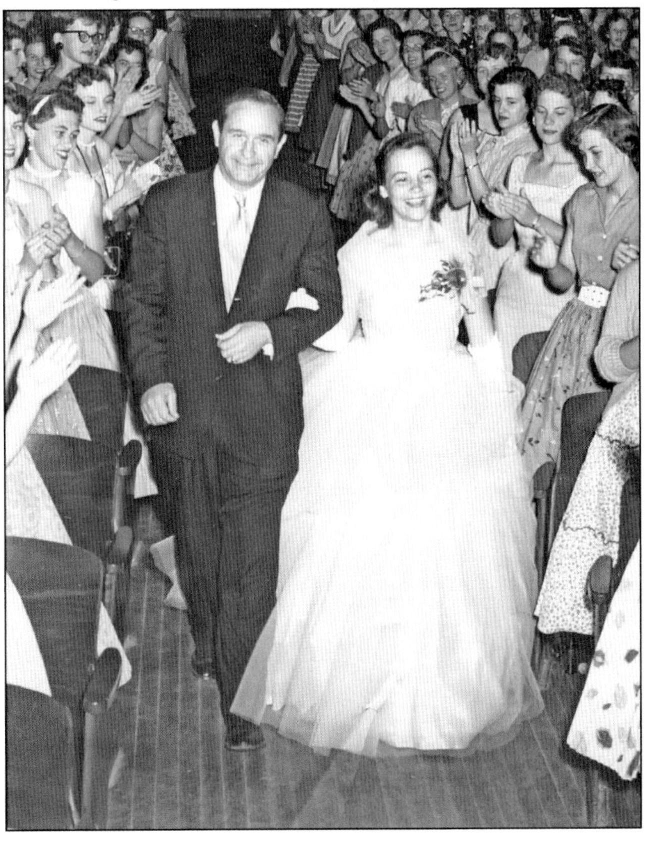

As the newly elected governor of Arkansas Girls State, Newport's Lindley Williams is escorted into her inauguration by Arkansas governor Orval E. Faubus in 1955. Outfitted in her prom dress, Williams was following the tradition of her day, which clearly did not regard women as potential executives. Williams later married her high school sweetheart, Kaneaster Hodges Jr., also of Newport, whom Gov. David Pryor appointed to fill the unexpired term of Sen. John McClellan. (Courtesy of Lindley Williams Hodges.)

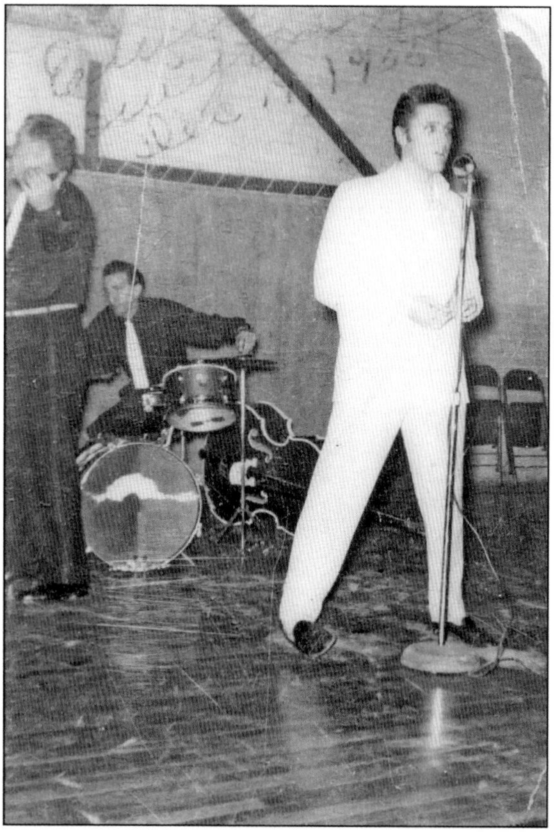

Elvis Presley warms up for a performance at the Swifton High School gymnasium in 1955. A 13-year-old Tara Chapman snapped this photograph with her Brownie camera; later, her father took her to Elvis's pre-Graceland house in Memphis, and the King came out and sang to her in his yard, giving her a chance to snap more shots. Tara keeps her Elvis images in a bank vault. (Courtesy of Tara Chapman Byrd.)

Jackson County native Sonny Burgess, in the dark coat, entertains the crowd at Farmers Day in 1956 with his band, the Pacers. Onstage with Sonny are Kern Kennedy on the piano, Bobby Crafford on drums, Jack Nance on trumpet, Joe Lewis on lead guitar, and Johnny Ray Hubbard on bass guitar. The Pacers went on to have an international following. Their most famous song was "We Wanna Boogie!" (Courtesy of Henry Boyce.)

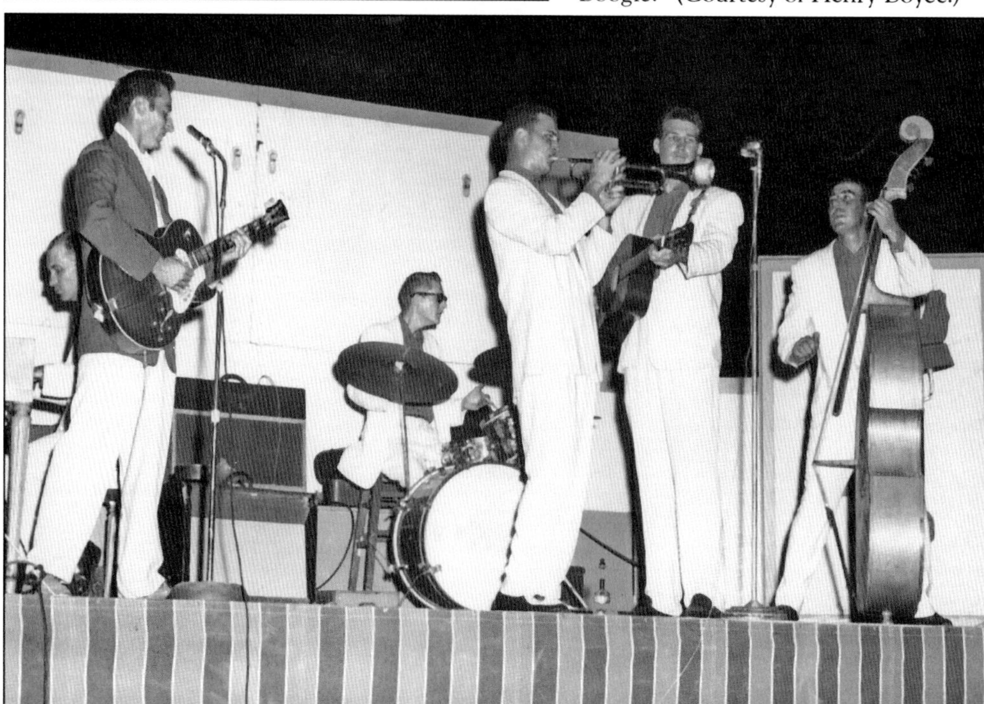

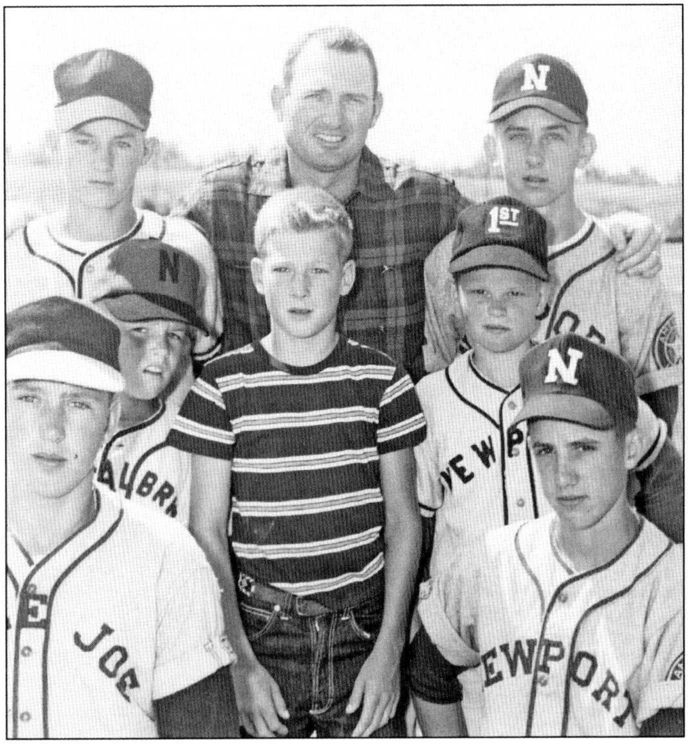

Baseball hall of famer George Kell of the Detroit Tigers, a native of Swifton, coached this all-star team in the mid-1950s. Clockwise from the bottom left are James McCoy, Mike Allen, Sonny Wayland, Kell, Crackie Parker, Chigger Jones, Dale Harrison, and George Kell Jr., team mascot. Swifton produced many baseball prodigies, perhaps because its young men were accustomed to such hard physical labor in the soybean and rice fields surrounding the town. (Courtesy of Ron Michaels.)

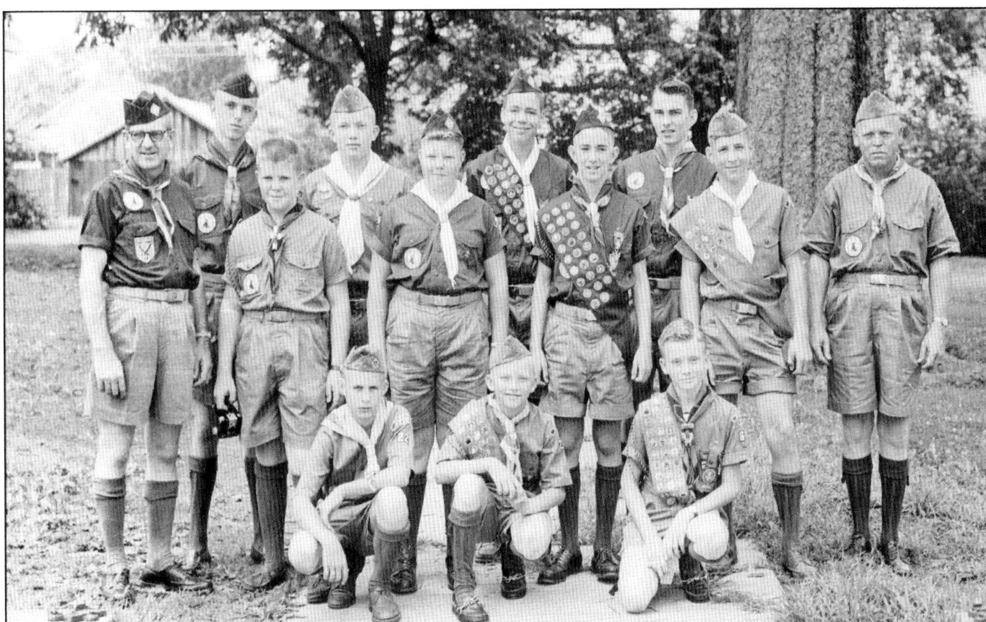

Boy Scout Troop No. 67 from Newport prepares to attend the National Jamboree in Valley Forge, Pennsylvania, in 1957. Pictured here are, from left to right, (first row) David Hare, Jim Carr, and Robin Carr; (second row) troop leader Ray Fann, Stanley Wilson, Cecil Gardner, Jim Brown, Marvin Hare, and troop leader Paul Young; (third row) Mike Buffington, David Hodges, John Purdy, and Gene Brownd. (Courtesy of John Purdy.)

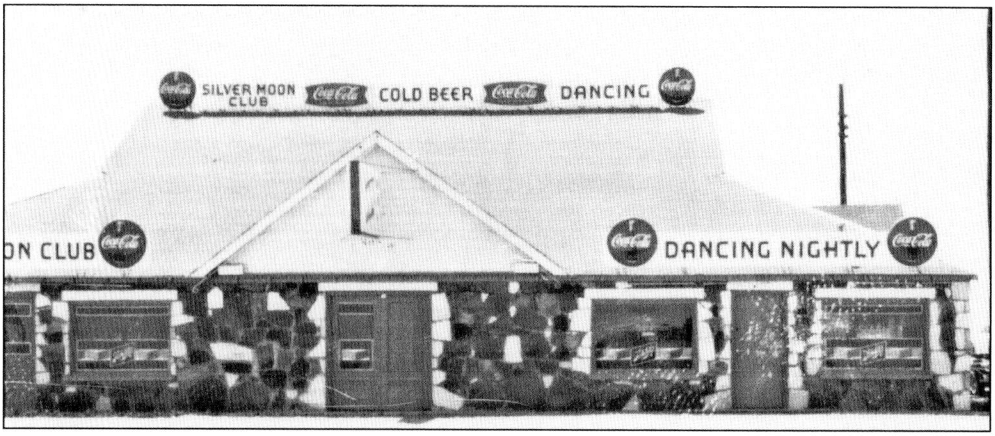

The Silver Moon in Newport, with a seating capacity of 800, was thought to be largest honky-tonk in Arkansas. People came from as far away as Memphis to hear Fats Domino, Louis Armstrong, Elvis Presley, Conway Twitty, Sonny Burgess, and many other rock-and-roll, jazz, and country-and-western greats in their early years. Live bands, alcohol, and gambling were the order of the day, and Newport was known far beyond Jackson County as a place to have a good time. (Courtesy of Frank Plegge.)

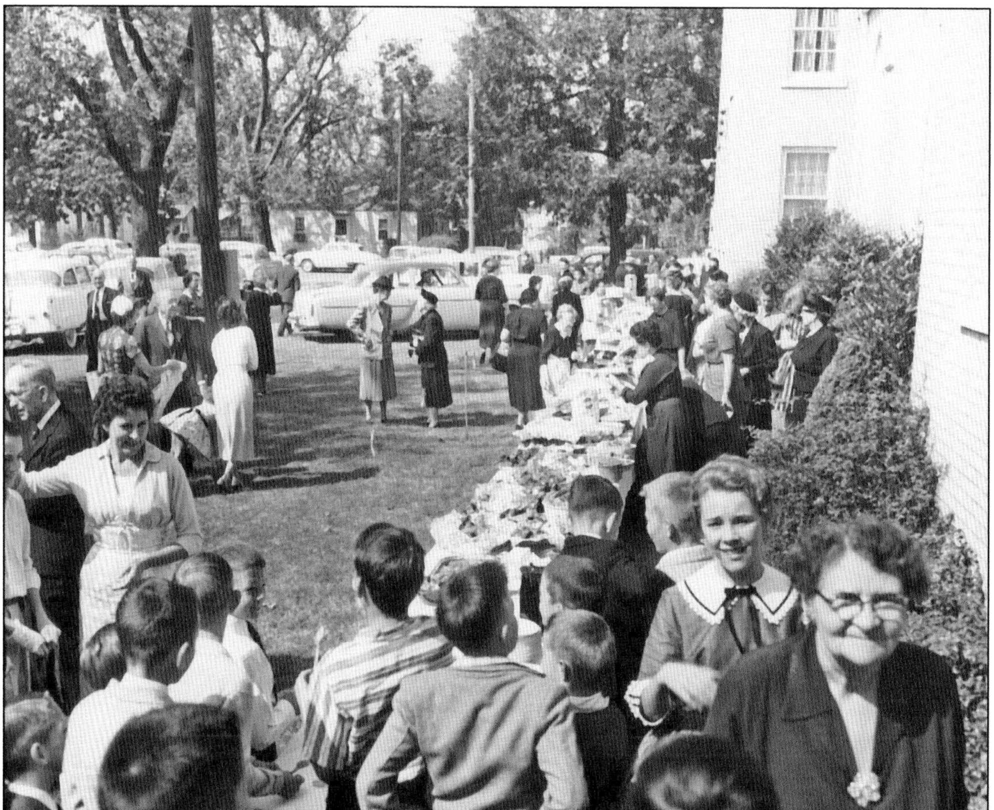

Dinner on the grounds at Newport's First Baptist Church was a favorite activity on pretty Sundays. The Reverend Ed McDonald thought it was a good idea and apparently so did a lot of little boys. (Courtesy of Jane Parnell.)

Nine

New and Old Together
The 1960s

The 1960s in Jackson County saw continued industrial expansion amid the general farm prosperity. New factories such as the outdoor furniture maker Brown Jordan and the new Brown Shoe Company added hundreds more assembly-line jobs, and the additional workforce required additional service industries such as insurance agencies, law firms, doctors, and hospitals.

The war in Vietnam seemed very far away to most people, and a general sense of economic well-being allowed more Jackson County residents to enjoy the wonderful natural resources of the area. The county was home to some 39 lakes for fishing, along with the two major rivers, the White and the Black. Duck hunting in the Cache River lowlands was second to none in the state. The opening of Jacksonport State Park in 1965 provided many more recreational opportunities as well as a new venue for learning the county's history in the old Jacksonport Courthouse Museum, set in the courthouse built in 1871, when Jacksonport was the county seat.

School consolidation and integration came in this decade, as African American children entered into the previously all-white public schools in the county, and many smaller outlying schools closed and the students moved into the larger schools at Newport, Tuckerman, Swifton, and Grubbs.

The national turmoil of the late 1960s did not touch Jackson County, and local citizens continued to work, play, and worship together without the anger and animosities created by the antiwar movement on many of the nation's college campuses. Whites and African Americans went to school together but remained socially segregated, and race riots were something inexplicable that happened far way, to other people.

By the end of the decade, the general prosperity of the last couple of decades seemed permanent. Newport and Jackson County continued to grow, and the stage was set for the expansive 1970s.

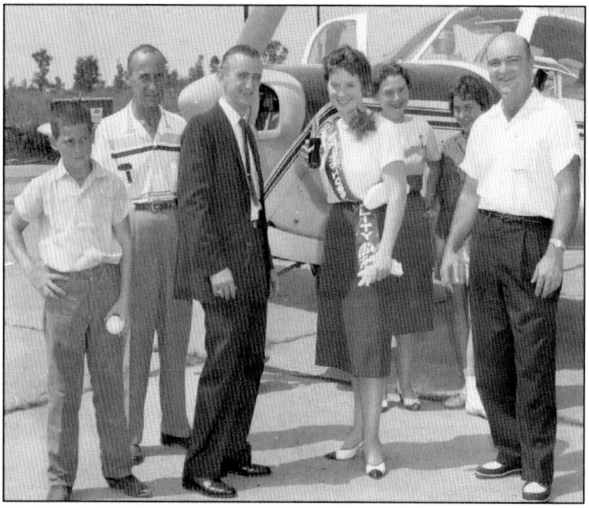

Pretty Jamie Umsted (later Castleberry) served as Newport's representative in the Arkansas "Miss Hospitality" contest. Here, she flew in for her Newport visit and is greeted by, from left to right, her little brother Mick; her father, Milton Umsted; Newport mayor Bill Duncan; her mother, Virginia; her sister Betty; and a representative of Arkansas Power and Light Company. The contest winner that year was Donna Axum, who, as Miss Arkansas, went on to become Miss America. (Courtesy of Jackson County Historical Society, Mildred Minor Gregory Collection.)

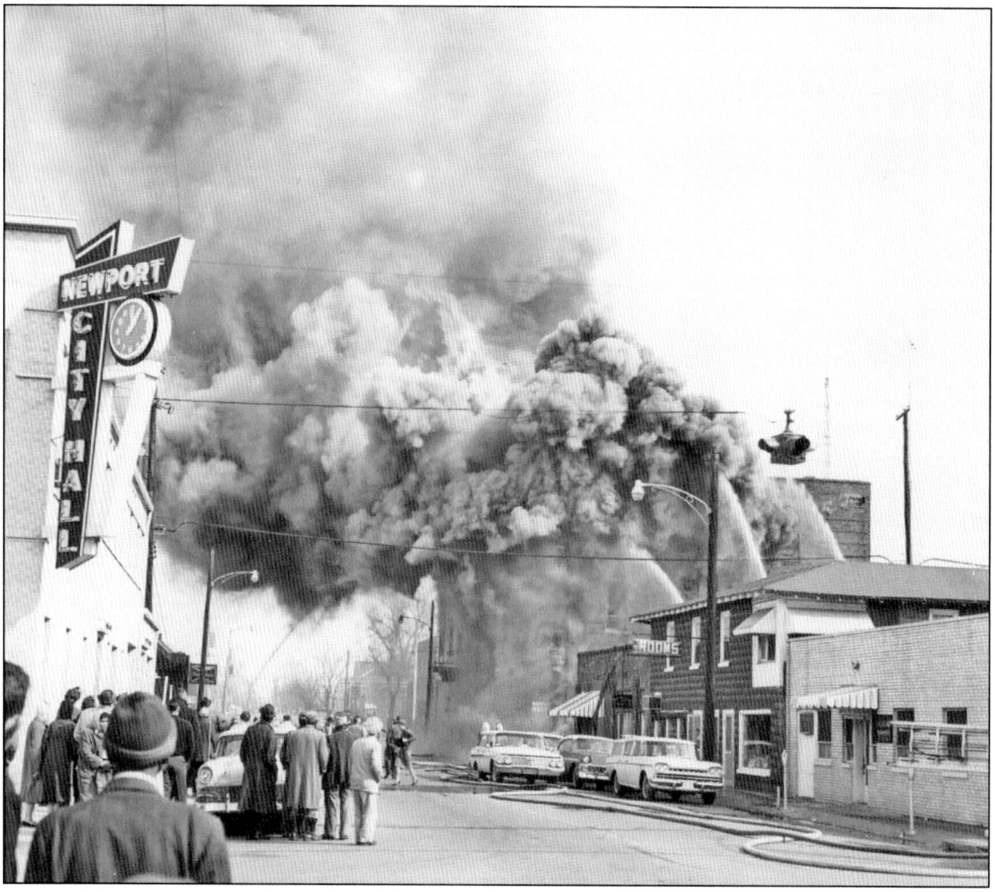

An exciting fire brought down the old Hazel Hotel in the early 1960s. Many people turned out to watch the blaze at Second and Hazel Streets, some of them undoubtedly remembering the terrifying fire of 1926. The Hazel was one of the last real hotels in Newport, all of which were downtown. The age of the motels out on the highway was fast approaching.

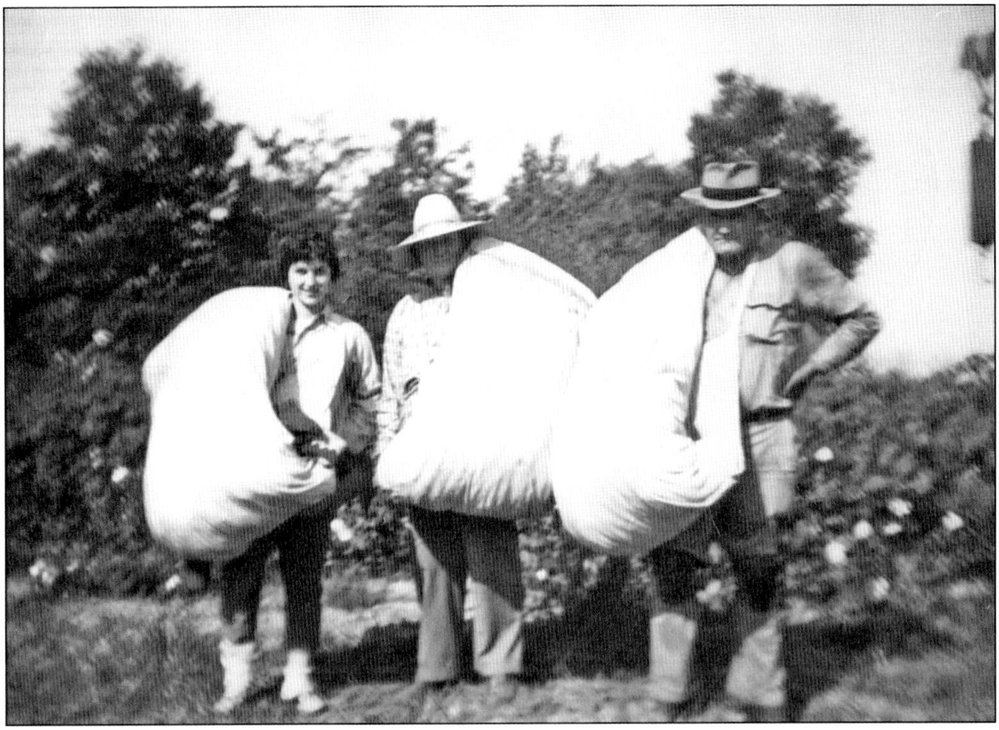

These cotton pickers in Swifton were proud of their day's work. Pictured here are Pam Swink Worthington and Mrs. and Mrs. Tom Gibbs. At this late date, cotton was still picked the way it had been for centuries: by hand, with the picked bolls stuffed in large sacks, pulled along the rows behind the cotton pickers. (Courtesy of J.W. Hulen.)

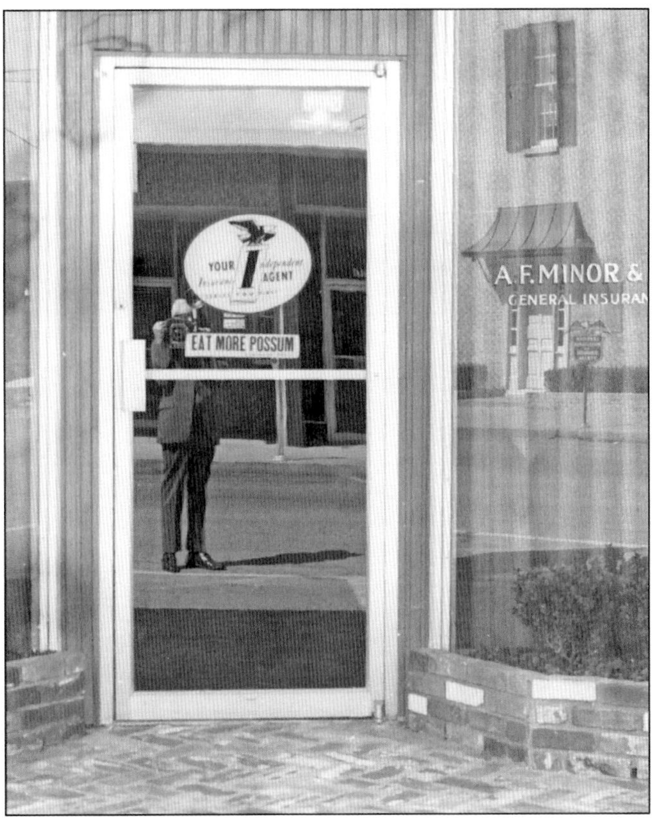

Alcorn Minor Sr. was one of the liveliest and most popular people in Jackson County. His zest for playing pranks and making people laugh was legendary, as is suggested by the "Eat More Possum" sign on his office door. Not many people ate possum in Jackson County. (Courtesy of Jane Parnell.)

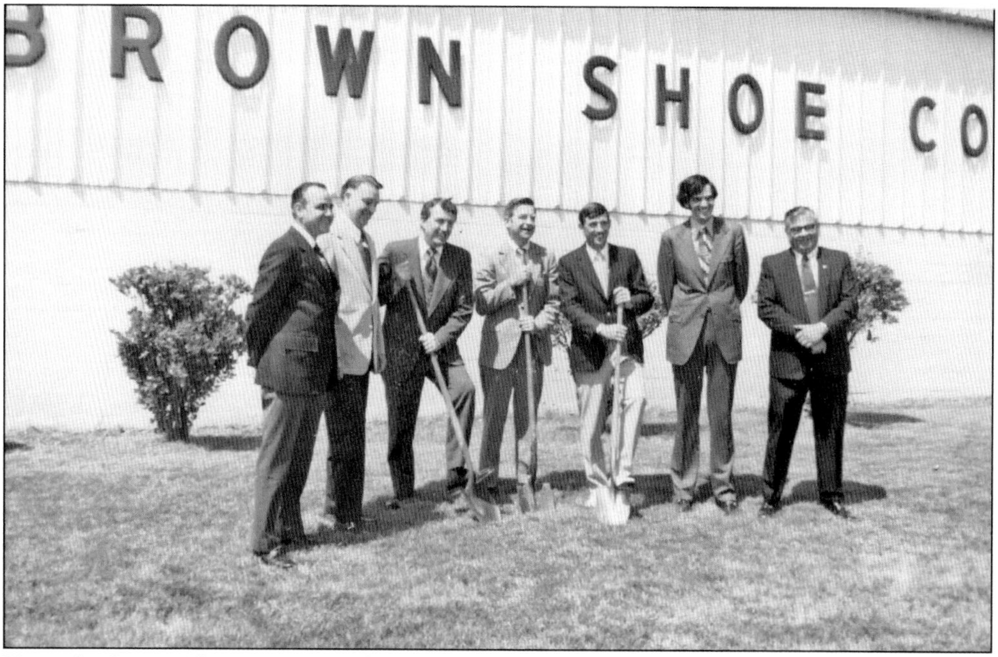

Here, the Brown Shoe Company christens its new facility. Among the citizens and dignitaries present that day are, from left to right, James A. "Jug" Wallace, P.K. Holmes Jr., Arkansas governor Dale Bumpers, an unidentified Brown Shoe Company official, John Minor, county judge Reuben "Buzz" Harper, and Rep. Tom Collier. (Courtesy of Jane Parnell.)

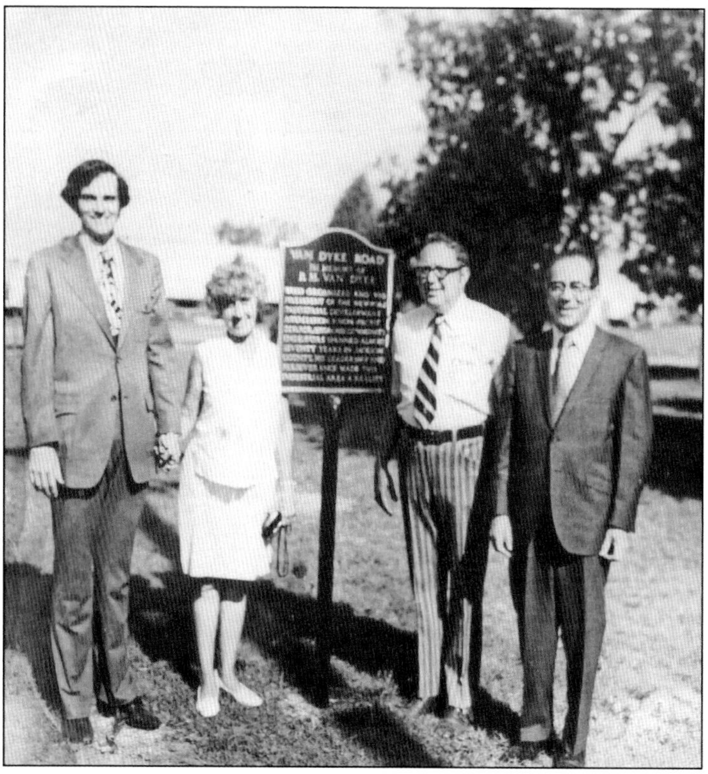

Margaret Van Dyke was one of the most beloved citizens in the county. Full of ideas and mirth, she wrote and directed plays, traveled extensively, and wrote a popular column for the *Newport Daily Independent* under the nom de plume Eliza Doolittle. Here, she participates in dedicating the Van Dyke Road in honor of her father. Standing with her are, from left to right, county judge Buzz Harper, engineer Albert Miller, and Robin Stamps. (Courtesy of Jane Parnell.)

Robert Harvey, a lifelong resident of Swifton, was a longtime member of the Arkansas General Assembly. Senator Harvey was one of the most influential members of the Arkansas legislature for decades and the author of the Revenue Stabilization Act, by which the State of Arkansas ended budget deficits. (Courtesy of Jane Parnell.)

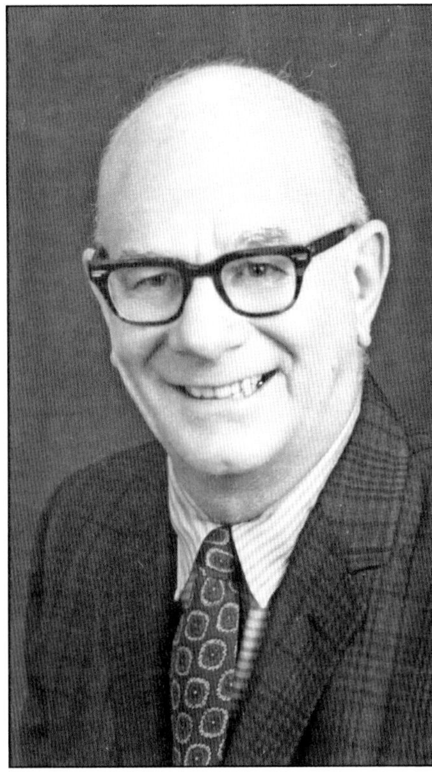

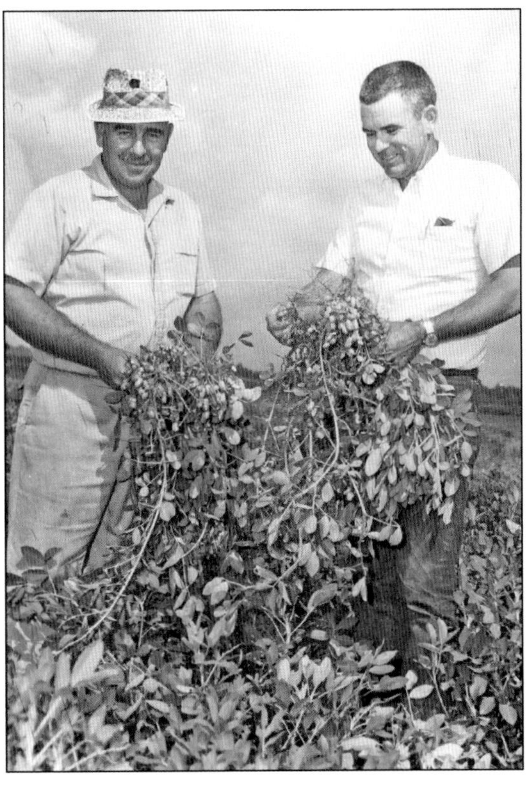

Two leading Tuckerman farmers, Bob Penix (left) and Jim Bailey, inspect a crop of peanuts. As intensive cotton farming robbed the soil of its minerals, farmers experimented with a wide variety of other crops in an effort to replenish the soil. Eventually, soybeans and rice became the money crops in Jackson County. (Courtesy of Jane Parnell.)

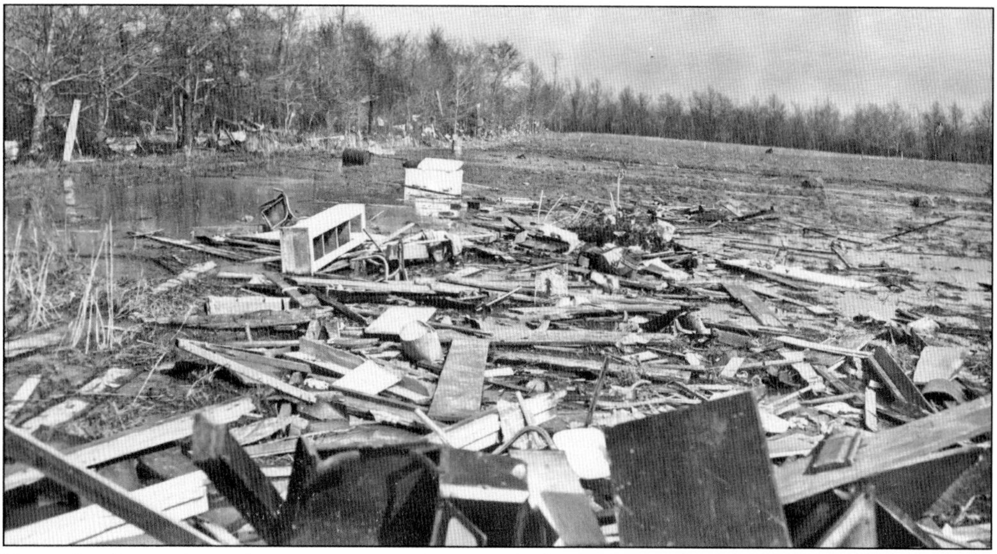

Tornadoes have always been a constant threat in Jackson County, as in much of Arkansas. The damage shown here reflects the incredible force of these storms, which generally track the old Southwest Trail from southwest to northeast through Arkansas. Although Newport is directly on this line, it has never been hit by a tornado, unlike the surrounding towns of Oil Trough, Jacksonport, and Tuckerman. (Courtesy of Farmers Electric.)

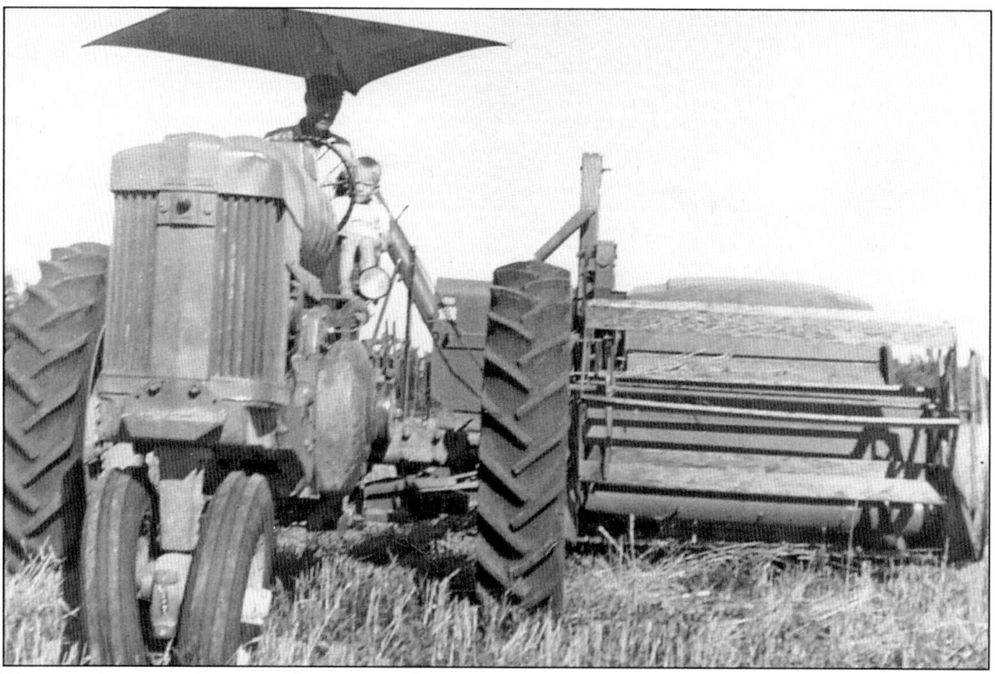

Tractors, large combines, and cotton-picking machines spelled the downfall of many agricultural towns throughout the South. As mechanization robbed laborers of their jobs, they moved away, taking their buying power with them. If towns could not generate other sources of income, they floundered, which is what happened to many of the farming towns in Jackson County. Here, Edgar Nicholson of Swifton holds his son Tim on a series 60 tractor pulling a combine. (Courtesy of J.W. Hulen.)

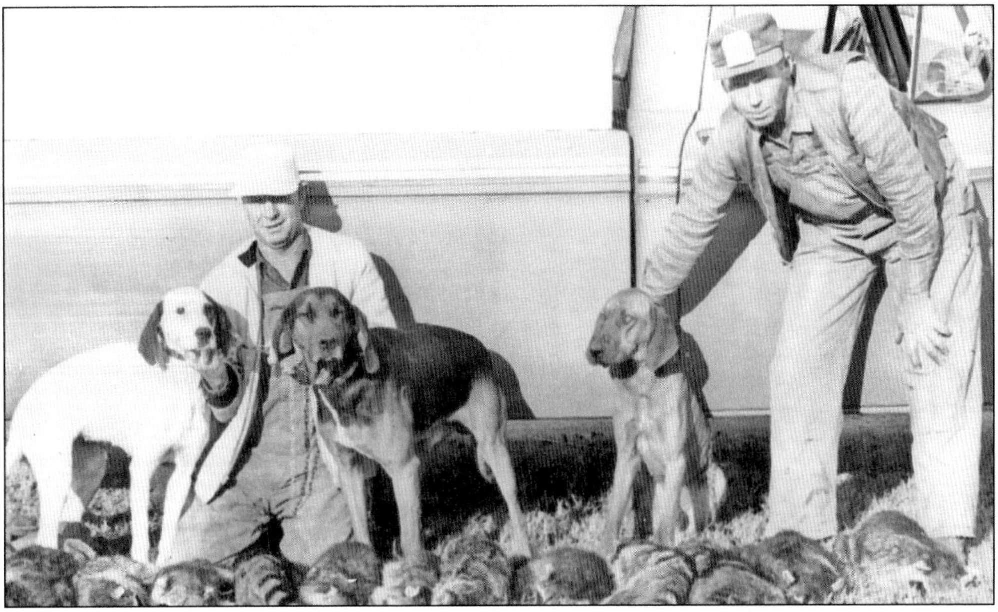

Hunting has remained a constant among the premier activities of Jackson county males over the last 185 years. Here, Jack Jimerson (left) and Claude Brown of Swifton display the results of their most recent raccoon hunt. Duck hunting is by far the preferred form of the sport, as so much of the county consists of marshes and rice fields that attract the unwary (and unfortunate) waterfowl. (Courtesy of J.W. Hulen.)

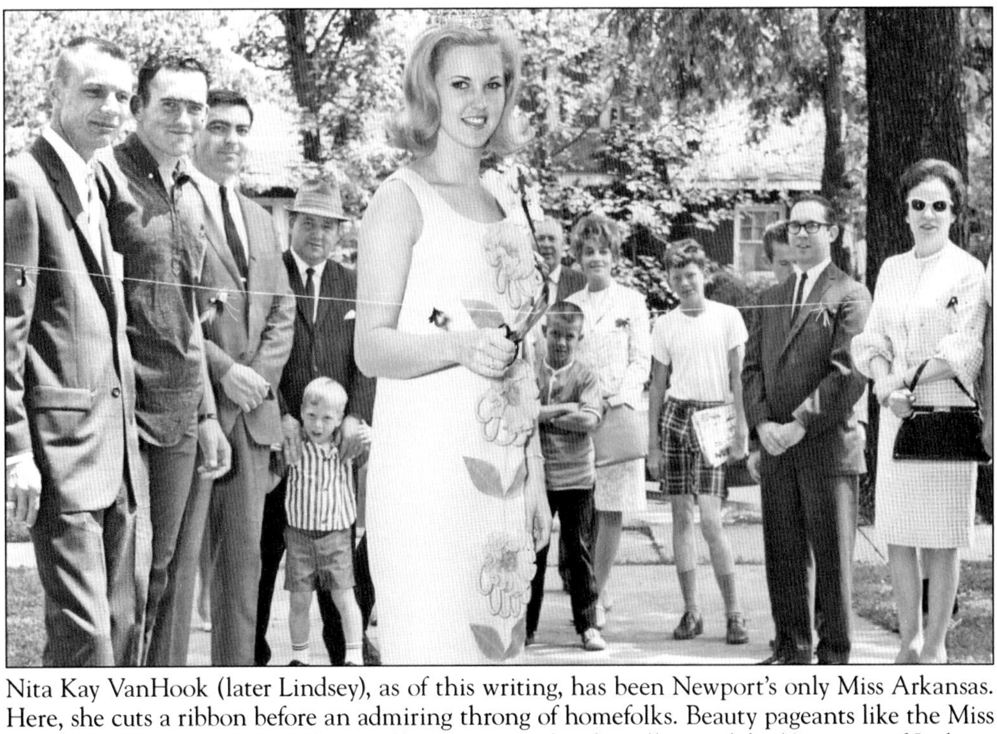

Nita Kay VanHook (later Lindsey), as of this writing, has been Newport's only Miss Arkansas. Here, she cuts a ribbon before an admiring throng of homefolks. Beauty pageants like the Miss Jackson County contest, held annually, were a staple of small-town life. (Courtesy of Jackson County Historical Society, Mildred Minor Gregory Collection.)

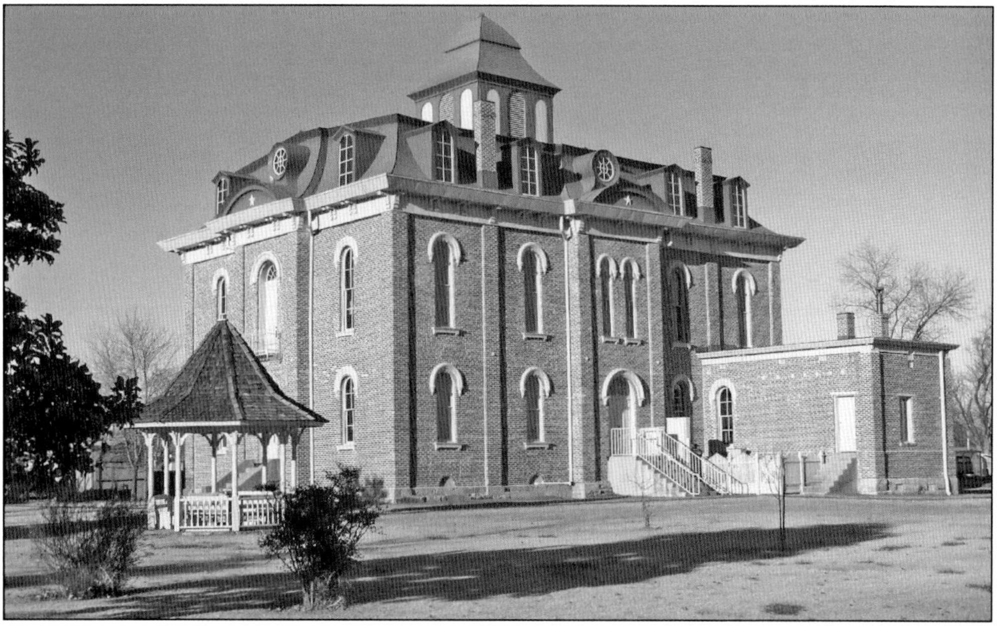

The 1960s saw the creation of the Jackson County Historical Society, the restoration of the old Jacksonport Courthouse, and its conversion into a museum that was then taken over by the Arkansas State Parks system, and the creation of a steamboat museum, the *Mary Woods No. 2*. Here, the old courthouse has been restored to its original splendor. (Courtesy of Frank Plegge.)

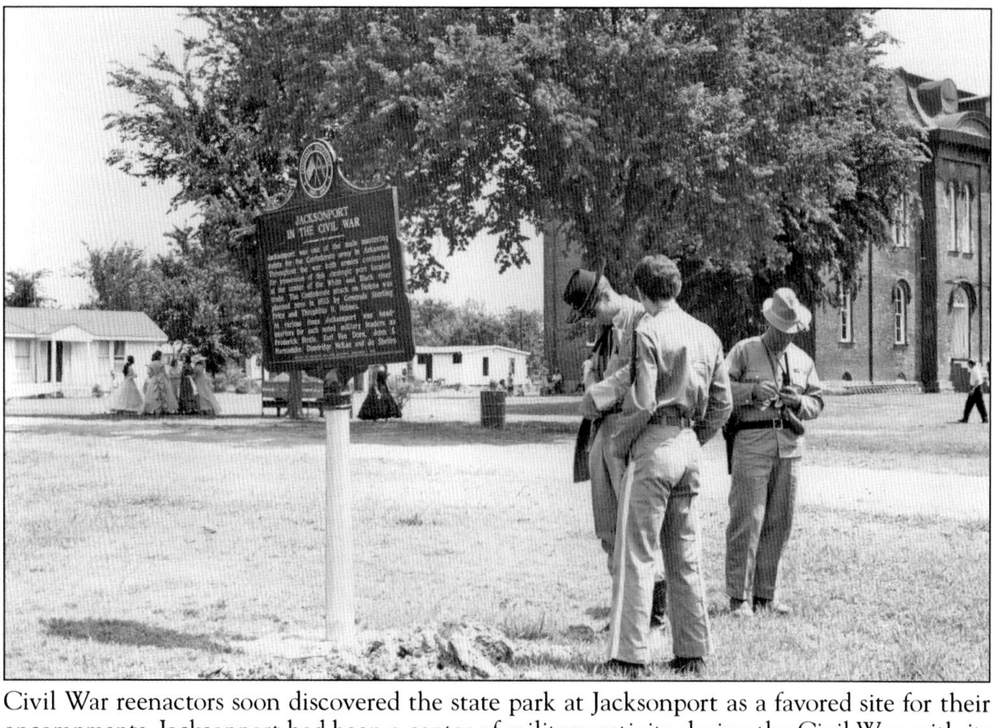

Civil War reenactors soon discovered the state park at Jacksonport as a favored site for their encampments. Jacksonport had been a center of military activity during the Civil War, with its prominent location at the head of deepwater steamboat activity on the White River. The town changed hands several times during the War between the States. (Courtesy of Farmers Electric.)

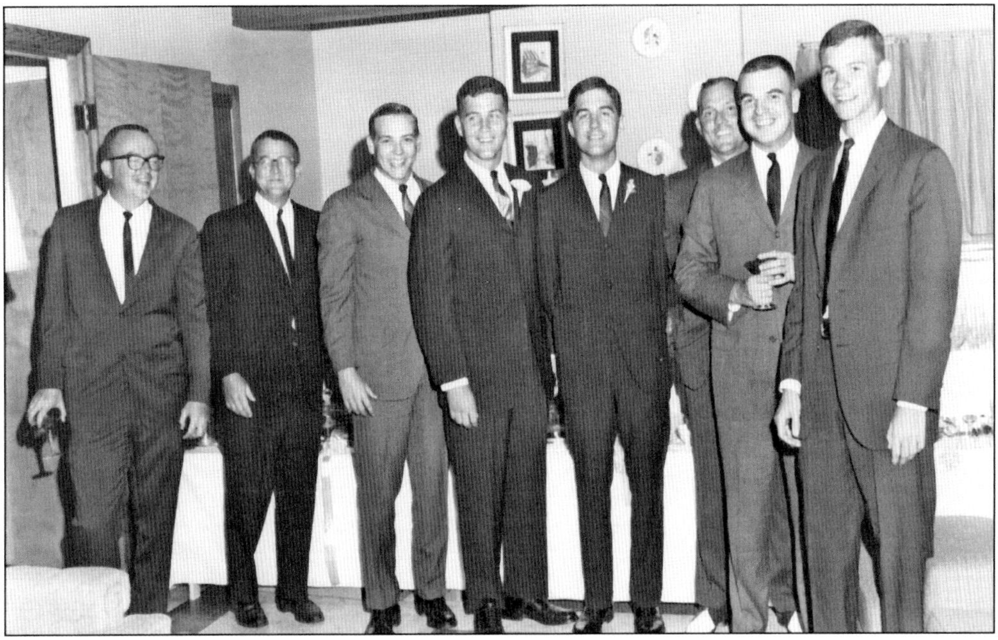

The Wilmans family was one of the oldest families in Jackson County. Here, the youngest generation of the Wilmans men gather for Jabie Jackson's wedding in 1965. Pictured are, from left to right, Dorsey Wilmans III, Stephen Graham, Rex Wilmans, Dorsey Jackson, Jabez F. Jackson Jr., Bobby Newell, Jimmy Wilmans, and Sam Freeman. (Courtesy of Rex Wilmans.)

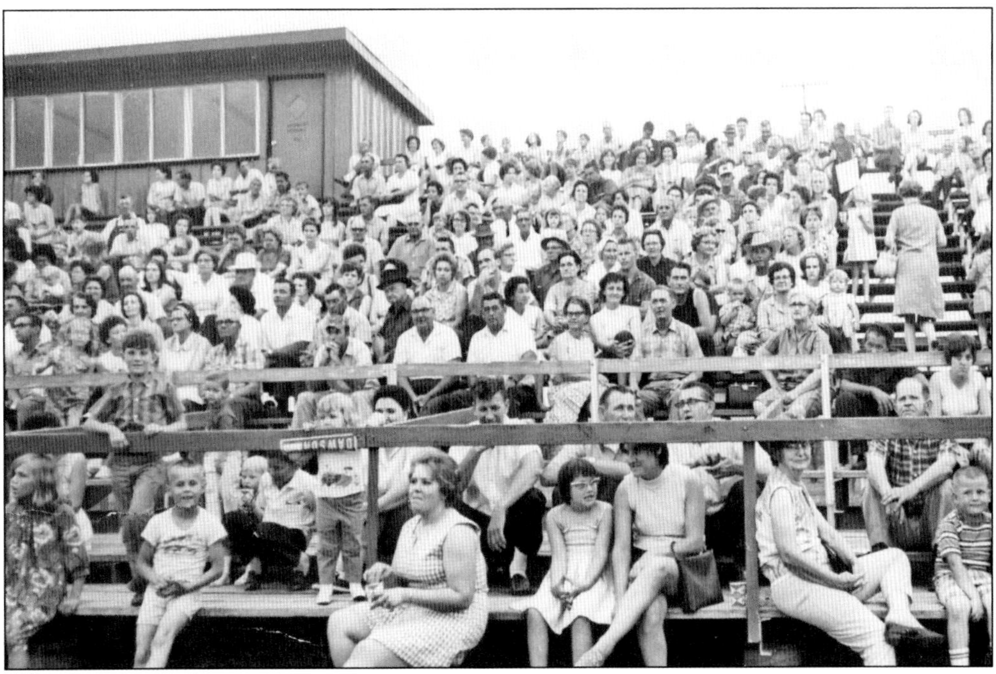

Farmers Day continued as an institution in Newport throughout the 1960s. The crowds were huge, and enthusiastic, but as racial tensions heightened throughout the country, the crowds at Farmers Day became increasingly segregated. (Courtesy of Farmers Electric.)

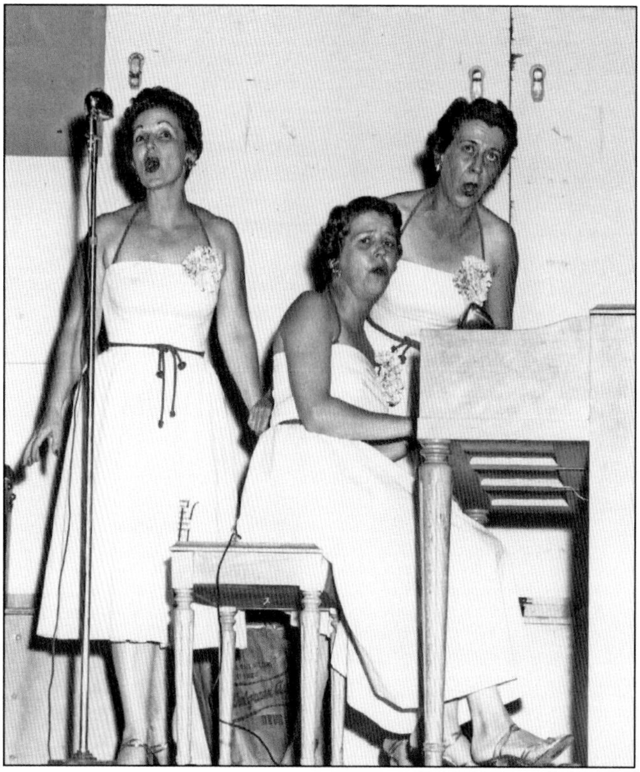

The Baguettes were an institution in Newport, singing often for civic groups and here at Farmers Day. Elaine Burton (left) and Eleanor Jowers (right) belt out a number, while Chris Cross accompanies them on the piano. Cross's husband, Carl Cross, was the general manager of Farmers Electric Company. (Courtesy of Farmers Electric.)

At Farmers Day in 1968, H.E. Satterfield of Beedeville took home one of the most exciting prizes, a new portable television. Farmers Day always included demonstrations on how to use the latest electrical conveniences, whether in the household or the barn. (Courtesy of Henry Boyce.)

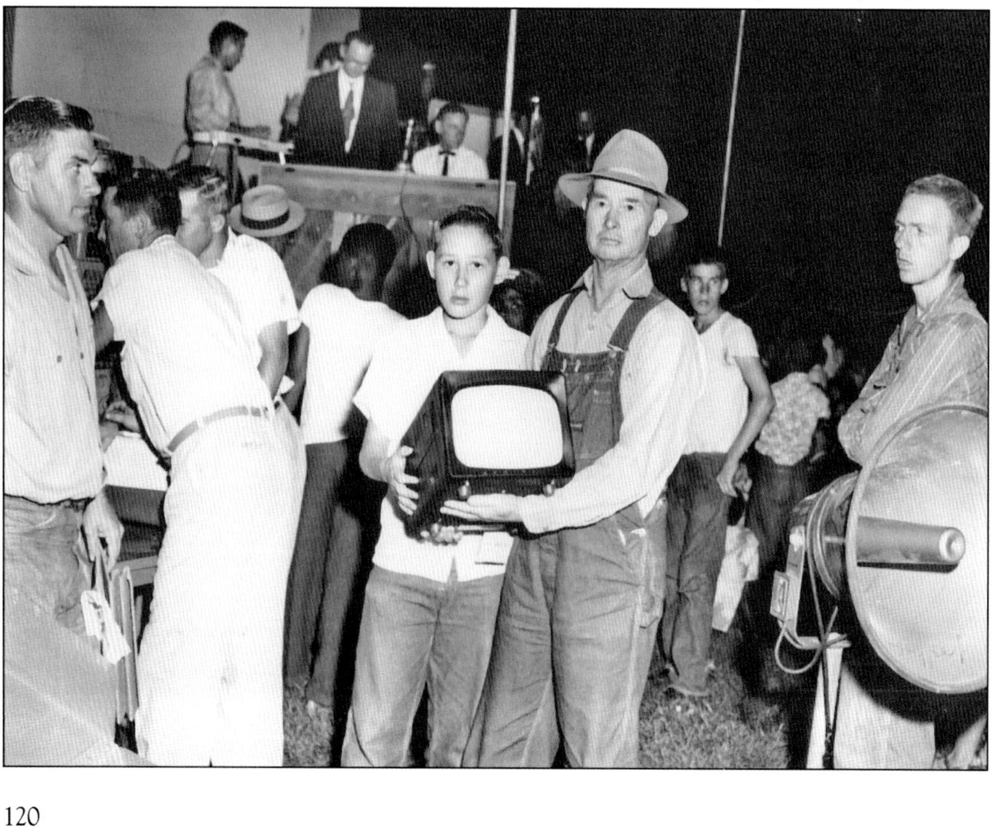

Ten

New Problems
the 1970s

The 1970s saw a heightened awareness of the war in Vietnam, with the loss of several of the county's young men in that conflict. The state park at Jacksonport expanded to provide even more recreational activities with the addition of a beautiful sand beach on the White River and many new picnic sites. There was still time for fun and frivolity, as were seen in the short but widely reported sightings of the "White River Monster," later debunked.

The opening of the Village Mall, the first indoor shopping mall in the county, was a major event in 1972, anchored as it was with one of the first Walmart stores, founded by former Newport resident Sam Walton. The movement of downtown residences and businesses eastward accelerated throughout the decade. The old cotton fields east of Highway 67 in Newport were transformed into tree-lined avenues with upscale residences and churches. The area south and east of the curve in Highway 67 developed, with a modern new Kroger store and new residential areas.

While Newport held its own in population in the 1970s, only Tuckerman among the smaller towns in the county could keep up. Swifton, Auvergne, Grubbs, Weldon, and Tupelo lost most of their citizens to Newport or to jobs outside the county. Olyphant had virtually ceased to exist, as had Grand Glaize.

As late as the 1960s, Newport enjoyed frequent and convenient passenger service on the new Missouri Pacific Railroad (successor to the Iron Mountain). As many as 10 passenger trains a day stopped at the depot in Newport, providing transportation south to Little Rock and north to St. Louis. The old Rock Island Line had ceased to exist in the county, and Highway 17 developed along its roadbed. In the 1970s, rail passenger service virtually ceased to exist in Jackson County, the victim of the automobile and new and better highways. Rail freight traffic was still brisk, but the old roundhouse and warehouses on the railroad side of Front Street were relics of the past.

Farmers and businessmen no longer utilized the river commercially, except for the last few barge loads of gravel taken to the Mobley Construction Company on the bluff bank of the White River at Newport. The Front Street fish markets closed, as commercial fishing in the White and Black Rivers had been supplanted by fresh fish in supermarkets and the new catfish ponds dotting the landscape.

Newport and the county had begun a slow decline by the late 1970s and early 1980s, a decline that continues to this day, although Newport has held its population steady for the last 15 years or so. In the interim, the county lost more than half its population.

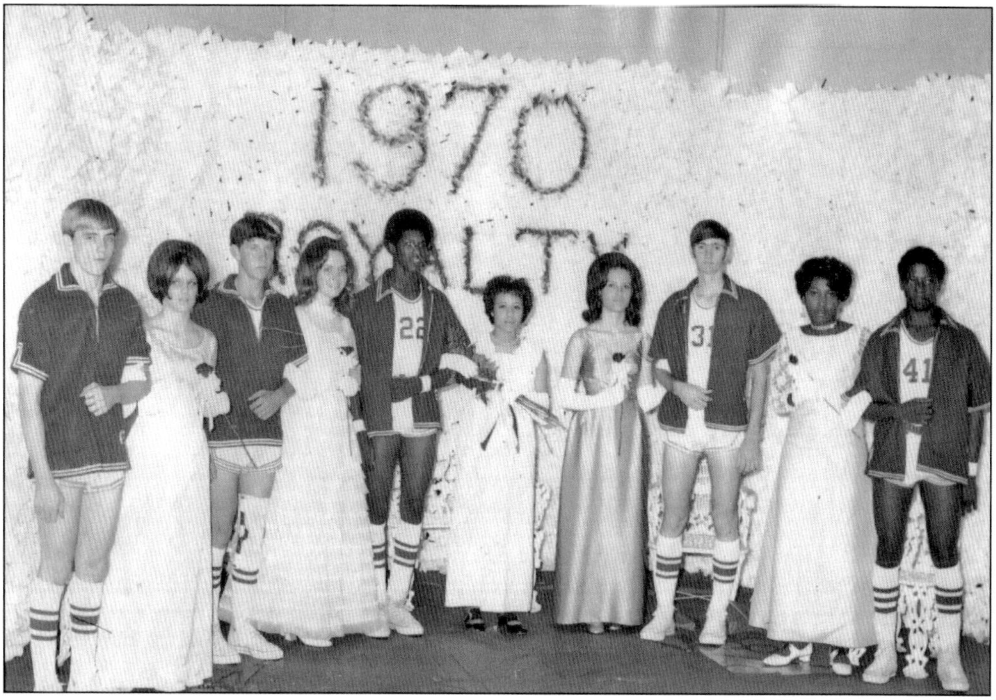

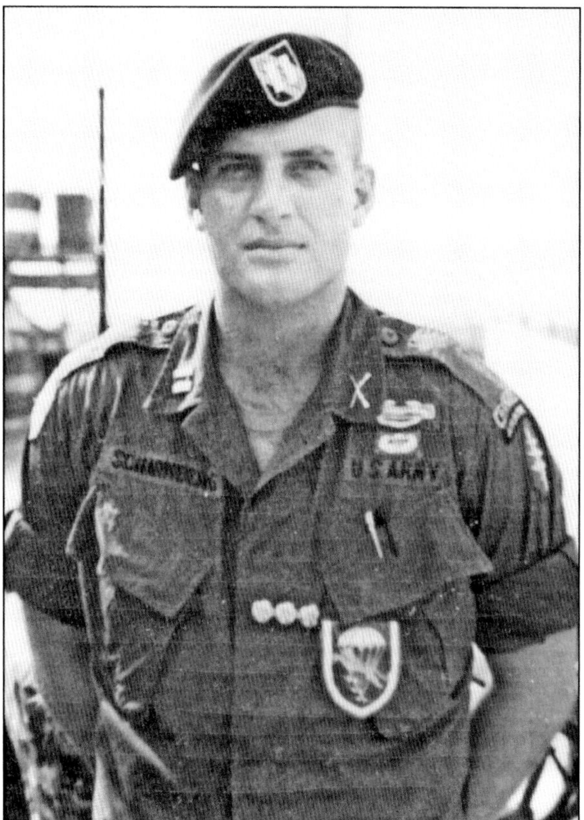

This homecoming court in 1970 demonstrates that integration was very much a fact of life in Jackson County public schools by the end of the 1960s. (Courtesy of Jane Parnell.)

US Army major Ronald Oliver Scharnberg was a Green Beret whose helicopter crashed in March 1971 in Vietnam, killing all aboard. Major Scharnberg of Newport, a career soldier, did his duty for his country. He was killed while serving his third voluntary tour of duty in the Vietnam War. He was the son of Lady Elizabeth Luker. (Courtesy of Tim Watson Sr.)

David Hodges served as prosecuting attorney of Jackson County from 1966 to 1972. Here, he is campaigning in an unidentified farmer's field. David and his brother Kaneaster were crusading lawyers who shut down much of the gambling in Jackson County. (Courtesy of Jane Parnell.)

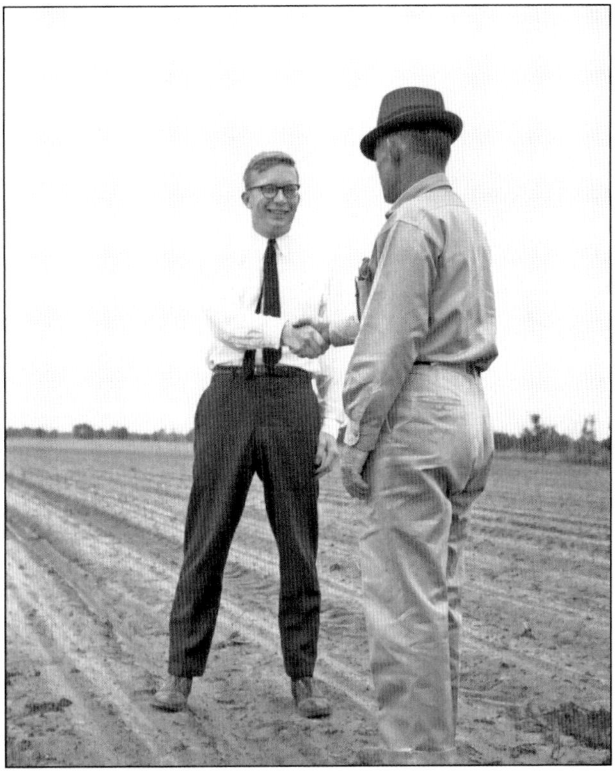

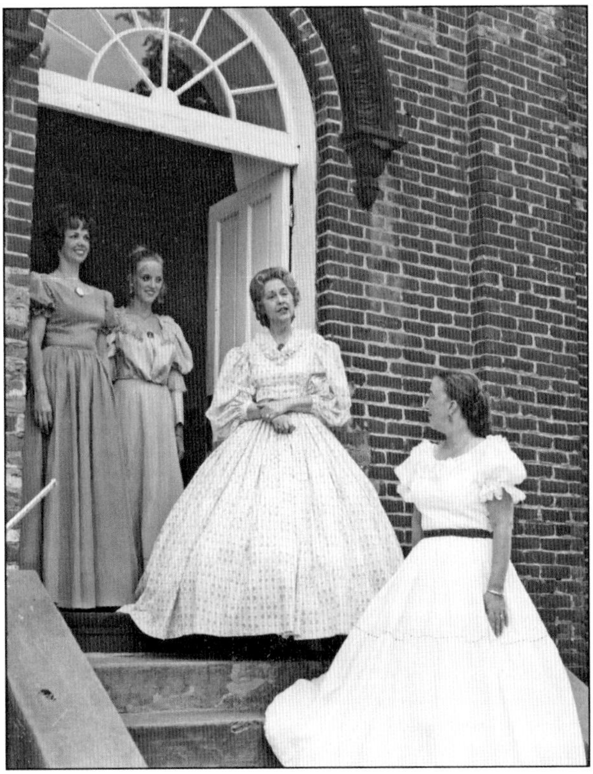

Lady Elizabeth Luker, center, poses as a Southern Belle for the 1973 Arkansas Educational Television special titled *Jacksonport Round the Bend*. On her left are Luckett McDonald Martin, left, and Cindy Hodges (later Burns), and on the steps below is Ann Price Ashley. (Courtesy of Tim Watson Sr.)

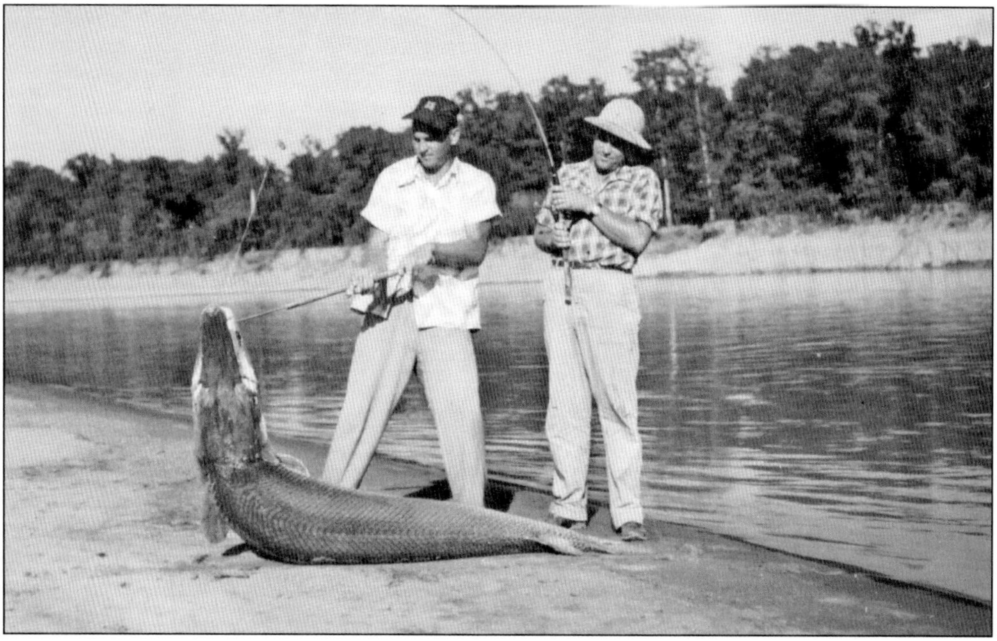

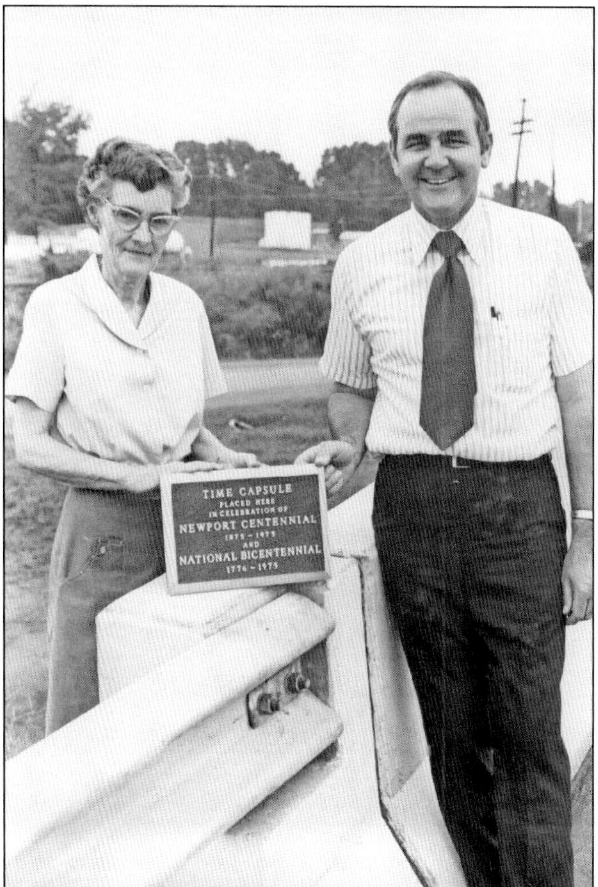

The "White River Monster" was a legendary creature reportedly sighted many times in the river close to Newport. This 230-pound eight-foot gar and his brethren may have been the source of that legend. The note on the postcard claims that fishermen in the area used deep-sea tackle to land these monsters, which have been recorded to weigh as much as 250 pounds. (Courtesy of Ray Hanley.)

Mildred Minor Gregory and J.A. "Jug" Wallace, representing Newport's Centennial Steering Committee, place a time capsule at the base of the Jacksonport overpass commemorating Newport's centennial in 1975 and the nation's bicentennial in 1976. Someone will have to remember to find this time capsule in 2075. (Courtesy of Jane Parnell.)

Kaneaster Hodges Jr. served as a US senator from December 1977 to January 1979. He was appointed by his friend Gov. David Pryor to fill out an unexpired term when Sen. John McClellan died unexpectedly. Pryor then ran successfully for the Senate seat and served three full terms. (Courtesy of Jane Parnell.)

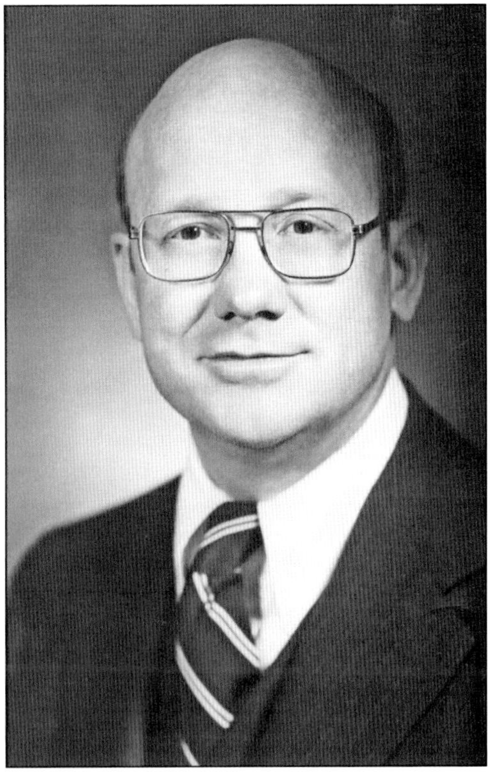

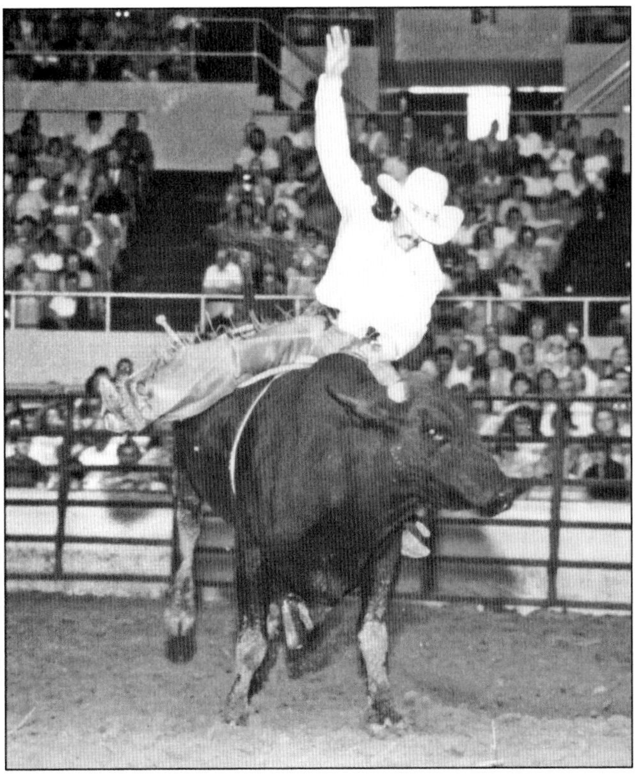

Robert Haas "Rob" McDonald, descended from several old Jackson County families, won the International Professional Rodeo Association's World Bull Riding Championship at Madison Square Garden in 1977. Competing for many years, McDonald also trained horses and performed in other rodeo events. His signature accessory was rose-colored glasses. (Courtesy of Luckett McDonald.)

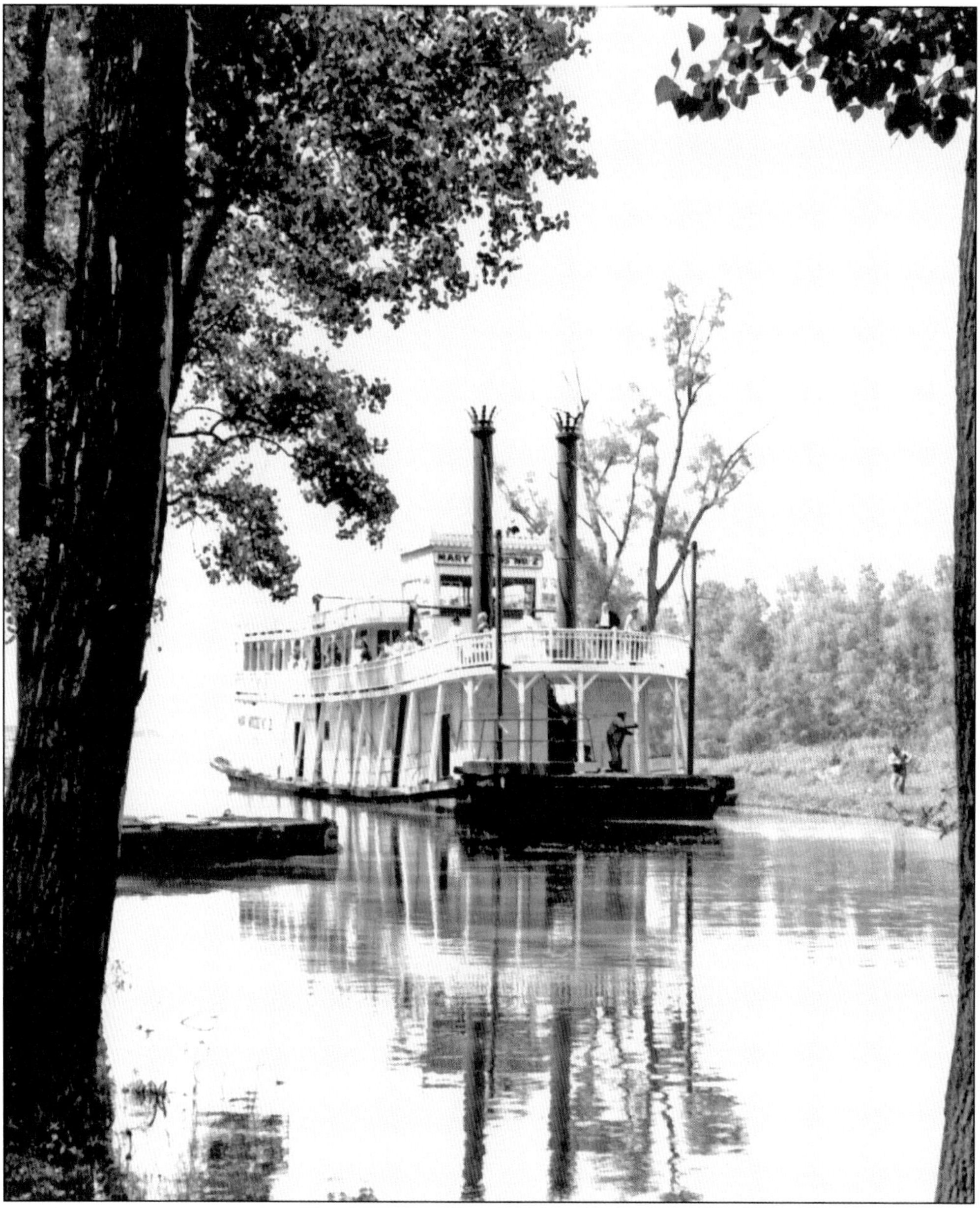

In 1967, the Potlatch Lumber Company donated the *Mary Woods No. 2*, a working paddle wheeler tugboat, to Jacksonport State Park. The boat then underwent major renovations and was refurbished to look like a steamboat of the 1860s. Here, it sits close to its berth just below the Jacksonport Courthouse, loaded with county residents dressed in 1860s garb, ready to participate in the 1973 educational film *Jacksonport Round the Bend*. Under the supervision of Lady Elizabeth Luker, museum curator, the *Mary Woods* became a steamboat museum, displaying at every turn what life would have been like for passengers and workers on a river trip. Staterooms and the main room were furnished with period objects, and in 1976 it opened as a floating museum and operated as such for 30 years. Unfortunately, the *Mary Woods No. 2* sank in an ice storm in 2010, and its superstructure was so heavily damaged that it could not be restored. This elegant paddle wheeler was a fitting symbol of the culture that grew up along the river it served.

Bibliography

Bevens, William E. *Makers of Jackson County: Short Stories of Early Pioneers, and Something about the Founding of Old Jacksonport*. Undated pamphlet, privately published.

Boyce, Wayne. *Best Little Town: Tuckerman*, Fayetteville: University of Arkansas Press, 2015.

Hanley, Ray. *A Journey through Arkansas, Historic Highway 67*. Charleston, SC: Arcadia Publishing, 1999.

McManus, Elliott McDonald. *A History of the First United Methodist Church of Newport, Arkansas, 1874–1984*. Newport, AR: privately published, 1985.

McKee, Daniel Deupree. *Laborers in the Vineyard: A History of St. Paul's Episcopal Church, Newport, Arkansas, 1861–1982*. Newport, AR: Craig Printing Company, 1993.

Morgan, James Logan, Ed. *Centennial History of Newport, Arkansas, 1875–1975*. Newport, AR: Jackson County Historical Society, 1975.

Newport Daily Independent. *A Century of Celebration, 100 Years*. Marceline, MO: D-Books Publishing, 2001.

———. *Reflections: A Pictorial History of Jackson County*. Marceline, MO: D-Books Publishing, 1996.

Schwartz, Marvin. *We Wanna Boogie: The Rockabilly Roots of Sonny Burgess and the Pacers*. Little Rock, AR: Butler Center Books, 2014.

Sutherland, Daniel E., Ed. *Reminiscences of a Private: William E. Bevens of the First Arkansas Infantry CSA*. Fayetteville: University of Arkansas Press, 1999.

The Stream of History: Volumes 1–42. Newport, AR: Jackson County Historical Society.

Watson, Lady Elizabeth. *Fight and Survive! A History of Jackson County, Arkansas in the Civil War*. Conway, AR: River Road Press, 1974.